THE FALL OF THE ROYAL GOVERNMENT IN MEXICO CITY

THE FALL
OF THE
ROYAL GOVERNMENT
IN MEXICO CITY

Timothy E. Anna

University of Nebraska Press ● Lincoln and London

This book has been published with the help of a grant from the Social Science Research Council of Canada, using funds provided by the Canada Council.

Publishers on the Plains

UNP

Library of Congress Cataloging in Publication Data

Anna, Timothy E   1944–
  The fall of the royal government in Mexico City.

  Bibliography: p. 263
  Includes index.
    1. Mexico—Politics and government—1810–1821.   2. Mexico—Politics and
government—1540–1810.   I.   Title.
F1232.A57   972′.03   77–17790
ISBN 0–8032–0957–6

To Mary Jadwiga

Contents

Preface

THE EXISTING HISTORIOGRAPHY of the fall of the Spanish royal government in Mexico City during the War of Independence (1810–1821) focuses almost exclusively upon the rebels. The fundamental premise of this study is that the vast bibliography devoted to the process of rebel victory tells only half the story of how Spain lost political control of its richest overseas territory. The success of the rebels and the failure of the royalists, though obviously related, are not necessarily the same stories. Before the Liberator, Agustín de Iturbide, could establish an independent Mexico, the three-hundred-year-old government of imperial Spain must first have faltered in some way. Historians in the past commonly have assumed that it was the rebellion that destroyed royal government in New Spain. The thesis I wish to present here is that the causal relationship is not that simple. Iturbide's Plan of Iguala provided the government that filled the void created by the viceregal regime's collapse, but Iturbide did not destroy the royal government. Nor did the revolts of Miguel Hidalgo and José María Morelos.

Historians who study the Mexican independence movement are faced with a central problem not previously isolated in the historiography: How could a regime that survived so many serious threats to its existence from 1808 to 1816 be overthrown so quickly in 1821? None of the existing explanations for independence answers this question. As this study seeks to prove, the answer lies as much with the viceregal regime as with the external forces that attacked it.

Related questions must be answered after the central problem is isolated. How did the viceregal regime survive the shocks of 1808 to 1816, when the ship of state was more severely battered than ever before in its history? What element of strength or determination characterized the regime in 1816 that was lacking in 1821? What role did the leadership of individuals play? When

ix

did Mexicans become disenchanted with their regime, and why? These essential questions, it seems to me, have been glossed over, because historians have been fascinated by the winners and have ignored the losers. We have let stand as if it were an explanation Lucas Alamán's rather vague statement that in 1816 the rebellion was everywhere defeated but the spark of independence could not be quenched.[1] While much attention has been paid to the movements of rebel and royal armies in rural New Spain, little has been paid to the political centrality of Mexico City, the head and heart of Mexico both before and after independence.

What was Mexico City doing in this period? Did its inhabitants ever express their wish concerning the burning question of the day? If so, why and how? To these questions I first turned my attention when I began this study. As time went on, however, I became aware that the matter of Mexico City's role in the War of Independence could not be separated from the viceregal regime's role, for the capital was the central strength as well as the center of that regime. In attempting to trace the shifting loyalties of Mexico City's policy-makers—both members of the royal government and civilians—I became convinced that in Mexico City tentative answers can be found to the broader interpretive questions underlying War of Independence studies. The broader themes at work in the independence period stand out once the focus is placed, not on the rural uprisings and individual rebels, but on the reaction of established power to them. The meaning of Mexican independence in the context of the wider Spanish-speaking world—where it should always be placed—becomes clearer.[2]

In this study two profound and troubling questions are presented and discussed; they will, I hope, encourage further debate. The first is: Was the final achievement of independence in Mexico the product of revolution or counterrevolution? The second is: Why did Spain lose? The first applies only to Mexico; the second might well have empire-wide relevance.[3]

The matter of whether Iturbide's success in 1821, after so many other insurrections failed, was the product of revolution or counterrevolution is basic and is essential to an understanding of the atomization of politics that characterized the early republic. The traditional thesis is that Iturbide's movement represented a counterrevolution in the Mexican context of the decidedly more radical insurrections that preceded it. This theory has received its most eloquent recent enunciation by John Lynch, who says that in the period 1815 to 1821 the royalists had come to depend entirely for the maintenance of their regime upon royalist creoles, who were intensely conservative. When, with the reinstitution of the Constitution in 1820, Spain neglected the interests of this group, they turned on the Crown and proclaimed independence. Romeo Flores Caballero also accepts the counterrevolutionary thesis, ascribing it almost exclusively to economic considerations. The work by Luis Villoro could also be placed in the counterrevolutionary camp on the basis of its conclusion, but on the grounds of its evidence it will be discussed with the other group.[4]

The other thesis, as yet only partially articulated, is that independence was the natural culmination of deep-seated economic and social disfunctions that characterized New Spain from the time of the Bourbon economic reforms of the 1780s. Florescano and Brading have shown, for example, the economic disfunction that existed in the provinces, the former concentrating more on the poor, the latter more on the wealthy.[5] Villoro has shown the real complexity of the social divisions in late colonial New Spain, adding a degree of sophistication and subtlety to the long oversimplified creole-versus-peninsular ethnic duality. Brading also has shown that for the mining and merchant elite of New Spain the creole-versus-peninsular problem was more than ethnic. Brading and Florescano, however, carry the narrative only up to 1810. They therefore provide only the initiating complaints, not an explanation of how independence came about.

Villoro, although he carries his reader through a detailed discussion of class conflicts at work in the War of Independence, confuses the issue by dividing the elite into two groups, concluding that the creole elite won and overthrew the peninsular elite with the sole object of avoiding change in order to preserve order, leaving the middle class with a mere foothold on political power, thus provoking the conservative-versus-liberal struggles of the early republic. While providing the interpretations needed for advocates of the revolution idea, Villoro ends up arguing the counterrevolution theory on grounds that are historically weak, since the Plan of Iguala did not, as he says, "abolish the Constitution with all its reforms."[6] The Plan actually reaffirmed the Constitution of 1812 for use in Mexico until such time as a new legal code could be written.

The revolution-versus-counterrevolution debate has recently been brought to its highest level in the work of Doris Ladd.[7] Arguing that independence was genuinely reformist, Ladd says that the nobility of New Spain, the cream of the elite, and their extended kinship group supported the Plan of Iguala precisely because it was both constitutional and monarchist. They desired reform within the context of a limited monarchy. Ladd reminds her readers that they must not define liberalism in 1810 from the point of view of post-1910 Mexico, in which case the creators of independence were staunch conservatives, but rather from the point of view of the late imperial system, in which case these same men were responsible for major changes in their world even if they did not advocate the social revolution of Morelos. The colonial era did not end in 1810, as much of the existing historiography concerned with the decline of the empire seems to suggest, but in 1821. Ladd suggests that the War of Independence should be studied by colonialists, who can view it as the end of something, rather than by historians of the national era, who must perforce see it as the very confused beginning of something else.

Ladd marshals a wealth of detail to support her argument, but she suggests that her study raises a number of questions. Her study substantiates its point that there were significant traces of liberalism in Iguala and that the extended kinship group of the handful of nobles in New Spain was more extensive, powerful, and tightly knit than previously known. Above all it proves its point that the nobles' role in the achievement of independence "suggests that the idea of autonomy represented more than a reaction to a few Spanish decrees of 1820."[8] But that still leaves the problem of transition from 1810 to 1821. During this period the net effect of the actions of nearly the entire elite was to uphold the royal regime, in spite of their support for autonomy; yet, in 1821, with an imperial government that should have answered their complaints, they abandoned the Crown. The problem of transition, the process of change itself, as Peter H. Smith has argued, is precisely the critical element to be dealt with in any study of the rise or fall of political legitimacy in Latin America.[9] This forces a return to the problem of how the royal regime failed.

As Hugh M. Hamill, Jr., has pointed out, independence was not inevitable; the royal regime was clearly capable of surviving and, indeed, responded vigorously to all challengers.[10] The new evidence indicating the extent of New Spain's social and economic problems can too easily be assumed to provide an explanation of how independence came about. In fact, this evidence only reveals some people's complaints—complaints which could be entirely lost sight of when the colony was faced with an overriding internal danger such as Indian rebellion. Social and economic problems alone do not explain how the balance of power in New Spain shifted from 1810 to 1821.

I would like to propose a refinement to the revolution-versus-counterrevolution debate. I believe independence was neither, but was, in fact, a massive compromise of such proportions that it satisfied no one beyond the immediate moment. Revolution is clearly too strong a word for the reforms sought by some of the elite, especially in view of their opposition to Hidalgo and the opposition of some of them to Morelos, though Ladd shows that some nobles actually favored Morelos. Only if Hidalgo or Morelos had won could we call Mexican independence a revolution. But counterrevolution is also too strong a word for the final solution because, as Ladd has made clear, many of the elite, the very people who established independence, favored limited reform. The Iturbide solution was, first and foremost, a massive compromise of the objectives of the long-time rebels with the more limited aims of the elite.

The interpretation of the Plan of Iguala as a compromise is closely linked to a slightly different, and I think a more important, question—why did the Spanish regime fail after overcoming all its enemies? An answer to that question would solve a related problem—why did the creole drive for autonomy result in outright independence? By 1816 the royal government had restored its control over the territory of New Spain. Peace prevailed, and some reconstruction was even implemented. The achievements of Viceroys Francisco Javier Venegas and Félix María Calleja were astounding. Yet, five years later, in 1821, a shocked Viceroy Juan Ruiz de Apodaca had no defenses against Iturbide, and admitted as much to Spain.[11] The regime collapsed with a suddenness that appears all the more stunning when viewed in the context of its newly revived strength. I believe the explanation for this paradox is that the Spanish imperial system and idea lost its authority.

My use of the term *authority* has been influenced by the semantic clarification provided by Carl J. Friedrich, who makes it clear that authority is not power but, rather, the foundation of power.[12] Much less is it "the established government" or "the authorities," for an established government may lose its authority to an opponent or another force without its immediately being clear to observers that this transition has occurred. I believe this is what happened in New Spain. The Spanish imperial government lost its authority in about 1816—as a result of events of the eight preceding years—but this fact did not become manifest until 1821 because, before the appearance of Iturbide on the scene, there was no one in whom, or no idea upon which, the nation could vest authority. *Authority*, as used in this study, is thus similar to the more widely recognized term *legitimacy* but is somewhat broader. Friedrich says, "Authority is not 'legitimate power' as is often claimed, for legitimate power may be without authority, a situation which arises in the approach to a revolution."[13] Authority is given by the nation, albeit unconsciously, to the state or the regime. It is the right to possess sovereignty, the right to govern. It is thus based upon the ability of the established authority to prove to the governed its right to continue governing them.[14] Friedrich's definitions go well beyond those of Max Weber—at least beyond the use to which Weber's definitions of political legitimacy have normally been put. It is essential to distinguish between authority and legitimacy in the case of the Mexican example because the royal regime remained the only legitimate regime for some years after it ceased to possess authority. As will be demonstrated, no acceptable blueprint for the creation of a new legitimate government existed between the destruction of the rebellions and the appearance of Iturbide.

While Friedrich provides us with the most flexible and usable terminology, there is a growing body of literature dealing specifically with the meaning and origins of political legitimacy in the Spanish American context. Frank Jay Moreno has clarified, for example, the fact that the Spanish imperial regimen in America—contradictory though it may first appear—was both a patrimonial authoritarian system and, simultaneously, a freely accepted system. That is, while the monarchy was authoritarian and patrimonial, it was also accepted, which is the only real basis for authority. Moreno says, "The fact that the system is *accepted* rather than *imposed* helps to distinguish an authoritarian regime from a regime of force. In the Spanish political formula, the basic ingredient was acceptance, not violence."[15] To this theoretical base Richard M. Morse adds the intriguing and essential thought that within the Spanish political philosophy of colonial times there existed the idea—based upon the interpretation of Thomas Aquinas provided by the sixteenth-century philosopher Francisco Suárez—that the rebellions against Spanish control were themselves also legitimate. That is, on the basis of Suárez's principle that the law of the prince loses its force if it is unjust, if it is too harsh, or if the majority has already ceased to obey it, Morse argues that the revolts experienced throughout Spanish American colonial history—revolts of conquistadors, uprisings of subject races, and creole movements of protest—all possess characteristics that could define them as "legitimate" rebellions within the framework of the Thomist, patrimonial state.[16] Finally, Peter H. Smith argues for the point of view that, in the specific context of the national era of Spanish American history, one theoretical type of legitimacy not conceived by Weber but particularly suited to the Latin American reality is that provided by success—what Smith calls *dominance*—the idea that those who hold power successfully are endowed thereby with some sort of legitimacy.[17]

These theoretical works provide us with two important foundations for studying a particular independence movement. On the one hand, they permit us to argue that the legitimate power of Spain collapsed because it lost its authority and that the regime that succeeded it was itself legitimate. On the other hand—and perhaps more important—they also clarify the fact that not legitimacy but authority is the critical variable. There can be a chronological difference between the moment Spain lost authority and the moment it lost legitimacy. It is the transfer of authority that is critical. Moreno has made it clear that this supposedly monolithic, absolutist regime was in fact based, however distantly in the past, upon "the consent of the governed," although great care must be taken not to use this term in the sense of Rousseau and Jefferson, for here we are dealing with a concept of consent that is more complex and subtle than that employed by the North Americans and the French. In Spanish law the monarch—rather than the people, as in the common-law tradition—was the core, the focus, of consent. The will of the Spanish monarch superseded the custom and traditions, even the folkways, of the people. The king was the creator of the law and could ignore the law in the name of equity if he chose. In his ultimate role of moderator, the king could, and did, hear petitions from any level of his subjects and address his subjects directly. As moderator, he could hear petitions against the actions he himself had taken as administrator and law-giver. This was made possible by the fact that the kingdoms were considered to be the patrimonial property of the Crown, of the *Señor*.

Moreno points out that this complex of direct and indirect channels of communication and power permitted great flexibility, allowing the Crown to govern its immense empire without force, and even at minimal expense. These several ideas reached their culmination in the long-standing tradition in Spanish America of the privilege exercised by colonial administrators of disobeying the edicts of the king if they found them unwise or unsuited to local conditions—the famous principle of *obedezco pero no cumplo* ("I obey but I do not comply"). Politically this privilege was a good bargain for all parties concerned, allowing colonial administrators to exercise local discretion and allowing the monarch, without the use of force, to govern millions of subjects spread over thousands of miles of territory.[18] The crucial point is that everything, from the authoritarian power of the viceroys to the role of the monarch himself, was based on the single principle—strong and weak at the same time—of the acceptance of authority, the right to rule, of the monarch. This was an authoritarian regime, but not a regime of force. The

Bourbons had even made considerable advances in converting it into an absolutist authoritarian regime on the model of their French cousins. And yet its very core, the genius that made it all adhere and function, was acceptance. Students of the legal and institutional history of British and North American common law will have no difficulty understanding this principle of acceptance, which is the core of Anglo-Saxon tradition and of the self-governing republic. The principle of consent was also the source of the authority of the Spanish and Spanish-imperial authoritarian state and thus is important in tracing the erosion of that authority in colonial New Spain.

An awareness of the centrality of the principle of consent in the Spanish tradition will help historians overcome any latent tendencies to ethnocentrism in their treatments of the process of Latin American independence and republic-building. Glen Dealy dealt with this problem in his discussion of the tendency of North American authors dealing with Spanish American independence to look for French and North American conceptions of power, the state, and democracy, and to conclude that South Americans were too politically naïve or inexperienced to adapt themselves to this imported ideology of republicanism.[19] However, when Dealy concluded that the opposite was true, that South America's early constitutions did not embody constitutional liberalism, he made the same mistake he properly accused others of making—he assumed that liberalism could not be indigenous. Charles A. Hale has cited a multitude of examples of liberalism but has noted that, as generally applied, the definitions of liberal and conservative are not specific enough and are too colored by later perceptions to be rigidly usable.[20] Jaime E. Rodríguez has demonstrated the existence of a powerful and persistent indigenous Spanish and Spanish American liberalism in Mexican independence.[21]

The theoretical writings of Friedrich, Moreno, and Brading provide a solution to the problems involved in defining and describing Spanish American liberalism. First, we must always define such relative terms as liberal and conservative within their own context. Second, and more important, is the point made by Brading in his discussion of the development of the Mexican nationalist thought of Servando Teresa de Mier and

Carlos María Bustamante: the two key founders of the ideology of Mexican nationalism—which, of course, was a major cause of the destruction of the Spanish power—did not base their writings on a Rousseau or a Jefferson, not for lack of awareness or understanding, but because they did not need to.[22] Besides, they hated the French republic and feared the North American republic. Spanish-Mexican legal, philosophical, historical and institutional traditions provided them with adequate substantiation for independence. The same traditions provided opponents of independence with adequate substantiation. Only when the process of independence—or the resistance to independence by the Spanish power and its supporters—is dealt with from the point of view of the historical-philosophical traditions of Spain will the full meaning of independence be clear. We must remember that the Spanish empire had existed for three centuries with no need to import foreign ideologies or rationalizations, because it provided its own. I am not arguing that the study of history should be internalized—Spain was, after all, a vast empire that sprawled across both of the world's great oceans and perforce had to respond to outside events—but rather that we should always look for internal origins before gratuitously importing the foreign. To do otherwise is to repeat the errors of some of the early students of pre-Columbian civilizations, and of many Enlightenment thinkers as well, in assuming that nothing significant in the New World could possibly have originated internally. Consequently, this book is a study of how the Spanish power declined from within.

Precision in the use of the terms *authority* and *legitimacy* is essential, because our task here is to assign a date to the loss by imperial Spain of its ancient mandate to govern New Spain. I believe the date of this event has been greatly confused in the existing literature. What is important is not when individual free-thinkers concluded Spain's hour in America had passed, but when a general consensus took place among the policy-making elite. Hence, I will argue that Spain's authority was still intact in 1808 when a handful of men who were truly ahead of their time attempted to coerce the viceroy into declaring autonomy, and in 1810 when Hidalgo and his Indian horde rebelled, and in 1813 and 1814 when Morelos's rebellion was at its height—because these were all external forces. The various threats to Spanish power prior to 1821 all failed because they could not take away from the legitimate possessor its right to sovereignty. Only Spain herself, through the actions of those who represented her in America, could prove the illegitimacy of her continued possession of sovereignty.

Thus it fell to Spain, to the imperial power itself, through its own confusion of goals and its own internal contradictions, to point the way for Mexicans to replace the imperial regimen with an alternative form of government. The military might of Spain, by eliminating many of the earlier antagonists, helped fashion Iturbide's final solution. The final solution, being a compromise of necessity rather than choice, proved profoundly unsatisfactory as the foundation for a new state.

Part I
WINNING THE WAR

Chapter 1

"This Most Noble City"

No OTHER PLACE in all the immense Spanish empire in America so completely represented both the strengths and the weaknesses of the Spanish imperial regimen as did Mexico City, the capital of New Spain. Here the visitor could see the imperial system at its very best, for from here three centuries of missionaries and conquerors had fanned out through the vast interior of Meso-America to spread Christianity, order, stability, government, and some of the missing arts of civilization. Like the kingdom over which it presided, the city was rich with the accumulated effect of the mixture of the Spanish and American Indian peoples and cultures. The imperial ethos—Christianity, civilization, and the monarchy—grew and multiplied. As Alamán said, the whole continent functioned "with uniformity, without violence, one can say without effort."[1] But there were problems, for the most acute of ancient grievances against imperial Spain also centered here. Mexico City was characterized by immense social cleavages and political tensions.

From the time of its foundation in 1325 to the present day, Mexico City has been more than a place, it has been a phenomenon. Before the Spanish Conquest it was the seat of a vigorously expanding Aztec empire, an indigenous American Rome with a population estimated by Charles Gibson at 250,000 to 400,000 and by Jacques Soustelle at 560,000 to 700,000. Most recently Jorge Hardoy has drastically lowered the estimate to about 165,000. After the Conquest, a rapid decline in population occurred, and by the 1560s the figure was reduced to 75,000, but the city was still one of the largest in the world. Throughout the colonial era, it gave an impression of such size and grandeur that in 1777 Juan de Viera incorrectly estimated its population as "bordering on one million individuals" and Antonio de Alcedo estimated in 1788 that it was 350,000. The actual figure was very much less, as Baron Alexander von Humboldt showed in 1803 when he produced the most accurate count up to that date— 137,000 persons. He said there were a mere 2,500 white Europeans (or gachupines, as peninsulars were called); 65,000 white creoles (Spaniards born in America); 33,000 Indians; 26,500 mestizos; and 10,000 mulattoes.[2]

During the War of Independence, two fairly accurate census figures were produced, though each is marred by temporary demographic fluctuations. One was given in the first annual report of the newly organized Junta of Police and Public Security in 1811. Based on reports from the Junta members for the districts over which they presided, it showed a total population of 168,811 (74,973 males, 93,838 females).[3] This statistic included the 16,179 Indians who lived in the jurisdictions of San Juan Tenochititlán and Santiago Tlaltelolco, separate Indian districts (*parcialidades*) dating from the post-conquest era.[4] As Fernando Navarro y Noriega attests, however, the 1811 figure included "many families" that had fled to the capital from towns occupied by the rebels, and it therefore represented an increase over the regular population.[5] The second statistic arrived at with sufficient care to make it reliable was the one submitted in 1813 by the newly elected constitutional city council, in obedience to a requirement of the Constitution. It showed a marked decline to 123,907. The decrease of approximately 45,000 persons from the 1810 figure is accounted for by the direct and indirect effects of the epidemic that swept the capital in 1813, in which 20,385 persons died, and by the return of thousands of refugees to their rural homes after suppression of the Hidalgo uprising. The constant population of the capital during the War of Independence, therefore, should be placed somewhere between these two figures—as the first United States minister to Mexico, Joel Poinsett, decided when he estimated in 1824 that it was 150,000.

It may be that none of these figures is absolutely accurate, because the city contained a large homeless population that no doubt shifted about in such a way that it could not be counted with precision. In addition, over 6,000 persons, mainly provisioners supplying the markets, entered and left the city every day.[6]

Mexico City, at any rate, was no sleepy colonial town. According to Humboldt, of all the cities of Europe in the first decade of the nineteenth century, only London, Dublin, Paris, and Madrid were larger. Thus, after Madrid, Mexico City was the second city in the Spanish empire. In America it was the undisputed champion. Its nearest competitors were New York (with 96,000 persons in 1810), Lima (with 53,000 at the turn of the century), Philadelphia (with 53,000 in 1810), and Boston (with 33,000).[7] Not until 1830 did New York City's population equal Mexico City's. However, the long-term demographic trend favored the north. With 168,000 inhabitants in 1811 and 150,000 in 1824, Mexico City clearly was declining in population or, at most, was fluctuating within a range of 15,000 or 20,000. In the same period, from 1800 to 1830, New York City's population expanded at the rate of 30,000 each decade. Mexico City would soon lose its preeminence in America, but during the War of Independence it remained what it had been for four hundred years, the major city in the New World.

The kingdom of New Spain, with a population in 1814 of 6,122,000, was second only to the United States (7,240,000 in 1810) among the New World countries. The Intendancy of Mexico, comprising the modern states of Mexico, Guerrero, and Morelos, had a population of 1,592,000, greater even than that of New York State (with 1,373,000 in 1820).[8]

Yet, while Mexico City was an important part of New Spain, it was quite different in makeup, as table 1 shows. Half of the city's population was white, while the country as a whole was only 18 percent white. Only 24 percent of the city's population was identifiably Indian, while New Spain as a whole was predominantly Indian (60 percent). More significant for future political developments is the fact that 48 percent of the capital's residents were creoles, while only 17.8 percent of the nation as a whole was creole. And the capital had proportionally ten times as many Europeans as the rest of the country. Mexico City, therefore, was creole and white in a country that was not, and that was its chief characteristic.

TABLE 1

Comparative Populations

New Spain, according to Navarro y Noriega, 1814			Mexico City, according to Humboldt, 1803		
Groups	Number	Percent	Groups	Number	Percent
White	1,108,000	18	White	67,500	50
Creole	1,093,000	17.8	Creole	65,000	48
European	15,000	.2	European	2,500	2
Indian	3,676,000	60	Indian	33,000	24
Mixed Castes	1,338,000	22	Mixed Castes	36,500	26
			Mestizo	26,500	19
			Mulatto	10,000	7
Total population	6,122,000		Total population	137,000	

Sources: Navarro y Noriega, "Memoria sobre la población del reino de Nueva España," AGN, Impresos oficiales, vol. 60, no. 48; Humboldt, *Ensayo político*, p. 129.

Mexico City came close to fulfilling the promise of its conqueror, Cortés, to make his capital "the noblest and most populous city in the occupied world." It was, in Doris Ladd's evocative phrase, a "pride of palaces."[9] It had over one hundred churches and chapels, twenty-three monasteries, fifteen convents, twelve hospitals, elaborate and ancient secondary schools (some in serious decline by 1810), an extensive system of markets and granaries (though the latter were also nearly defunct by 1810), an Academy of Art, the world's most advanced school of mining, one of America's greatest universities, and a botanical garden. Its public buildings, such as its great cathedral, the viceregal palace, the municipal palace, the mint, the Inquisition, the University, the customs house, were impressive. The few foreign visitors who saw the city just before or just after independence freely attested to its size and beauty. Humboldt, Poinsett, and Madame Calderón left records of their astonishment, marveling at the city's seven causeways, its two aqueducts, its wide and well-lighted streets, its boulevards and markets, and the vestiges of the ancient Aztec canal system still in use in the late colonial period. Spanish visitors were moved to hyperbole in their descriptions of it. Alcedo called it "the most beautiful, grand and sumptuous city of the whole of the Spanish monarchy." Juan de Viera could not resist speaking of "this new Babylon."[10]

Two authors in particular are responsible for adding a human angle to the general picture of late colonial and early independent Mexico City: Fanny Calderón de la Barca, the wife of the first Spanish minister to independent Mexico, and José Joaquín Fernández de Lizardi, a late colonial satirist and Mexico's first novelist. These two left vivid pictures of the elegance and classicism of Mexico City, together with its hypocrisy and poverty. Madame Calderón filled her pages with accounts of murders on her doorstep, beggars at her windows miming every human woe in order to gain alms, armed guards protecting the ambassador or his wife whenever they left their house.[11] Lizardi left in his works a clear picture of the brutishness of life for the poor, the emptiness of wealth, the pride of the Spaniards, and the aspirations of the creoles. In *El Periquillo Sarniento* (1816), his novel of social satire directed against the colonial regime, he characterized the city's white population as composed of hypocritical old ladies; priests who exploited the faithful; self-interested doctors and lawyers; usurious merchants; neglectful mothers and fathers; superstitious religious fanatics; venal judges; bullying officers and soldiers; avaricious rich men; fraudulent mendicants; and girls for hire. Lizardi showed the pretentiousness of colonial life, which he thought extended even to the highest levels of officialdom. In his journal, *El Pensador Mexicano*, published at various times during the War of Independence, he described the government as composed of a viceroy who thought himself an absolute sovereign, oidors who were no less arrogant, secretaries who thought they were something more than ministers, alcaldes de barrio who thought they were at least alcaldes de corte, and their servants who thought they were alcaldes de barrio. He reminded the viceroy not to be lulled by the sycophants who surrounded him, but to remember he was "a miserable mortal, a man like all others, an unimportant atom in the face of the All Powerful." And he wondered how Mexico City, blessed by nature with sunshine, water, a perfect climate, and an abundance of fruits and flowers, could be so filthy and filled with so many beggars and thieves.[12]

The elegant façade that the capital revealed to the world was the result of its being the chief residence of the nation's wealthy. While the precepts of imperial absolutism and a vigilant vice-regal government worked constantly to check the political power of the domestic plutocrats, there were no limitations on their economic or social power, and that, in turn, meant that they inevitably had great indirect political influence on the government. As it turned out, the chief limitation on their power was their frequent inability to agree on objectives.

Mexico City's rich citizens were the wealthiest of all Spanish Americans, some having fortunes of over a million pesos. Ladd has found record of seventeen families in New Spain that were millionaires and nine that had fortunes of 500,000 to 900,000 pesos. Some sense of the immensity of these fortunes in a preindustrial society can be gained from realizing that the Mexican peso of 1810 was the equal of the United States dollar of the day. These colonial plutocrats owed their wealth to a variety of sources, although usually, as Brading has shown, large fortunes were originally made in merchant speculation or mining, or both, and in the second generation were diverted partly into entailed agriculture. The most stable fortunes represented investment in all three activities. Fortunes fluctuated wildly, especially if heavy investments were made in mining or agriculture, but the general picture is of a group of wealthy extended families, some noble, some not, whose fortunes had increased steadily because of the commercial and mining reforms dating from the 1780s. The domestic titled nobles of New Spain invariably came from this group. Ladd points out that not every rich man was a noble, but almost every millionaire was noble. Membership in this domestic elite was, however, tenuous, as great family fortunes rose and disappeared, sometimes in the space of three generations.[13]

Though not always born in Mexico, these plutocrats made their fortunes there and were not absentee grandees. The wealthy, in short, were neither exclusively Spanish nor exclusively creole, but mixed. They functioned out of large extended family groups, so that many people might share in the status of great wealth and power attained by a particular man. These families were so thoroughly mixed that they cannot be identified merely as peninsular or creole, as though their birthplace determined their political opinions and objectives. The typical wealthy family, modeled on the findings of Brading and Ladd, was founded by a gachupine immigrant who made his fortune and left it to a creole first generation, the daughters of which married newly arrived gachupines, producing a mixed second generation. Ladd found, in addition, that probably half of the resident Mexican nobles at the time of independence were mestizo—that is, they traced their families back to Indian nobility, though they were white in terms of their social status.[14]

Much has been written about the social cleavages characterizing late colonial Mexico, especially the creole-gachupine struggle for power, which was once said to be the fundamental cause of the movement for independence.[15] However, a new picture is beginning to emerge. The most important aspect of the work of Brading and Ladd on the "really rich" is the suggestion that these people, so powerful in local economic and political affairs— through their ability to loan huge sums to the government, to sway public opinion, to build their own clientele of extended family and employees, even to create their own militia and picket corps—do not fit the stereotypical view of creole-versus-gachupine conflict that continues to dominate War of Independence studies. The elite families were so thoroughly mixed that the antagonism between creole and peninsular was muted in favor of the advancement or protection of the family. In tracing the genealogy of Guanajuato's social elite, for example, Brading found that "in many cases the division between gachupine and creole was soon resolved into little more than a distinction of generations: creole lawyers were often the sons of gachupine merchants and gachupine merchants were equally often the sons-in-law of creole miners."[16] Finding similar genealogies for the titled nobility, Ladd eliminated the elite from the creole-peninsular dispute: "Creole-peninsular strife was evidently a class interest sustained by the petite bourgeoisie to protest immigrant preference in office and in managerial positions. It was clearly an interest that was not shared by the elites."[17]

Villoro had previously made it clear that place of birth was less important in determining the political objectives of various groups in New Spain than class, income, associations, and kinship and compadrazgo loyalties. Now, with the genealogical clarification provided by Brading and Ladd, a revision of the traditional view of the social classes that existed in New Spain at the outbreak of the insurrection is necessary. The following review of Villoro's social classifications—the ultimate statement of the classes involved in the "independence as counterrevolution" thesis—will be useful in determining what modifications or refinements need to be made.

Villoro specified and described four classes existing during the War of Independence: the ruling class, which he called the "administrative and commercial class"; the domestic elite, whom he called "proprietors and military"; the lesser business, professional, and clerical class, which he called the "middle class"; and the "poor," which he said was composed of Indians, mestizos or castes, and blacks.[18]

The ruling class, Villoro's administrative and commercial class, had governed the colony for three centuries, although it was numerically tiny. Villoro said these were the people whose interests conformed to those of the Crown. He identified them as the royal administrators of the colony, the monopoly merchants associated with the Consulados and other aspects of the import-export business that supplied the colony, and the great land owners and mine owners. He said they were all peninsulars and owed their status and social position entirely to the metropolis.

The second class—proprietors and military—differed, according to Villoro, from the first in that their social predominance was only "partially dependent on the metropolis." This class consisted of the high clergy, the "great proprietors," and the army officers, and their unifying characteristic was an "ambiguous feeling concerning their dependence on the Crown." Though they owed their original appointment or position to the Crown, they depended on domestic sources of income for their wealth. The high clergy were deeply involved in Mexican property transactions and banking. Military officers owed their capacity to function to their soldiers, who were Americans. The miners, chiefly creoles, were increasingly restive in the face of metropolitan economic decisions antagonistic to their interests. The great land owners were unhappy because their control over the rural Indians was constantly thwarted by the Crown. Some members of the domestic elite were peninsular and some were creole, but all were rich, and all suffered from what might be called a "revolution of rising expectations." The expanding wealth of New Spain and the general optimism of the era in economic affairs made them rebellious under the conservative commercial system of the Crown; all favored local control of the economy so that they might make as much money as possible. Villoro identifies this domestic elite as the key group that brought about the counterrevolution of 1821.

The third group Villoro called the middle class. They were, he said, white creoles, but of limited wealth. Unwilling to engage in business but not rich enough to be great land owners, they were usually lawyers and clergy (*letrados*). These lesser creoles did not share the views of the propertied creoles and never would. After independence they were the liberals and federalists. They most keenly resented Spain's restrictive legislation barring them from high administrative and clerical positions, and they suffered from a lack of employment commensurate with their pretensions and training. "The [members of the] middle class, more than any other, were conscious of not being able to achieve in society the function to which their vocation oriented them." This numerous class, economically unproductive and hampered by limited horizons, occupied the lesser magistracies and curacies "and almost all the administrative posts of the small cities." This strangely "displaced" population, "living in a world in which they did not participate," fell back upon intellectual pursuits, dedicated themselves to reading of juridical and theological texts, and became the provincial intelligentsia.

Villoro's fourth class is the working class, composed of Indians, mestizos, castes, and blacks. These were the ranchers, farmers, artisans, and members of Indian communities, who were subjected to an oppression scarcely softened by royal paternalism. Numerically the largest, they were not expected to participate in politics. Although as a class they had the same ultimate goals, they were too racially disparate to be aware of their similarities, and, as is common, they hated each other more than their real but unidentifiable oppressors, who were the great proprietors. They were the most useful element of the population, the producers, workers, and soldiers—the proletariat. Living in misery, they bore the brunt of the economic and social inequality of the imperial system. They were also the vast majority of the national population, comprising 82 percent of it according to Humboldt's statistics. Hungry and desperate, they provided the cannon fodder for insurrection, only to be betrayed at the last moment, according to advocates of the thesis, by an elitist counterrevolution.

Villoro's social categorization is helpful because it focuses attention on social perceptions and economic fears rather than upon the creole-versus-peninsular struggle as the basic explanation for independence. It is also appealing because it reaffirms the view that independence was a betrayal—without which many explanations for the chaos of the early republic would fail. But it does not fit the new data, and consequently now appears to be weakened by hypothetical inductiveness.

Brading and Ladd have convincingly shown, for example, that it would be an error to identify the interests of the mixed creole-Spanish merchant, mining, and hacendado elite too closely with those of the royal administrators; to forget that after the decree of Comercio Libre the Consulados were as much dependent on Mexican as on Spanish trade (though the Consulados still aspired to monopolize transoceanic trade and were still controlled by peninsulars); or to overlook the facts that the very rich had many complaints about the economic system, that they were not invariably white, and that they were not purely peninsular. It seems, therefore, that the great monopoly merchants and the mining elite—the plutocrats—do not belong in the same category as the royal administrators, largely because many of them favored autonomy. Similarly, Ladd has thoroughly disposed of the theory that Villoro's second class, the domestic elite, turned to counterrevolution, for she has shown that they consistently and logically favored limited reform. It would seem to be an error to classify all less wealthy whites (Villoro's third class) as a single group, much less to assume they would all be creoles. As Ladd and Brading have shown, there were many poor peninsulars—recent immigrants who had not yet prospered—while at the same time the oldest elite creole families were constantly losing their fortunes and being cast down among the lesser creoles. Moreover, the extraordinary complexity of the extended kinship groupings meant that many people took their social position not from their own accomplishments or income or life-style, but from that of their cousins, in-laws, compadres, and spouses. There is also some question whether the term *middle class* can even be applied in a country where, according to Manuel Abad y Queipo, bishop-elect of Michoacán, society was divided in two groups: "those who have nothing and those who have everything."[19] Finally, to identify all poor as nonwhite does serious violence to the fact that some of the poor were white while some of the more prosperous were not entirely white, although, certainly, all whites had built-in privileges in matters of status.

What is needed, therefore, is a revision of the conventional theory of the makeup of the social classes existing in New Spain. In place of Villoro's four classes—administrative and commercial, proprietors and military, middle class, and working class—a slightly revised four can be proposed: royal administrative and foreign elite, domestic elite or plutocrats, petite bourgeoisie, and poor.

These four classes can be characterized by the type of dwelling each occupied in Mexico City, for life-style was the most obvious indication of disparity among the classes. The royal administrators lived in official residences in state buildings; the domestic elite lived in privately-owned palaces and self-contained houses; the petite bourgeoisie lived in rented houses, rooms, or quarters attached to places of business; and the poor lived in hovels, shacks, and slums—or had no place at all. The city showed on its face the disease of inequality that festered in the body—not simply the difference that separated rich from poor, but rich from rich, and poor from poor.

The astounding disparity is most clearly revealed in an important article by María Dolores Morales, who found that, according to an 1813 census of real estate in the capital, only 2,207 persons or institutions owned the total of 5,520 pieces of real estate that existed in Mexico City. That is, only 1.68 percent of the total population owned property. Of these proprietors, 75 percent owned only one house, while 1.15 percent were major proprietors, some owning more than 100 houses. The church was the city's greatest landlord. Regular and secular orders together owned 47.08 percent of all properties, including most of the valuable ones, and those located in the urban center, where property values were highest because municipal services were most fully developed. Most renters lived in habitations owned by the church. Among private individuals who owned property (the private sector possessed a total of 44.56 percent of the properties) 80 percent owned only the one house in which they lived. The 41 private citizens considered to be great proprietors owned an average of eleven properties each. Morales also found a group of 370 proprietors, owning an average of two houses each, who would be considered upper class as well. Most private houses belonged to artisans or workers and were small adobe structures on the underdeveloped outskirts of the city. While some private proprietors owned properties valued up to 827,730 pesos, most private properties were worth less than 2,000 pesos.[20] There is, unfortunately, one major gap in these important statistics. The 1813 census apparently did not list government properties, convents, and church properties not rented out—for example, residences of government officials and convents actually occupied by the orders that owned them. Private properties not rented out but occupied by owner were included. It should be emphasized that the distinguishing characteristic between classes was not so much the ownership of a house but the type of house occupied.

Since the political masters of New Spain were transients representing the Crown, they lived well but impermanently. The majority of the administrative elite—viceroy, bureaucrats, prelates, officers—lived in houses or rooms provided for them but which they did not own. As a general rule, most government personnel were prohibited from owning property in the territory they administered, in order that they might remain disinterested in local affairs. There were, however, some exceptions: Brigadier Calleja had been allowed to acquire Mexican property because his wife was Mexican, and the magistrates of the audiencia, because they were civilians theoretically permanently or semipermanently settled in the city, had to find their own residences. A handful of Spaniards who were unattached to the government—such as commercial agents—also functioned in Mexico and did not have governmental accommodations; these were the "foreign elite." Some of the colonial administrators lived very lavishly; most did not. The viceroy, who received a salary of 40,000 pesos a year with an additional allowance of 20,000 pesos a year for his "table of state," lived with his retinue of officers and secretaries in the viceregal palace.[21] The directors of government offices often lived in rooms within official buildings. The intendant of the province of Mexico, Ramón Gutiérrez del Mazo, who simultaneously served as corregidor of the capital, lived in splendid rooms in the municipal palace, from which he was unceremoniously evicted in 1820 by an angry and aggressive elected city council. Officials such as Inquisitors, prelates, directors of the customs and the mint, taxation officers, army commanders, and directors of the state monopolies lived in official rooms within state buildings. In a few instances, noble residences were rented to officials, but on the whole the state residences of government figures were the open symbols of their positions.[22] They more than represented the state, they were the state. As a matter of long-established policy, Spaniards monopolized high offices in state, army, and church. Since the 1780s, the Crown had renewed its efforts to limit the number of nonpeninsular high officials throughout the empire as a whole, cutting down on the proportion of creole-born oidors, for example, that had existed earlier in the century.[23]

It is still not possible to estimate accurately how large a group this administrative and foreign elite was. The famous census figure of Fernando Navarro y Noriega—that there were no more than 15,000 Europeans in all of New Spain in 1810—does not tell us exactly what we wish to know, because not all 15,000 peninsulars were necessarily members of this elite. Indeed, Ladd and Brading have shown that some peninsulars were not part of any elite. It is clear, at any rate, that the number could not have exceeded 15,000 in 1810.[24] Of this number, about half were soldiers and 1,500 were clergy.[25] There could have been, therefore, no more than 6,000—of whom a very few were female (Humboldt, for example, showed 217 *españolas* in Mexico City)— who engaged in the civil service or in trade. This tiny number of people controlled the government, the army, the church, most external trade, and the wine and textile industries in the internal trade.[26] That so few people, most of whom were not as well educated or as wealthy as the domestic elite, could continue their peaceful domination of a country with a population of over six million is stunning indication of the extent to which Mexicans consented to and collaborated in—or at least did not oppose—Spanish suzerainty.

The chief thing that distinguished the domestic elite from the administrators—for they were closely allied in most regards—was the extent of ownership of all kinds of property. Hence, some of the peninsulars—for example, those engaged in Mexican trade or amalgamated with creole families—might well be counted among the domestic rather than the foreign elite. What was important was not birthplace but the extent to which one's orientation was national or internal rather than imperial. The domestic elite lived in Mexico and made their fortunes there. When the insurrection came, the administrators could go home, but the domestic elite had to survive. Ownership of property, and the local influence that entailed, was the domestic elite's most important characteristic. It set them off from the poor and the royal officials alike, while the amount and value of their property distinguished them from the bourgeoisie. Their property might be in any form—houses, haciendas, mines, mercantile enterprises and inventories, government bonds or investments, shares of pious funds and chaplaincies, equipage, furniture, clothes, jewels, plate, or currency. But in the capital it was their houses, both those in which they lived and those they rented to others, that most distinguished them.

The houses belonging to the richest of this domestic elite were famous. The most elegant residential streets in Mexico City were the Calle San Francisco, Calle Capuchinas, and Calle Cadena. In a nation where an income of 300 pesos a year was a decent living,[27] the wealthiest residences were built at outrageous cost. Ladd cites examples: the mansion that the marqués de Jaral rebuilt as a wedding gift for his daughter cost 100,000 pesos; the house of the great silver miner José de la Borda cost 300,000 pesos; the house of the conde de Jala cost 107,000 pesos; and the house of the marqués de Prado Alegre cost 37,000 pesos just to furnish.[28] Revenue town properties were also extensive. In Mexico City the conde de Santiago owned 31 houses; the mariscal de Castilla owned 28; the Guerrero mayorazgo, 24; the conde de la Cortina, 18; Estevan Escalante, 30; the marqués de Salvatierra, 17; the marquesado del Valle, 37. Of course, members of the most prestigious regular orders would derive from the domestic elite, and these prominent orders were the city's greatest real estate owners.[29]

The ostentation of the domestic elite was partially imposed upon them by a society that measured status by jewels, horses, and houses. The titled nobles, at least, were required to live in the manner of great nobles in order to maintain their titles. Still, they seem to have entered into it with a little extra enthusiasm. The residences of the great families required large retinues to maintain. Ladd cites examples of families with fifteen to thirty-two servants. Besides servants, there would be poor relatives, orphans, and clerics living in their houses. Most of the rich people also maintained, in addition to city residences, one or more haciendas employing hundreds of people and valued at hundreds of thousands of pesos. The marqués de Aguayo owed mortgages equal to nearly double the yearly income of Mexico City.[30] Some of the spectacular fortunes required for this life-style were associated with mining. Brading cites several great eighteenth-century mine owners who invested millions of pesos for reconstruction and drainage of their mines, in return for which the lucky ones made further millions.[31] These pluto-crats were unique in the colonial empire, for wealth such as theirs did not exist in other parts of Spanish America.

It would be a mistake to suppose that these plutocrats and domestic elite were in total agreement with the viceregal admin-istrators. They had many complaints against the imperial re-gime. Some of their complaints, which were chiefly economic, are enumerated by Ladd. The elite sought the abolition of the mayorazgo, the foundation and maintenance of which had become a burdensome expense. They objected to the Bourbon administrative reforms that eliminated ancient hereditary offices that had served the elite as important social distinctions. They objected to the heavy "taxes, trammels and duties" imposed by an empire constantly involved in war and heavily dependent on New Spain's contributions. Brading has shown the extent to which the great families faced absorption of their fortunes by peninsular upstarts who carried off the creole heiresses in marriage while the creole males entered religious life. Brading, Michael Costeloe, and Ladd have shown the extreme dependence of the rich on mortgage capital from the pious funds of the church and from silver financiers and merchants.[32]

Most of all, the elite objected to the Decree of Consolidation of 1804—the nineteenth-century equivalent, in terms of its impact upon the colonial elite, of the New Laws of 1542. The Decree of Consolidation was designed to sequester the funds of pious capellanías, the nation's major source of mortgage capital, to pay for the peninsular wars.[33] This would have required the paying of all outstanding mortgages owed to the church funds, which in effect would have siphoned off perhaps two-thirds of all the capital in New Spain.[34] Most of the rich would have been ruined, for nearly everything they owned was mortgaged. Ladd shows how opposition to the Consolidation, universal among the rich, brought together for the first time the bourgeois proto-nationalist sentiment and the grievances of the elite in a "dramatic incident that the masses could identify with."[35] The amortization was never carried to completion, however, because few of the Mexican debtors could pay their mortgages in full. The collection of Consolidation funds was suspended in New Spain in July, 1808, by a nervous viceroy who was aware that it could provoke revolution, and it was abolished throughout the empire at roughly the same time by the Junta Central, which knew that Spain needed friends and voluntary contributions more than amortization. Its effect, however, was massive, for it convinced many of the elite of the "bad government" of Spain in America. It provoked a desire for autonomy among the plutocrats so that they could guarantee themselves in the future against the danger of such ruinous legislation from Spain. Since they feared the masses and depended upon the ancient traditions of Church and state to maintain social order, the plutocrats did not advocate independence, only autonomy.

Important evidence that extent and type of ownership separated the social classes can be seen in the circumstances of the bourgeoisie. They, like the domestic elite, were predominantly creole, often well educated (indeed, sometimes better educated than the elite, for they were the professionals), and shared with the elite a dependence on internal Mexican political and economic development that made their concerns national rather than imperial. Because they shared so many common concerns with the elite, they have usually been classified simply as creoles, but the gulf that separated them from the elite was immense. It was the difference between an income of thousands of pesos a year and 300 to 500 pesos a year, between owning or renting a house valued at thousands of pesos and renting rooms at a cost of half one's annual income, between constantly expanding horizons and constant frustration of ambition. The petite bourgeoisie aped the elite in clothing and manners but retired from an afternoon at the cafe to dingy rooms, cluttered offices, cramped quarters, unimportant curacies. Villoro brilliantly portrayed them as men without a future—scholastics constantly preaching or talking, unwilling to work with their hands, unable to find the sort of government employment they incessantly sought. Included among them, in addition to that group Villoro discussed, would be the important group, recently isolated by Ladd and Brading, that included ruined mayorazgos, families whose fortunes had fallen, poor peninsular immigrants or creoles who kept shop for the rich, and merchants who had not yet inherited wealth, married into wealth, or purchased their own establishments. They were clearly distinct from the rich in the status-conscious society of New Spain, but it is inappropriate to call them middle class, for they were not in the middle of anything and in comparison with the masses might be viewed as a type of elite. They were not among the dispossessed—except in the sense that they thought the whole country should belong to them by right—but, since they knew what they wanted, they perceived themselves to be burdened with the deepest grievances of any portion of the population. They were barred from fulfillment of their ambitions by a series of glaring inequalities: they were born in the wrong country to achieve high governmental or clerical office, yet they lived in a country where one already had to be very rich to make more money. They were the creators of that proto-nationalist sense of identity that is termed creolism, the first to realize that they were not simply Spaniards living in America, but Americans. Nonetheless, when the insurrection began, they, like the elite, recoiled with horror from the specter of Hidalgo's Indian horde and Morelos's radical social reform. Yet, unlike the elite, they more readily assented to the proposition of independence itself, and some provided the propaganda expertise and other types of leadership for the rebellion that developed out of the first insurrections.

How many of them were there? It is not possible to make a precise estimate, but they probably constituted over half of those 65,000 creoles living in Mexico City, plus some of the 2,500 gachupines, depending on status and kinship group. But their numbers had no direct bearing on their social, political, or economic power, for the handful of Spanish administrators and the small group of domestic plutocrats controlled politics and economic affairs. It would not be surprising, therefore, to find the petite bourgeoisie in conflict with the domestic elite in 1808 and throughout the war years. Nor would it be surprising to find them temporarily allied in 1821 for the achievement of what briefly became common objectives. As shall be seen, the city council of Mexico represented both these groups, which was a fundamental cause of its frequent confusion and inability to act.

In the tense political atmosphere of early nineteenth-century Mexico, the domestic elite and the bourgeoisie did have one important characteristic in common. They shared a sense of identity as creoles that, not yet sufficiently cogent to be termed nationalism, is best called proto-nationalism or creolism. The best treatment of this subject is by David A. Brading, who finds its essential elements to be the native Americans' patriotic dedication to the idea that the Europeans who held most of the important offices in late colonial New Spain were outsiders, foreigners who were mere travelers in the land that the creole called his own.[36] Throughout the three centuries of Spain's colonial rule, Europeans had denigrated the abilities, talents, physical vigor, and mentality of the Americans, while the Americans, in self-defense, had created a series of counter-myths about themselves. By the 1780s creole patriotism in Mexico had assumed a unique and particular form not seen in any of the other Spanish American territories. Mexican creoles were dedicated to three chief myths—that they were the heirs of the Aztecs, a thoroughly civilized and cultured society unjustly snuffed out by the invasion of the Spaniards (this was called Neo-Aztecism); that their population was a unique blend of the Indian and European cultures personified in the mestizo, and that this new people had received the direct and immediate protection of the All Powerful in the appearance of the Virgin of Guadalupe; and that the Spanish Conquest was an unjust and illegal act, therefore Mexico still belonged to the Mexicans, not to the Spaniards. Mexican creolism received its most important prerebellion summary in the *Historia antigua de México* of the exiled Mexican Jesuit Francisco Clavijero. The various reforms of the Bourbon monarchs in the last century—the expulsion of the Jesuits, the improved fiscal exploitation of the colonies, the gradual replacement of creole office holders with peninsulars, the attack on the privileges of the clergy, the new wave of immigration from the peninsula, and the general reinvigoration of the economy and administration—all served to strengthen the creoles' sense of self-identification as Americans, distinct from the peninsulars and with differing political objectives. However, not until the War of Independence was this proto-nationalism converted, particularly through the political writings of Fray Servando Teresa de Mier and Carlos María Bustamante, into a full-fledged anti-Spanish nationalism. The niceties and complexities of this growing sense of Mexicanism were, in all probability, unknown to the lower strata of Mexican society, and yet it was to them that the *Grito de Dolores* of Father Hidalgo, framed in the very symbols and myths of this intellectual proto-nationalism, would have its most emotional, and most destructive, appeal.

On the bottom of the social ladder were the poor, who lived so horribly in Mexico City that every visitor commented upon it. Poinsett, while finding Mexico City in general more grand and imposing than any city of the United States, went on to say: "With us, however, a stranger does not see that striking and disgusting contrast between the magnificence of the wealthy and the squalid penury of the poor, which constantly meets his view in Mexico."[37] The most fortunate poor owned their own adobe houses on the outskirts of the city or were attached to the establishment of their employers—servants living in the great and small houses, employees living in their master's shops, day laborers living in accommodations provided near public works, inmates of sweat-shops sleeping next to their machinery, or-phans and servant children living in schools, foundling homes, or convents. Some thousands of conscripts lived in army barracks. At any one time a few hundred of the poor lived in

municipal, ecclesiastical, and viceregal jails. But the vast majority of the poor were not as fortunate. They lived in multiple-
dwelling vecindades, slums, hovels and lean-tos thrown up
beside fences and walls, in dumps for night soil and animal
waste, in the open pastures and parks, in flop-houses, in stables
and barns, in the stalls at the public markets. Dr. Luis Montaña
in 1813 ascribed the rapid spread of the devastating epidemic of
that year to the fact that the poor "live like prisoners in shacks
hidden away in a maze of alleys and lots, which are surrounded
by rubbish, manure piles, and puddles."[38]

The most shocking fact of life in Mexico City was not how
many poor there were, but how many were utterly indigent.
Poinsett estimated that at least 20,000 of the capital's 150,000
inhabitants had no permanent place of abode and no means of
gaining a livelihood.[39] These were the so-called léperos, largely
mestizo, mulatto, or Indian, who earned their living from
begging or from sporadic employment. They were the largest
single identifiable group among the poor. They constituted a
serious threat to social order, not only because of their drunk-
enness and crime, but because of the strain they put upon
institutions of charity and government. Enrique Florescano says
that in the periodic cycles of skyrocketing maize prices and
agricultural crisis that swept New Spain in its last century,
perhaps a majority of the population of Mexico City were
léperos.[40] Madame Calderón's hair-raising stories of beggars at
her windows and murders on her doorstep illustrate that there
were still many léperos after independence.

There were, of course, great differences among the poor in
income and standard of living. The léperos had no fixed income.
Better off were the many half-rural, half-urban peons—Indians
and castes—who lived in the city but worked in the farms on the
outskirts. Florescano says their salaries at the end of the
eighteenth century were 1.5 to 2.5 reales a day (for a total of 60
to 114 pesos a year). In addition, they received a weekly maize
ration, which Florescano estimates was enough to feed a family
of four for three days. These were the people who kept Mexico
City fed. Approximately 6,000 of them traveled in and out of the
city every day, supplying the markets with fresh produce and
charcoal for cooking. Among the poor, the best situated were

artisans and workers in specialized trades, with average salaries of 3, 5, or even 8 or 10 reales a day (or 100 to 300 pesos a year).[41]

The poor lived on the margin of survival, totally dependent on the maize crop to provide their staple food. In the last century of the colonial regime, New Spain suffered ten major cycles of agricultural crisis, price increases, and economic decline and disruption. The last occurred in 1808, 1809, and 1810, and Florescano believes it was the match that ignited the insurrection. In these periods of crisis the price of maize in Mexico City would increase from 100 to 300 percent, driving the léperos to starvation, while the working poor were forced to spend the major part of their income on mere subsistence. These agricultural crises were characterized by a decline in maize production and a corresponding increase in price, leading to the death of work animals in mining and farming, causing widespread unemployment, and sending thousands of homeless, destitute people flocking to the cities, especially the capital. This in turn caused major outbreaks of social unrest and, more disastrous still, of disease. Florescano has shown that, of the ten major epidemics in Mexico City in the last century before independence, seven occurred in conjunction with agricultural crises. The 1808–1811 agricultural crisis was followed by the 1813 epidemic in Mexico City, which killed over 20,000 people, mostly the poor. In the 1736–1739 epidemic, Mexico City lost nearly 50 percent of its population; in 1761–1762, more than 25 percent; in 1772, 1779, and 1797–1798, between 10 and 15 percent.[42]

The statistics concerning increases in the price of maize for the last two decades before independence largely tell the story of what was happening to the poor in that period. In 1790 maize sold at a low of 16 and at a high of 21 reales per fanega; in 1811, at the height of the last price and production crisis, maize sold as high as 36 reales per fanega for months on end, and the median price for that year was 36. This last spiral of prices represented increases of over 300 percent compared to the 1790s.[43]

The immense social and economic differences that prevailed in late New Spain can best be seen in a comparison of incomes with cost of living. The working poor had cash incomes of about 60 to 300 pesos a year. Many received income in kind or accommodations that cannot be computed, but such income is relatively unimportant because Mexico City had a cash-market economy and the poor had to buy most of their needs with cash rather than by barter. The petite bourgeoisie income started at about 300 pesos a year, though 500 pesos a year was probably the margin of comfort. Among royal administrators, the ordinary bureaucrats and functionaries earned 500 to 1,000 pesos a year, while canons and departmental directors or ranking members of the bureaucracy received from 1,000 to 10,000 pesos yearly. Many officials also received noncash remuneration, chiefly housing. It is not possible to compute annual incomes for nonsalaried members of the plutocracy, but 5,000 to 10,000 pesos a year would be a conservative estimate, while some received upwards of 100,000 pesos a year. The income difference between working poor and rich was as great as the ratio of 1:1,000. For the poor, the basic essentials of survival could absorb nearly all their income. Humboldt said that Mexico City, with a population in his day of 137,000, had consumed 352,000 fanegas of maize a year as of the census of 1791.[44] Though this was the staple of the poor (the whites consumed wheat), the figures still reveal a median per person consumption in the city of about 2.6 fanegas of maize a year. Since the 1811 price was 36 reales a fanega, a family of four would spend about 374 reales (or 46.7 pesos) a year on maize alone. This sum represents perhaps the entire income of many destitute families, nearly half the annual income of a peon family, and a fourth or more of the annual income of a lower-paid artisan family. This can be expressed in per capita terms as well. Clark Reynolds, using the figures of Henry Aubrey and Fernando Rosenzweig, reasons that the per capita income of New Spain at the close of the colonial era was 20 to 32 pesos a year.[45] In 1811 the per capita cost of maize alone was 11.7 pesos a year, or close to half the per capita income. There can be no doubt that, in spite of the multitude of real or imagined complaints of the elite and bourgeoisie alike, it was the poor who paid the price for the failures of the royal system.

In short, all the social inequities and political tensions that characterized New Spain in general in the late colonial era were present in Mexico City, but in a more concentrated form. The city's rich lived at the highest level of ostentation and expenditure. Its poor lived marginal lives, since many did not have small farm plots for sustenance in time of high prices and depended upon a highly concentrated, and thus susceptible, market system. Its frustrated bourgeoisie, envious of the affluence of the elite creoles, found excuses for their status anxieties in the restrictions that were in turn imposed upon the imperial regime by the political necessity of preserving the country in unquestioned Spanish control. The city even had a higher death rate and lower birth rate than New Spain as a whole because of the much greater density of population and the higher proportion of celibate men and women.[46]

Reformist or insurrectionary tendencies were also highly concentrated in the capital, but they could not break out there as freely as they did in the provinces because the capital was the royal regime's center of strength. All the trappings and symbols of a living and functional imperialism were highly articulated in the capital. The city itself was the grandee of all colonial cities, and knew itself to be. It was granted by royal command the right to be called "imperial, significant, loyal, and most noble city," and bore in addition the official titles of "capital, court, and head" of New Spain. In official documents and public propaganda it was never referred to by any sobriquet other than *este N.C.* (*Nobilísima Ciudad*)—this most noble city. The high point of the city's official calendar was August 13, the day of San Hipólito, anniversary of Cortés's conquest. On that day the city celebrated the ceremony of the royal pendant (*real pendón*) and renewed its vows of grateful subservience to the monarch.[47]

Mexico City was thus the center and chief focus of that majestic authority upon which Spanish political control depended. No mere handful of transient colonial bureaucrats or prelates could artificially create that authority, for it rested upon the willing grant of the right to govern to the Spanish Crown and its constituted representatives. The residents of the capital obviously collaborated in and helped sustain imperial authority. They did so not only because it seemed in their best interests, but also because they believed in it. Such faith and loyalty to the regime was a force that no amount of grievances, no amount of social or economic inequality, could automatically or instantly disrupt. This strength of authority in Mexico City was behind the city's long hesitation to choose one of the many alternatives for change, any one of which would have carried the nation if

the city had chosen it. There were massive and pent-up grievances against Spain, to be sure, but any alternative would have
to be acceptable to the people who controlled Mexico City's
economy and society—as well as to the provincial elite—before
it could succeed.

The local government of Mexico City was vested in its city
council (cabildo or ayuntamiento). As the only governmental
institution in which the city's 65,000 creoles were represented,
the council served throughout the War of Independence as a
focus of the struggle between domestic and imperial priorities.
The cabildo was composed of hereditary members—hence,
creoles—whose families had often purchased their seats nearly a
century ago. It therefore stood for the creole point of view and
often came into conflict with the other branch of the royal
government in the capital—the viceregal power.

One should not, however, leap to the conclusion that the
cabildo represented directly the interests of only the domestic
plutocrats, for family wealth rose and fell so rapidly in New
Spain that some of the proprietary councilors—men whose
families had been the richest of the elite a generation earlier—
were now ruined mayorazgos, as Alamán said.[48] In the person
of some of its members, therefore, the cabildo also represented
the bourgeoisie.

There were fifteen hereditary regidors (aldermen) on the city
council. They were always creole, except in the rare case where
a proprietary seat lapsed and the closest heir was a peninsular.
The council exercised general direction of the city, and each
member was assigned supervision over two of the thirty-two
wards into which the town was divided (the remaining two
were assigned to either of the two alcaldes during the half-year
when he was not serving as chairman of the council).

There was a separate system of alcaldes de barrio under
auspices of the audiencia's Sala del Crímen. Created in 1782 by
Viceroy Martín de Mayorga, it consisted of eight major districts
supervised by members of the audiencia (calling on the corregidor or cabildo magistrates, or alcaldes ordinarios, if extra
judges were needed), and thirty-two minor quarteles supervised by thirty-two alcaldes de barrio appointed without pay
from among residents of each district. The alcalde de barrio

conducted court of first instance in criminal matters and was directly responsible to the audiencia. This was a simple and mutually agreeable division of duties between the audiencia and city council that was disrupted in 1809 by the creation of the Junta of Security, which was superseded in 1810 by the Junta of Police and Public Security, a paramilitary police force.[49]

The leadership of the city council was a source of constant complaint from viceroys and audiencia alike. The many accusations of inadequacy, ignorance, senility, or conflict of interest were probably true—the cabildo gave more than adequate sign of functional senility—but underlying the superior authorities' complaints was their suspicion of the politics of these fifteen aldermen. The chief complaint was that no peninsulars served in the entailed proprietary chairs, for as long as the old families could produce an heir who had the money to pay the purchase price, be he son, grandson, nephew, cousin, or even in-law of the incumbent, there was no legal mechanism by which the administration could impose peninsulars upon the cabildo. Proprietary chairs were also inherited by women, who transferred them to male relatives, including in-laws (thus causing name changes). There was, however, a check and countercheck in the system: the aldermen were creole and deeply entrenched, but they were also usually unable to provide aggressive leadership to the creole majority; on the other hand, the viceroy and the audiencia could not alter the proprietary membership.

The only significant reform in the cabildo structure occurred in 1772. As one of the major Bourbon reforms in local government, the cabildo was required to elect six honorary regidors from among the leading local citizens. In Mexico City three of these had to be peninsular. These men helped provide fresh leadership in an organization that might otherwise have died from inbreeding. They not only were better councilors than the hereditary members, but consistently provided aggressive leadership. There was the rub. The proprietary members almost always chose the honorary members from among the upwardly mobile elite—new rich or well-entrenched old rich. Three of the six had to be peninsulars, but as members of the domestic elite, they were rich men whose interests and homes were in Mexico and who agreed to serve on the cabildo to protect those interests. They identified with creole political objectives. In the cabildo, too, the creole-peninsular dichotomy was muted by commercial or business interests and kinship. When peninsular Bassocos, Yermos, or Fagoagas served on the council, they were usually advocates of limited autonomy rather than peninsular absolutism. In the long run what was important was whether a man was concerned with the advancement of national interests or imperial interests, and in that context the cabildo was the focus of Mexican domestic goals rather than international imperial political goals. The very election of Bassocos, Yermos, or Fagoagas by creole aldermen shows that they viewed them as kindred spirits. And why not? The Bassocos and Fagoagas, though peninsulars, were married to the Villaurrutias and Castañizas, while the Yermos owed everything to Mexican property.[50] Mere place of birth would not override self-interest in determining their political priorities. Gabriel de Yermo, leader of the 1808 coup, never served on the cabildo, but his nephew, Gabriel Patricio, was elected in 1820–1821.

The 1772 reform thus had not accomplished one of its objectives—the injection of administration sycophants into the city council—but it did succeed in making the cabildo a rather more aggressive focus of national interests than it might have been otherwise. When the cabildo worked well, which was rarely, it was often because of the leadership of the honorary aldermen.

The cabildo elected at the beginning of every year two alcaldes ordinarios and two syndics or attorneys (síndicos procuradores). The alcaldes served as chairmen of the council and had charge of municipal affairs in general. In Mexico City, one of the two alcaldes had to be a peninsular. The man who received the highest number of votes (the "alcalde of the first vote") presided in the first six months, and the man who received the next highest (the "alcalde of the second vote") presided for the last half of the year. These positions carried tremendous local prestige. If their possessors were men of great ability, they could also carry considerable power, but the office was what a man chose to make of it. The syndics, or city attorneys, were also chosen yearly, often for repeating terms if they had done their job well and could afford to continue. It was a good way to augment their legal trade. They represented the city in legal statements to the higher authorities, provided internal opinions, and also had the traditional task of safeguarding the rights of the citizenry. They were always professionals, and their opinion was almost always followed by the council. Usually both syndics were creole, since there was no regulation to the contrary.

Except for two major but very short-lived reforms under the Constitution of the Spanish Monarchy in 1812 and 1820, the council remained in this form until independence. With fifteen proprietary members, six honorary members, two alcaldes, and two syndics, it was as large a cabildo as allowed by law. Of this total of twenty-five, four (three honorary regidors and one alcalde) had to be peninsular. In 1813 and 1814, and again in 1820 and 1821, the membership was elected. In other years there was often confusion as to membership resulting from deaths or the inheritance of proprietary chairs.

A peculiar anomaly of the Mexico City council was the presence, as a sort of ex-oficio chairman, of the intendant of the province of Mexico, who simultaneously held the title of corregidor of the municipality. Throughout the War of Independence the office was held by Ramón Gutiérrez del Mazo. He was a strange figure, a professional bureaucrat who collected a salary of 7,000 pesos and lived free of charge in the municipal palace, but had little to do either in the city or the province because his powers were regularly and naturally preempted by the viceroy—after all it was the viceroy's royal capital. In addition, the councilors loathed him as a royal toady imposed upon them, the viceroys resented his duplication of powers, and the ministers of the audiencia thought he usurped some of their prerogatives. He was a focus of the tension that existed between the superior authorities and the city.

The city council did not object to the intendancy, but to Mazo's simultaneous possession of the corregimiento. While Mazo served continuously as intendant from 1810 to 1826, there were periods when he was simultaneously corregidor. For several years before Mazo's original appointment, the corregimiento of Mexico City had been vacant. During that period the alcalde of the cabildo served as chairman of the city council "with the powers of the corregimiento," while supervision over the city's property was temporarily vested in an oidor of the audiencia. This was a fairly logical division of powers, acceptable to both. On August 1, 1810, Mazo was granted the offices of intendant and corregidor by the "provisional government" of Spain (as the audiencia insisted on calling the regime at Cádiz). So from 1810 to 1812 he held the corregimiento. In 1812, however, the Cortes disestablished the corregimiento in Mexico City and distributed its powers back to the cabildo and audiencia. The situation became intensely confused when, upon Ferdinand VII's restoration to the throne in 1814, all enactments of the Cortes were abolished, and all governmental positions were ordered returned to the men who held them as of March 18, 1808. In 1808 Mazo had not held the corregimiento, yet the clear intent of the king's order was to restore the old forms of absolutist royal government, one of whose chief creatures was the corregimiento. Was Mazo corregidor or not? The viceroy and the audiencia decided in January, 1815, that Mazo must give up the office and that its powers would be divided again between the cabildo and audiencia as they had been in 1808. As a result, the city council ordered Mazo to pay rent of 1,000 pesos a year on his free apartment in the city building. He refused on the grounds that it had been granted by the Crown as an emolument of the intendancy, not of the corregimiento. The audiencia had to agree because of the clarity of wording in Mazo's cedula of appointment.[51] At any rate, from 1812 to 1817 Mazo was not corregidor, though in the constitutional period he served as chairman of the Provincial Deputation and was briefly imposed by Viceroy Calleja as chairman of the elected city council. Having decided Mazo did not possess the corregimiento, the audiencia referred its decision to the king for approval in 1815. Typically, the king reversed everything. In 1817 he replied that Mazo should regain the office on the grounds that a city council contract of 1738 to buy off the corregimiento for 200,000 pesos had not been fulfilled. The city had paid only 10,000 pesos of that sum. Ferdinand offered to allow it to pay the remainder within a year, otherwise the corregimiento would remain. Unable to pay, the city council let the matter drop.[52] From 1817 to 1820, therefore, Mazo again served as corregidor. Then in 1820, upon restoration of the Constitution, the whole matter was again opened for debate, revolving around the question of whether the Constitution meant the city council to be chaired by the intendant in his role as political chief of the province, the viceroy in his role as political chief of the kingdom, or the alcalde. The cabildo said alcalde, the viceroy said viceroy, and the intendant lost the battle. Though expelled from his free lodging this time, he remained as intendant and presided over the Provincial Deputation. In September, 1821, when Iturbide triumphed over the city, Mazo was given the powers of local political chief to supervise the transition of power, though this was done as a matter of convenience and was not meant to be a precedent for restoration of the corregimiento.

In short, the corregimiento was an anomaly, a historical problem inherited from the past that no one seemed able to remedy. It was a grievance that the cabildo—whether proprietary or elected—always complained about, as did the city's first deputy to the Cortes of Cádiz.[53] In general it might be said that, although Viceroy Calleja used Mazo to help soften the blow of the Constitution, Mazo was not a very effective city official because the duplication of authority that his office entailed lessened the strength of his position.

At any rate, the three most important characteristics of the cabildo were: (1) the extent to which it was the focus of nonimperial, or local and national, concerns, whether its members were exclusively creole or not—in this it sometimes provoked great tension with viceregal authorities; (2) its frequent confusion or inability to act—partly its own fault, partly imposed upon it; and (3) the fact that within the total population of the city it represented two constituencies. The cabildo was a center of privilege and everyone knew it, but its constituency consisted of both the domestic elite and the creole bourgeoisie. On certain issues, this double constituency would cause considerable confusion in the cabildo, and it was more often the focus of conspiracies in support of autonomy than outright independence. While its bourgeois members favored more radical action, its elite members kept its objectives limited to autonomy. When it made an aggressive bid for leadership of the creole population as a whole, as in 1808 and again under the Constitution, its own internal inconsistencies did as much as viceregal pressure to nip any extremism in the bud. The several shifts in cabildo policy— its radicalism in 1808 followed by a period of dormancy up to 1812, then a second attempt to exert itself on the national political scene, followed by another period of dormancy, then a flowering of the autonomist urge in 1821 quickly converted to a desire for independence—were all due to this combination of external opposition and internal confusion. At all times, the city council also took very seriously its professed role of speaking for all of Mexico City and even for the kingdom as a whole.

Although the cabildo had charge of a vast number of local activities and services, its freedom of action was severely limited by the audiencia and the viceroy. The audiencia, the chief court of the kingdom, was granted extensive power to intervene in local finance and public works.[54] Theoretically it was required to approve all ordinances passed by the cabildo, and in many cases it legislated directly in matters of local interest. Its appellate jurisdiction as a court of law in cases originating in municipal courts meant that it often overshadowed the cabildo in local judicial matters. Much of the history of the city council during the War of Independence can be told in terms of its increasingly bold struggle for autonomy against the powerful and conservative audiencia and its loyalist magistrates or oidors.

The power of the viceroy was even greater than that of the audiencia, especially because during the War of Independence the office was held by three of the most vigorous and effective men in its history—Francisco Javier Venegas (1810–1813), Félix María Calleja del Rey (1813–1816) and Juan Ruiz de Apodaca (1816–1821). The viceroy exercised personal supervision over the governmental and military affairs of his capital. He controlled its purse through his power to grant, with royal approval, rights to various sources of income (*propios*). The viceroy and audiencia acting together—the so-called real acuerdo—constituted the highest political or legislative power in the kingdom outside of royal intervention.

What then were the duties of the city council? A set of trimesterly reports of income and expenses published by the cabildo in 1820 reveals the following: Most of its revenue was spent in maintenance and repair of city property, for it had charge of the upkeep of causeways, bridges, aqueducts, and drainage ditches. The largest single expense in 1820–1821 was garbage collection and cleaning. In the last years of the War of Independence garbage services were in the hands of a private contractor, though at other times the municipality itself managed the service. The city also spent a good deal of money on maintenance of the public paseos and the Alameda park, although this too was sometimes given over to private contractors. In health and education, it helped to support a number of hospitals and schools. At the end of 1820, because the liberal constitutional government in Spain had abolished several religious orders, it was required to support four of the city's hospitals. It had charge of the preservation and distribution of the lifesaving smallpox vaccine. In times of epidemic, as in 1813, it was responsible for meeting most of the expenses of emergency measures, treatment centers, and medicines. It supported two schools directly, both ancient institutions for the care of mestizo and foundling children. It was also required by royal order to pay for the education of a number of children enrolled in other schools and to give an annual contribution of 1,000 pesos to the Royal Academy of San Carlos, the Mexican school of fine arts.[55]

The cabildo maintained its own jail and court and a standing constabulary force, which by 1820 consisted of a chief and lieutenant, eight sergeants, and ninety-four guards. The reflecting oil lamps that lighted the municipal squares, including the purchase of oil and employment of lamplighters, were also a city responsibility. Maintenance of the publicly owned markets, which were strictly supervised even to the point of regulating prices, distribution, quality of products and hours of sale, was a municipal activity absorbing the energy of several aldermen. The cabildo also supervised slaughterhouses and the sale of meat. For regulation of market practices it maintained an office of weights and measures.

One of the council's chief functions was the arrangement of a bewildering array of ceremonial affairs. It paid for special bull fights, religious ceremonies, and public acclamations honoring significant events in the empire. Special illuminations of the viceregal palace and municipal buildings were invariably required. These ceremonial functions were important, but the cost was a burden that often required sacrifice in some other public service. As the war years progressed, the royal ceremonies were cut to a minimum.

The operating costs of the council—salaries, upkeep of the municipal palace, secretarial supplies, the cost of elections, and travel expenses for Cortes delegates—absorbed the last major portion of its income. The city had a huge debt by 1820, hovering between 640,000 and 680,000 pesos, which it serviced in an ad hoc fashion whenever spare funds were available.[56]

The council derived the often insufficient revenue to meet such varied expenses from two major sources and a variety of lesser ones. The largest single source was municipal taxes (derechos municipales) over specified articles of the national customs. Among the items on which taxes were collected by the viceregal government on the city's behalf were European and domestic liquor, vinegar, wheat, corn, barley, pulque, sheep, cattle, and goats.[57] In the first full year of published financial reports (June, 1820–June, 1821), this tax netted over 108,000 pesos, accounting for over 46 percent of that year's income. The other major source of revenue was property. The municipality owned the major markets, the largest of which was the Parián, and rented concessions to merchants. Other property included a number of houses, corrals, and municipal commons (ejidos) rented out as pasturage to finish animals destined for city markets. In all, the city's property was valued at approximately 750,000 pesos.[58] Minor and subsidiary sources of revenue during the War of Independence included a tax on carriages for hire, the sale of water through the municipal aqueducts to outlying farms, and the deposit of trusts from citizens. In 1820 the city's total income was 230,000 pesos, or about 1.5 pesos per inhabitant. The yearly total varied considerably, and during the worst years of the war income was insufficient to meet municipal needs.

This, then, was the most noble city of Mexico, in 1810 the largest municipality in the New World. With such inequalities among the various classes and such political grievances and tensions, one is inclined to assume that independence was inevitable. And yet, when confronted over the next few years with a series of threats that would destroy many political systems, the royal regime survived and emerged apparently stronger than ever. The problem of how it survived is just as important as how it eventually failed.

Chapter 2

The Main Threat: Autonomy

THE MAIN THREAT to royal sovereignty throughout the War of Independence was the desire for autonomy among both the bourgeoisie and the elite. Autonomism received its first major enunciation in 1808 but was rapidly and skillfully suppressed by friends of royal absolutism. In 1810 it was superseded by the outbreak of violent insurrection. Miguel Hidalgo's *Grito de Dolores* of 1810 was a natural result of the suppression of the autonomist drive two years earlier, but it represented a very different constituency and called for very different objectives. The elite autonomists could not support it, nor could many of the creole bourgeoisie autonomists. Thus the idea of limited autonomy within the imperial system was shunted aside by the sound and fury that followed the *Grito*. Autonomy remained, however, the principal objective of the domestic elite and bourgeoisie, resurfacing during both constitutional periods. Finally Spain so discredited itself that autonomists converted to the Plan of Iguala, calling for very much the same reforms as before, but within the context of total separation from Spain. The autonomist program is the one constant that runs throughout the War of Independence period. It succeeded where waves of revolution failed because it acquired the support of the policy-making elite; it was the only alternative that could succeed.

35

When first presented in 1808, however, the autonomist formula fell short of victory because its supporters were confused and factionalized by the catastrophic events in the mother country. It was suppressed by a group of peninsulars who overthrew Viceroy José de Iturrigaray on the night of September 15–16, 1808, in a coup d'état designed to preempt further developments by neutralizing the supporters of autonomy. The events of September, 1808, are usually oversimplified as the classic confrontation of creole versus gachupine. There were creoles and gachupines on both sides, and the confrontation was actually one of domestic political objectives versus imperial political objectives, rising out of the imperial government's decadence in the Manuel Godoy era and the accumulated grievances of New Spain's inhabitants of every class and color. It was the beginning, however inadequate and confused, of the struggle for national self-determination.

The urge for autonomy was motivated, on the part of the elite and other property owners, by opposition to the 1804 Decree of Consolidation, which attempted to amortize all outstanding loans owed to pious funds and collect them for transfer to the peninsula. The disposal of the 10.5 million pesos actually collected in New Spain from the Consolidation, of which 2.5 million pesos came from the archdiocese of Mexico alone, was the ultimate sign of the decadence of the Spanish administration of King Charles IV and Manuel Godoy. More than half a million pesos collected in New Spain were absorbed by graft on the part of Viceroy Iturrigaray and others, while five million pesos of Consolidation funds were turned over to Napoleon by Godoy's agent in Paris.[1] The elite's grievance against the Consolidation, as has been said, combined with the proto-nationalist grievances of the creole bourgeoisie to unite both classes briefly in common recognition of the extent to which imperial government was potentially harmful to colonial interests. This discontent, reaching its peak between 1804 and 1808, characterized gachupine and creole alike.

For a brief span of time, the majority of literate people in the viceroyalty of New Spain could and did define their common enemy as 'bad government' and their common cause as Mexican development. . . . It was articulated by nobles, by entrepreneurs, by reform-minded clergymen and lawyers, by threatened property-owners, large and small. . . . It did not divide Spaniards and Creoles.[2]

In short, an alliance of interest was beginning to form between the elite and bourgeoisie, one that disregarded the traditional creole-gachupine division. This incipient alliance, however, was broken up by the reaction of various parts of the politically active population to the crisis that swept metropolitan Spain in early 1808. For years Spanish foreign policy had been a game of cat and mouse, with Charles IV's chief minister, Manuel Godoy, attempting to maintain the friendship of Napoleon. The game ended in the spring of 1808 when Napoleon's troops poured into Spain, by permission of Godoy, on their way to occupy Portugal. This event led to a coup by which the king's son, the prince of Asturias, forced the abdication of his father and assumed the throne as Ferdinand VII.[3] This change was announced to the people of Mexico City on June 9, 1808, in the official newspaper, the *Gazeta de México*. In the same *Gazeta* the people read that the Portuguese royal family, fleeing the French armies, had arrived in exile in Brazil. The progress of the new king to the city of Bayonne to meet with Napoleon was also announced. The cabildo prepared a letter inviting the king to emulate the Portuguese and take up residence in Mexico City, "where with open arms your loyal vassals will receive you."[4] It had no time to send the offer, for on July 16 the *Gazeta* carried the stunning news from Bayonne that Ferdinand had returned the crown to his father, who then renounced it in favor of Napoleon. Joseph Bonaparte, brother of the French emperor, usurped the throne of Spain and the Indies. On July 29 Mexico City heard the news of the uprising in Madrid against the French conquerors—the *Dos de Mayo*—and of the creation of a junta of loyalists in Valencia to resist the usurper. On August 1 the creation of another junta at Seville was announced.[5]

These calamities provoked massive political crises in all parts of America, especially in Mexico City, where the regime was totally unprepared. Viceroy Iturrigaray and many other royal officials were appointees and friends of Godoy, who was now hated as a traitor. Their discredit intensified. The mother country was conquered by its former ally while England, Spain's former enemy, now became its friend. In less than two weeks, as Mexicans saw it, they lost two monarchs, while the definition of sovereignty itself was cast into total confusion. Rival juntas in Spain claimed to possess legitimate authority in the absent monarch's name. A former Mexican viceroy, Miguel de Azanza, helped proclaim the French takeover in Spain and was made Joseph Bonaparte's minister of the Indies. For a time, confusion and shock were universal. What does a country that is governed by an absolute monarch do when the former king, his heir, and the entire dynasty fall captive to a foreign enemy while a usurper takes the throne?

Three basic points of view began to emerge. One, proclaimed on July 15, a day before arrival of the news of the usurpation of the throne by Joseph Bonaparte, was formulated by two members of the city council, the syndic José Primo Verdad and the honorary regidor Juan Francisco Azcárate. This plan was a call for autonomy in the form of the creation of a Mexican provisional government to rule in Ferdinand's name. It was not a call for independence—though it could easily have developed into one, as the establishment of provisional governments did in Caracas, Santiago, Buenos Aires, and Bogotá—but to political conservatives, it seemed to be just that. The second plan, advocated by the most conservative members of the audiencia and of the elite, was simply to wait and see what developed in Spain, meanwhile maintaining the absolutist form of government in New Spain with no alterations. The third plan, advocated by other members of the audiencia and elite, was to recognize the Junta of Seville as the legitimate representative of the absent king. They favored Seville over its rival juntas largely because of Seville's long history of involvement in American affairs and because it lay in a part of the country that was not at first overrun by the French and was close enough to the sea to maintain communications with America.

In the next three months these three contradictory plans contested for dominance. In the process, the developing alliance of domestic elite and bourgeoisie collapsed, and a new emphasis was given to place of birth. Mexicans struggled to take advantage of Spain's paralysis and move toward autonomy, while peninsulars, conscious that Mexican resources could keep Spain from defeat, struggled to reaffirm the mother country's control over its richest colony. The elite-bourgeoisie alliance would not form again until 1821.

At the center of the struggle was Viceroy Iturrigaray, who had been in office since 1803.[6] Owing to the suspicion in which he was held by many inhabitants, peninsular and creole alike, because of his long involvement in graft and his close attachment to the party of Godoy, his position was particularly vulnerable. On the eve of this unforeseen crisis Tomás Antonio Campomanes, a cousin of Spain's great liberal statesman the conde de Campomanes, expressed in a letter to the prince of Asturias the misgivings of the peninsular elite about Iturrigaray. He urged the prince to assert his influence against the party of Godoy, which in America was personified by Iturrigaray. In a cover letter to his friend the duke of Medinaceli, Campomanes warned, "A very strong revolution is at hand" unless Iturrigaray were removed from power, for the viceroy was "the worst of the evils [*el mal de los males*] among all the inhabitants of America."[7]

This widespread contemporary suspicion of the viceroy still leads some modern authors to conclude that he was the leader of a conspiracy for independence or a conspiracy to make himself king of Mexico.[8] In fact, there is no substantial evidence that he had any aspirations to independence or to establish a throne for himself. He was not an initiator of these events but was, rather, caught up in them and destroyed by them. What can be said of him—and given his powerful position, it is just as damning as accusing him of treason—is that he allowed himself to be so compromised in the crisis that he became vulnerable, both contemporaneously and historically, to any accusation. His vulnerability paralyzed his ability to provide leadership in the crisis. He is a perfect symbol of the decline of viceregal administration, a decline that was to be ably reversed by Venegas, Calleja, and Apodaca.

It is not that Iturrigaray was inactive in face of the July crisis; indeed, the conservatives might have preferred him to be. He continued to use his full powers as viceroy, inspite of the fact that the *rey* to his *virrey* was in dispute. On July 22 he suspended Consolidation collections, probably in order to assure the loyalty of the proprietors. He instructed military commanders to buy arms from the United States in case of French attack. Most important of all, he listened with care to the autonomists, which to the absolutists was the equivalent of treason. Every act of the viceroy, many of which were not compromising in themselves, provoked further hostile suspicion.

Conservative oidors, for their part, suspected Iturrigaray's loyalty from the moment they heard of the abdication of Charles IV, or so they later claimed in their testimony at his residencia (the legal review of his term of office). They declared that the viceroy at first ordered no public acclamation of Ferdinand VII's accession and that he was only moved to do so after the regent Pedro Catani personally asked him to. The audiencia reported that Iturrigaray was defeatist, believing the Bourbons would never return to the throne. This defeatism alarmed the ministers, although it would have required the blind faith of a fanatic in July, 1808, to foresee that Ferdinand would ever be restored. In addition, the oidors remembered that the creole councilor Azcárate, a notorious proponent of autonomy, frequently visited Iturrigaray and was considered his protegé. It was, in their view, just plain bad politics. "As a result of the viceroy's bad politics," they attested, "all types of conspiracies for independence began to originate in the capital."[9] A resident of Jalapa wrote only three days after receipt of the news of the usurpation that since that day "nothing is whispered in this kingdom except independence."[10]

Still further suspicions were created by the viceroy's month-long delay in announcing to the city council the accession of Ferdinand VII. He made the announcement on July 14.[11] Only two days later, news arrived of the usurpation by Joseph Bonaparte, completely confusing the picture again. In an effort to pressure the viceroy into declaring his undivided loyalty to the new king, the audiencia on July 15 asked him to announce that New Spain would recognize only Ferdinand. The editor of the *Gazeta*, Juan López Cancelada, was ordered to publish such a resolution. However, he showed the draft of the statement to the viceroy, who refused to approve it and ordered it not to be printed. How was the viceroy's action to be interpreted? The oidors ascribed it to his unwillingness to swear allegiance to Ferdinand. Indeed, as a protegé of Godoy and a servant of

Charles IV, Iturrigaray might have been ambivalent toward Ferdinand. However, the more likely reason for his delay was the sheer confusion of the moment. It was not clear, even to the viceroy, whether the royal father or son was king, and the fact that the son traveled freely into French captivity while the father abdicated no less than twice, both times against his wishes, further confused the matter. All the audiencia knew for certain was that beginning on July 15 the viceroy was in close consultation with the more suspicious members of the city council.

There was the heart of the matter. At a meeting of the cabildo on July 15, Azcárate presented for discussion a draft resolution that called upon the viceroy to assume direct control of the government of New Spain in the crisis. It proposed, in other words, autonomy. The council debated the matter on July 15 and 16, passed it, and agreed to present it to the viceroy at the next public court. During this debate, the regidor Azcárate was in frequent and intimate communication with the viceroy.

The resolution was presented to Iturrigaray in a meeting on July 19. The meeting was notable, among other things, for the fact that the councilors, wearing full dress uniforms and carrying their maces of office, were honored with formal military salutes as they entered and left the viceregal palace. This unaccustomed reception astounded and alarmed the audiencia. After the leading gentlemen of the city gathered in the viceroy's presence, Azcárate publicly read the city council's resolution. "This most noble city," it said, "by itself and in the name of the public, petitions Your Excellency . . . to maintain these vast dominions under your wise and just control, in the name of and representing the king and dynasty." The central argument was notable as a precise and clear restatement of sovereignty in the Spanish corporate tradition: "In the absence or during the impediment [of the king], sovereignty lies represented in all the kingdom and the classes that form it; and more particularly, in those superior tribunals that govern it and administer justice, and in those corporations that represent the public."[12] The council, which incidentally was the foremost of those corporations "that represent the public," later asked Iturrigaray to call a convocation or junta of the most distinguished citizens to hear his orders and give their opinions. Ultimately, a representative assembly would meet, composed of delegates from all the cities. Following the public reading, all the aldermen placed their hands on their swords and swore allegiance to Iturrigaray.

The chief advocates of this plan, which would have created a provisional junta to govern Mexico, were all creoles. Azcárate, Primo Verdad, and the marqués de Uluapa were from the city council; other supporters were the creole nobles the marqués de Rayas, the conde de Medina, and the conde de Regla; the creole oidor Jacobo de Villaurrutia (born in Santo Domingo) was its strongest advocate in public discussions.[13] The most extreme ideologue of autonomy was the exiled Peruvian friar Melchor de Talamantes, a confidant of the marqués de Uluapa. Talamantes, although he never mentioned republicanism in print, was the chief advocate of calling a Mexican congress which would promote radical reforms, including abolition of the Inquisition and ecclesiastical fuero courts, free trade, and mining, agricultural, and industrial reforms. This congress would assume a multitude of powers, including the right to name a viceroy, to fill all civil and ecclesiastical positions, to manage the treasury, and to send ambassadors to Europe and the United States.[14] He advocated this program in a paper entitled *Congreso Nacional del Reyno de Nueva España*, addressed to the cabildo on July 28. Though Talamantes clearly represented the extreme of creolism, apparently advocating outright independence, it is not clear to what extent he influenced the cabildo.

That is precisely where the problem of interpretation of this request for a Mexican junta, and of Iturrigaray's role in it, lies. To the extreme conservatives it seemed a treasonous call for independence. The mere idea of popular sovereignty, in however limited a form, was heresy. When Iturrigaray's residencia was conducted, everyone (with one exception to be noted) testified that the proposal meant independence. When the plan was first presented, the audiencia informed Iturrigaray that it would be illegal unless the audiencia consented, which it had no intention of doing, for the plan "would attribute to Your Excellency the honors of sovereignty." The lawyer Juan Martín de Juanmartineña stated the conservatives' suspicions most clearly; "The intimate union of Sr. Iturrigaray with the city and the conformity of their methods, made us believe that they were planning to usurp the sovereignty of these dominions and declare it independent of the Metropolis. We did not doubt his treasonous intentions."[15] After the viceroy's overthrow, many people—from the Junta of Seville and its representative in Mexico City to the king's sister, Carlota Joaquina, wife of the prince regent of Brazil—heaved a sigh of relief and congratulated his enemies on their foresight in rescuing New Spain. The fact that identical provisional juntas created in other colonial capitals proceeded eventually to a proclamation of independence adds strength to the assumption that the Mexican cabildo's proposal had the same objective.[16]

While it is true that the plan might have been radicalized subsequently, as originally presented it was a proposal for the return of power to its origin—the cabildos of Mexico City and Veracruz. These bodies were the first legal governmental agencies created by the conquerors in New Spain and, in the view of the creoles, the original center of Mexican, as opposed to purely Spanish, legitimacy.[17] Sovereignty would thus devolve to the functioning agents of royal authority, and, even then, would do so only on a temporary basis pending restoration of some member of the Bourbon dynasty. While one cannot know the secret objectives of the various supporters of this proposal, what is known is that none of them, except perhaps Talamantes, ever spoke of independence.[18] Indeed, some of the same aldermen who passed this resolution, notably including Azcárate, strongly opposed the Hidalgo uprising. That Primo Verdad, for his part, never doubted the king's authority, is indicated in his statement that "authority came to the king from God, but not directly, rather through the people." Azcárate, too, was clear in his understanding that there existed an irrevocable pact between the nation and the king: when the king was impeded from ruling, the nation assumed authority, but upon the king's return to power, the people's direct exercise of authority would cease automatically.[19] Legally and technically, in view of the absence of the monarch and the claim by various Spanish juntas to possess authority in his name, the Mexican proposal was not treasonous. It was a proposal for autonomy, not independence. It was consistent with the most ancient Spanish political philosophy, in which New Spain was never considered a possession of the Spanish nation but only of the king. To view the proposal as an outright call for Mexican independence is simply to fall for the audiencia's point of view, for the absolutists defined autonomy as if it were the same thing as independence. Brading points out that the cabildo's representation was not a revolutionary statement taken from Rousseau, or even from Suárez, but was simply the application of the conservative theory of natural law propounded by Puffendorf, as translated and popularized in early nineteenth century Spain by the Madrid professor Joaquín Marín Mendoza.[20] Villoro best summarizes the subtle forces that were at work and the established authorities' rigid opposition to any change: "[The creoles in 1808] did not aspire, for the moment, to anything but a reform of scant importance. . . . But once the will for change were introduced, would it be possible to halt it?"[21]

Viceroy Iturrigaray's position was precarious. He could not fail to listen to the cabildo's proposal, because he had long curried the favor of prominent creole activists like Azcárate, whose friendship was beneficial to the very self-serving viceroy. Yet, even discussing the idea of a convocation of prominent leaders, much less of the cities, fired suspicions against him to full steam. Hatred for Iturrigaray among the peninsulars and conservatives was so intense that in the formal review of his term of office, only one person testified in his behalf. As early as October, 1808, the secretary of the viceroyalty, Manuel Velázquez de Leon, testified that, having observed the viceroy closely, he saw no indication that Iturrigaray desired to crown himself king nor that he was anything other than a complete patriot. Iturrigaray himself denied that he had ever aspired to independence.[22]

Iturrigaray's great fault, it should be repeated, was that he laid himself open to such widespread and uncontrolled suspicion that he was hopelessly compromised in the eyes of the very men who would ordinarily have been his strongest supporters. The only course of action he could have pursued that would have allayed these suspicions would have been to fight resolutely for maintenance of total absolutism—as his single-minded colleague, Viceroy José Abascal of Peru, was doing at that very moment under similar circumstances. Iturrigaray failed to do this and has been damned ever since.

Both Iturrigaray and the city council have been presumed guilty of treason on the basis of suspicion, partisan testimony, and, most important, future developments. Clearly, Iturrigaray's motives must be separated from the cabildo's. It appears that Iturrigaray, while certainly not blameless, was innocent of treasonous intent. He was only a self-serving cynic, too frightened by the danger of having his graft and corruption exposed and too confused by the overthrow of his protector Godoy to concentrate his attention on any objective other than remaining in office. The cabildo's motives were mixed. The extremists may have wanted to see an eventual declaration of independence, but, since events never got that far, independence can only be assumed to be their objective. The majority of the advocates of the cabildo's plan to call a national congress—including Azcárate and Villaurrutia—were talking about autonomy first and foremost, not independence.

Since as yet New Spain had not been informed of the uprisings of the Spanish people nor of the creation of juntas in Valencia and Seville (news of those events arrived on July 29 and August 1), the viceroy proceeded on July 23 to call for a convocation of the chief gentlemen of the city to discuss the crisis. No doubt he felt in need of advice. On that same day, the aldermen Primo Verdad and the marqués de Uluapa presented Iturrigaray with a second cabildo representation, which argued that the abdication of Charles IV and Ferdinand VII had no effect on New Spain, which might be considered one of the constituent kingdoms of which the Spanish monarchy was comprised. Thus, while Ferdinand and his father may have abdicated the throne of Castile, they had not abdicated the throne of New Spain, and Iturrigaray could legally establish a provisional government in the king's name.[23] Though a dubious argument, it is entirely consistent with the creole autonomists' view that New Spain was not legally or constitutionally a colony. According to the testimony of the conservative alcalde José Juan Fagoaga, Uluapa returned from this meeting to the municipal chambers, repeating twice during the day that "this most noble city in more than two hundred years had never accomplished as much as it had that day."[24]

The invitation for a convocation of prominent citizens to discuss the crisis was enough to convince many influential conservatives that the nation was drifting toward rebellion. Gabriel de Yermo, the oidor Ciriaco González Carvajal, and the inquisitor Bernardo del Prado, all peninsulars, were convinced that the very idea of a meeting was treason. The creole regidor Agustín del Rivero said that "to call the cities is to initiate civil war." The audiencia repeated on August 8 its feeling that "there is neither any urgency nor need to call such a junta," saying that the Laws of the Indies did not allow for it and that it constituted a dangerous precedent.[25]

In spite of all objections, however, four convocations met as a result of the viceroy's invitations, on August 9 and 31, and on September 1 and 9. Eighty-six persons attended the meetings. They were representatives of secular corporations (audiencia, ayuntamiento, Consulado, Mining Guild, the military, and the fuero courts of the royal treasury), Church corporations (Inquisition, university, cathedral chapter, and the principal monasteries of Guadalupe, Santo Domingo, and Carmen), the nobility, and three Indian governors of metropolitan barrios. Ladd identifies thirty-nine of them as creoles and twenty-nine as peninsulars; eighteen could not be identified by place of birth.[26] The first meeting was sufficient to convince the conservatives in their suspicions of Iturrigaray. When later asked to permit the viceroy to expand the junta to include representatives from all the cities—the cabildo's original plan—the audiencia refused, saying that such a meeting bore too close a resemblance to the French Estates General of 1789.[27]

The first meeting was stormy and inconclusive. Primo Verdad read the city council's representation that sovereignty was now in the hands of the people. Peninsular oidor Guillermo de Aguirre wanted to know "who are the people?" to whom sovereignty supposedly now devolved. Primo Verdad answered that the constituted authorities represented the people, to which Aguirre replied that they were not the people at all and warned that this seditious and subversive liberal doctrine of popular sovereignty would return power to the Indians, the original Mexican people. The real question of the meeting was whether to recognize the Junta of Seville. Iturrigaray's opinion was clearly that the Seville government should not be recognized, because it did not represent the monarch. No vote was taken on this crucial question at the first meeting, and the convocation broke up, having decided only that Ferdinand VII would be recognized as king.[28] The formal celebrations in honor of Ferdinand's accession to the throne occurred on August 13, day of the royal pendant. Meanwhile, conservatives flocked to join militia corps called Volunteers of Ferdinand VII.

Shortly after the first convocation, two commissioners of the Seville junta, Juan Jabat and Manuel de Jáuregui, arrived in Mexico City. Jáuregui was Iturrigaray's brother-in-law. They came armed with orders to depose Iturrigaray if he did not recognize the Seville government, which adequately accounts for the viceroy's hostility toward them.[29] Fabián de Miranda, in Seville, later reported to the Supreme Junta that, as far as most royalists were concerned, there were no real grounds for suspicion of Iturrigaray's loyalty until the viceroy heard of the establishment of a new legal Spanish regime; thereafter his refusal to recognize it constituted treason. Miranda wrote, "Iturrigaray attempted then [to establish] independence," and "the union of the viceroy with the city of Mexico confirmed this fear."[30] Such evidence has often been deemed sufficient to convict Iturrigaray, yet it is clearly partisan. Miranda was simply repeating Jabat's reports. Seville desperately wanted to be the recipient of the Mexican Consolidation funds that were even then waiting in Veracruz for shipment to whichever authority New Spain decided was legitimate. Jabat told Iturrigaray that Seville had already been recognized by the rest of Spain, which was simply not true.[31] The viceroy's refusal to recognize Seville was well grounded and does not convict him of treason.

Tensions immediately led to violence during the ensuing weeks. A private citizen wrote to his brother that after the first junta "the Europeans immediately bought all the arms and ammunition they could find in the capital." The purchase of powder was so heavy that the director of the monopoly warned the viceroy about it. Two persons were shot to death in a political argument.[32]

The viceroy and virreina made themselves further suspicious by distributing money to the crowds on August 15. The audiencia interpreted this "as an effort to gain the support of the common people, who were so well protected that day that they insulted various important personages by throwing rocks at their coaches." These stormy events culminated in the viceroy removing the oidor Aguirre from his job as censor of the *Gazeta* and threatening to remove the editor, Juan Cancelada, for having published reports earlier in the month of the king's return to Spain.[33] Iturrigaray assumed censorship of the *Gazeta* himself.

The arrival of the Seville commissioners necessitated the convocation of a second meeting on August 31 to consider the question again of whether New Spain should recognize the Junta of Seville. At this meeting, the supporters of Seville carried the day, voting forty-nine "yes" to twenty-nine "no." Leading supporters of the recognition of Seville were peninsulars: the oidor Aguirre; Fausto de Elhuyar, director of the Mining Tribunal; retired general Pedro de Garibay; the merchants Antonio de Bassoco, the marqués de Castañiza, and the conde de la Cortina; and the marqués de San Román, a councilor of the Indies. Some creole aristocrats, including the conde de Santiago, the conde de Aguayo, and the mariscal de Castilla, also supported recognition. The opponents of recognition were divided, fourteen favoring autonomy and twelve favoring watchful waiting.[34]

Another meeting had to be held the next day. The entire situation changed upon the arrival in Mexico on August 31 of delegates from yet another peninsular junta, this one at Oviedo, who carried promises of a British alliance. At the meeting of September 1, Viceroy Iturrigaray forcefully declared, "Spain is now in a state of anarchy, there are Supreme Juntas everywhere, and we should therefore not obey any of them." His thinking carried the meeting, as fifty-four of the gentlemen now voted to recognize no one, while seventeen still sided with Seville. A few persons still voted for Mexican autonomy (Villaurrutia, Rayas, Regla, Uluapa, Medina, Azcárate, Primo Verdad—all creoles); a few still supported Seville (the Spaniard San Román and the creole conde de Santiago); but most delegates preferred watchful waiting (including among the nobles the Spaniards Bassoco, Cortina, and Pérez Galvez, and the creoles Aguayo, Castañiza, and the mariscal de Castilla).[35]

The ruling class was radically divided into three contradictory factions by the pendulum of peninsular events. The most dramatic example of how this question divided the elite is the case of the Fagoagas, perhaps New Spain's premier mining family, all of whose members were politically active. José Juan, the first alcalde in 1808, José Mariano, and the old marqués de Apartado supported Seville. The young men of the family, Francisco, heir to the title, and a cousin, José María, supported autonomy.[36]

By the first week of September it was clear that a stalemate existed. Since the junta of September 1 had decided against recognizing any government in Spain for the moment, Iturrigaray proceeded to ask the audiencia for its approval to call the general meeting of the cities. On September 6 the audiencia strongly urged him to desist.[37] This first week of September was the turning point; in continuing to consider a general convocation of the cities, Iturrigaray was defying the audiencia and ignoring the sense of the junta, which, although it had voted against recognition of Seville, had certainly not voted in favor of calling the cities. The conservatives were enraged. Were Iturrigaray's actions treasonous? The answer in view of the September 1 meeting, seems to be no. All Iturrigaray was doing was considering the possibility of further developments, perhaps searching for wider consensus within New Spain. His refusal to abandon the idea of a general convocation, however, determined his fate.

One further event occurred in this bizarre process leading to the first violent overthrow of a Mexican viceroy. On September 5, Iturrigaray offered to resign in favor of Mexico's elder statesman, the octogenarian retired field marshal Pedro Garibay. The viceroy had originally broached this possibility in the first junta of August 9; now he formally requested the audiencia's opinion on whether any legal impediments prevented his resignation. Alamán admits that he was unable to determine the viceroy's motive.[38] That it probably was an attempt to gain public sympathy is indicated by the fact that viceregal secretary Manuel Velázquez de Leon wrote a secret letter to the city council ordering it to oppose the resignation publicly and loudly at the forthcoming junta of September 9. A request by the junta that the viceroy not resign could be interpreted by his friends as a vote of confidence in his personal leadership and his plans for calling a general assembly of the cities. It backfired mightily, however, for the oidors themselves later admitted that the viceroy's offer was "a light that clarified everything." His resignation would be a singular solution to the conservatives' dilemma.

The viceroy showed by his actions, at any rate, that he had no intention of resigning. Two days later, on September 7, he sent orders to two military units whose commanders were his intimates and who he no doubt thought would be loyal to him personally—the Dragoon Regiment of New Galicia and the Infantry Regiment of Celaya—to converge upon the capital. Was he preparing military support for a coup? There is no evidence one way or the other, but it is certain that a man who is about to retire peacefully with a designated successor on the scene has no need for troop reinforcements. The audiencia was frightened by the mere thought; his enemies made up their minds to depose him.

At the fourth and final junta on September 9, Iturrigaray was made forcefully aware of his lack of support. Part of the stormy meeting was open to the public, and both conservatives and liberals marshalled their rhetoric to sway the people who stood at the open doors watching the fate of the kingdom being debated. The archbishop and the marqués de San Román asked that their opinions supporting recognition of Seville be read from the minutes in full. The viceroy then asked the secretary to read the full opinions of the marqués de Rayas and Dr. Felipe Castro Palomino, who opposed recognition. Then the regidor Agustín del Rivero created an uproar by asking who would represent the castes in the meeting of the cities, causing many delegates to rise to their feet objecting that the meeting of the cities had been vetoed by the audiencia. In the confusion of many voices someone was heard to say that "if the cities are not asked to meet together they will meet together themselves," to which an oidor replied in the strongest terms that this would be treason.

Finally the doors were closed and the cabildo members enacted their charade of begging the viceroy not to resign. The regidor Antonio Méndez Prieto rose and asked the viceroy if the rumor of his intended resignation were true. In a carefully worded statement Méndez Prieto begged him to consider the consequences of such action. The viceroy answered, gravely admitting he had indeed contemplated resignation because at the age of sixty-six he was tired and beset by many woes. The assembly, which was supposed to be shocked by the threat, said not a word. After an embarrassing silence of some moments, three more members of the cabildo (Primo Verdad, Uluapa, and Rivero) spoke for the viceroy. It was clear that the junta was being invited to render a vote of confidence in Iturrigaray, but no one except members of the city council did so. The audiencia later testified, "Everyone remained in the most profound silence for about six or eight minutes," which "was interpreted as a desire of the members that His Excellency should put into effect his contemplated resignation."[39]

With the ruling class paralyzed by disagreement over the future course of action, it fell to individuals to force a resolution of the crisis. Between September 5 and 7, a conspiracy for Iturrigaray's overthrow was launched under the personal leadership of the peninsular merchant and hacendado Gabriel de Yermo. The conspiracy had the fullest connivance of the audiencia, the archbishop, and other prominent peninsulars, but it was entirely planned and organized by Yermo and merchant and hacendado friends from the Consulado. Yermo's chief motivation was his fear of popular unrest among the mulattoes and castes. He also had many reasons to dislike both the viceroy and the city council. He had served for years as contract supplier (*abastecedor*) of the capital's markets, in which position he had suffered losses, harassment, and insults from both the cabildo and viceroy. As an hacendado, owner of many slaves and large haciendas, he resented new taxes on brandy, meat, and pulque. He also suffered from the Consolidation. He hated Iturrigaray's corruption and the harmful example it set. He later wrote the Seville government criticizing the audiencia judges Aguirre and Miguel Bataller, who claimed to have planned the coup. He testified that they had been hesitant when he broached the idea with them, for they feared a creole uprising in support of the viceroy. Yermo calmed their fears by insisting that it remain a civilian action and that the troops quartered in the city be kept in their barracks. Yermo strongly distrusted any creole regiment and in the months ahead even opposed the creation of regiments of creole aristocrats in the capital. After the coup was successfully completed, he requested Seville not to honor the audiencia, for he insisted it had all been his idea and that of a few other private citizens.[40] Direct support of his contention came from the Seville commissioner, Juan Jabat, who said Yermo had been "the head of the revolution," and for a service "of such singular merit to the king," he requested Yermo be ennobled.[41] Two years later a title was offered to Yermo, but he declined it. Peninsulars all over the country knew that the coup was the exclusive work of peninsulars. Faustino Capetillo told his brother that the 15,000 or 16,000 peninsulars scattered over 1,000 miles of territory had reacted to the autonomist threat in total unanimity. He testified, "The firmness of *our* character intimidated the creoles."[42]

The coup occurred after midnight on the morning of September 16. Yermo's supporters consisted of about three hundred clerks and militiamen associated with the Consulado. The fact that the plotters were almost entirely merchants closely associated with the transatlantic trade, and therefore with Cádiz monopoly merchants as well as with the Veracruz Consulado, is well worth emphasizing. Brian R. Hamnett has illustrated how extensive their network of business associates and clients was within New Spain. Officers of the palace artillery corps, of the Commercial Regiment and of the Urban Cavalry Regiment were also in on the plot.[43] After being permitted entry into the palace by the officer of the day, the plotters overpowered the Corps of Halberdiers, arrested Iturrigaray in his bed, rounded up his family, arrested his personal secretary, Rafael José de Ortega, and impounded his belongings. The virreina's brother, Colonel Jáuregui, was heard to exclaim to his sister: "You well know that I prophesied . . . that your husband would follow the same path as Godoy."[44] Years later the viceroy's son Vicente, who was scarcely six years old when his father was overthrown, told the emperor and empress of Mexico about the insulting language the captors used toward his mother and sister.[45]

At two o'clock in the morning the archbishop and audiencia gathered in the palace to pass formally on Iturrigaray's removal from office. The Laws of the Indies granted the audiencia the right of interference in the government when the viceroy exceeded his powers, and on that basis it removed him and appointed Garibay as viceroy.[46] The conservatives hoped Garibay would serve as a puppet. Carlos María Bustamante, the rebel publicist and historian, said Garibay was "so stupid" that the oidors manipulated him easily.[47] Garibay's distinguished military career and his independence of mind tend to contradict the charge, although it is true his short administration failed to come to grips with the dangers facing New Spain.

During the predawn hours, as the viceroy and his family were being lodged in various convents and in the residence of the inquisitor Bernardo del Prado, the conspirators arrested the most prominent supporters of the provisional-government idea—Talamantes, Azcárate, and Primo Verdad. In the morning they arrested the abbot of the Convent of Guadalupe, Francisco Beye Cisneros, the canon of the Cathedral, José Mariano Beristain de Sousa, and the auditor of war, José Antonio Cristo y Conde. The last three were held only a short time, since suspicions against them were based mainly on rumor. Beristain, indeed, became the leading creole propagandist of the royal cause in the years ahead. Primo Verdad, Talamantes, and Azcárate fared not so well. Primo Verdad died after a few days in custody. Talamantes died of yellow fever in a Veracruz prison in April, 1809. Creolism had its first martyrs. Primo Verdad is now honored as the city's sacrifice on the altar of independence and is remembered by a handsome statue near the Municipal Museum. Azcárate stayed in prison for three years, but he survived and even reclaimed his honorary city council seat in late 1814.[48]

When the audiencia met again on the morning of September 16, it heard many witnesses testify that Garibay would be acceptable to both civilian and military branches of the government. Juan Jabat testified that Garibay's selection and Iturrigaray's overthrow would be perfectly acceptable to Seville. At no time did the conservatives receive anything less than public approval for their actions. Though the Garibay government did not formally recognize any Spanish government until March, 1809, when it did the newly elected Junta Central in Seville in turn recognized Garibay and thanked those persons who had overthrown Iturrigaray. Doña Carlota Joaquina, sister of Ferdinand, also sent her approval.[49]

And Yermo got his reward. With almost unseemly haste, on September 16 he presented to the audiencia and new viceroy a series of eight tax revisions, all benefitting merchants, Consulado members, and hacendados. All were approved, including abolition of the meat tax, reduction of the brandy tax, and suspension of a proposed new tax on pulque—"this healthful regional drink" as Yermo called it. Interestingly, Yermo also requested and received from the audiencia permission for New Spain to produce goods, notably grapes and olives, previously preserved as a peninsular monopoly. In a letter to Seville, he explained that this would obviate one of the chief popular grievances of Mexicans, many of whom were already planting vines and olive trees, and that, as neither plant grew well in New Spain, it would not harm the market for Spanish produce. The ever-willing Yermo even advanced the money needed to pay for the trip of Iturrigaray and his family to Veracruz.[50] The troops called by Iturrigaray to the capital and the large canton that he had built up in Jalapa were dispersed, the more dependable Dragoons of Mexico were summoned, and Consolidation funds were freed for shipment to Spain.

Iturrigaray's motives have always been in dispute, largely because he himself was so confused following the abdications. One motive, however, was paramount. He wanted to stay in office, if for no other reason than to continue enjoying the fruits of what was the most extensive viceregal corruption in history. When he was overthrown, he was found to be in possession of over two million pesos in jewels and plate, in addition to deposits of over 400,000 pesos in the Mining Tribunal. This was a genuine scandal for a man who earned 60,000 pesos a year and who was not supposed to amass personal profit from his office, but it was certainly not a secret. Every important person in Mexico City—officials, hacendados, merchants, miners, property-owners, the entire elite, whether creole or peninsular—knew of his corruption. Yermo charged that any office or career could be bought from the viceroy, his wife, his children, or his servants.[51] Iturrigaray's wife, Inez de Jáuregui—herself the daughter of a former viceroy of Peru—was directly involved in his illegal activities. The viceroy's addiction to gambling, particularly evident at the annual fair at San Agustín de las Cuevas, was also widely known. Iturrigaray, through his own corruption, was responsible for his untenable position at the outbreak of the 1808 crisis.

After returning to Spain, Iturrigaray was submitted to a legal review on charges of graft and treason. (He was the last Mexican viceroy to undergo such an investigation.) The final verdict, rendered in 1810, was appealed by Iturrigaray and, after his death in 1814, by his wife and sons; it was finally confirmed by the Council of the Indies in 1819. He had been found guilty of corruption, and his estate was fined the immense sum of 435,000 pesos.[52] He was excused from the charge of treason by the general political amnesty declared on October 15, 1810, to celebrate the installation of the Cortes. Consequently, no decision was ever arrived at concerning his political actions, and the question of whether he was a traitor has remained in dispute. The men who overthrew him were convinced he was a traitor or, at least, that his continuation in office would lead to revolution. Yet, once shorn of the circumstantial evidence, partisanship, and sensationalism that surrounds his actions, the evidence seems clear that he was not a traitor, but merely a victim of the suspicion and hatred created by his own corruption.

The preemptive coup was a complete success. It cut through all the entanglements in a single deft blow. It eliminated Iturrigaray and replaced him with an old man under the control of the conservatives. It forestalled the drift toward creole domination, scattered the autonomists, and chastised the cabildo. Most important, it was now impossible for New Spain to follow the path to creole provisional governments and then independence that most of the continental South American kingdoms pursued in the period from 1808 to 1810. In one sense, the royal cause could not have been better served.

Yet, while the drift toward creole domination over the government was suppressed, this first violent overthrow of a viceroy in New Spain's history had profound repercussions on the country's struggle for autonomy. It was so exclusively the work of Europeans that, as Ladd says, "legitimacy, popular sovereignty, and prejudice against peninsulars assumed explosive relevance."[53] The delicate balance of privileges and interests under the watchful eye of Spanish absolutism, which heretofore characterized the regime, was profoundly unbalanced by the success of a group of self-willed local proprietors in ousting the viceroy. Even while possession of the Crown itself was in question, the legitimacy of its agents in New Spain was cast into disrepute. Powerful creoles within the royalist camp, men like Jacobo de Villaurrutia and the marqués de Rayas, became champions of autonomy, convinced that something desirable and entirely reasonable had been high-handedly suppressed. They remained royalists, though suspicious authorities now viewed them as revolutionaries, and their sense of grievance increased, as did the grievances of all creoles.

Most important, this capture of the government by a handful of peninsulars was the first of several profound contradictions that began to corrode the legitimacy of royal authority even as it reaffirmed royal power. Authority and power are not the same thing.[54] From the point of view of the maintenance of authority, although no one at the time saw it, the selection of a new viceroy by initiative of local conservatives differed little—except in being conservative—from the cabildo's proposal to create self-mandated autonomy under the incumbent viceroy. Both constituted corrosion of imperial legitimacy, unavoidable though it might have seemed under the circumstances. This was the first of a number of contradictions that eventually destroyed the regime. The ultimate cost to the imperial system was clarified several years later when Servando Teresa de Mier, in his book *Historia de la Revolución de Nueva España*, justified American independence on the basis of the overthrow of Iturrigaray and the refusal of the conservatives to allow a representative Mexican assembly. Mier claimed that this had destroyed the social pact or contract that had been established at the time of the Conquest between the Spanish kings and their American subjects.[55] For years afterward the overthrow of Iturrigaray would be cited by creoles as the single event that proved their right to self-government.

The city council, the focus for autonomist aspirations, was severely chastised. From this point on, its every political action was closely watched and countered when necessary by an ever-vigilant superior government. For the moment, it was so thoroughly subdued that from 1808 to 1812 it played the role of sycophant to the superior government. But the peninsulars were correct in assuming its incorrigibility, for in 1812 the proclamation of the liberal constitution provided it a second opportunity for initiative in the achievement of autonomist aims.

A lively controversy raged in the years ahead concerning the extent to which the city council had actually been making a bid for independence. Juan López Cancelada, former editor of the *Gazeta* and proclaimed enemy of Iturrigaray, claimed in two published diatribes that the cabildo and viceroy together had plotted independence. Friends of Iturrigaray and friends of the cabildo found themselves defending both simultaneously in response to Cancelada's allegations. José Beye Cisneros, Mexico City's delegate to the Cortes in 1810, published a reply to Cancelada, as did the city council.[56]

The audiencia, Yermo, and Juan Jabat, for their part, clearly recognized the cabildo as the enemy. In a report to Seville, Jabat set forth a number of recommendations that exactly duplicated those made by Yermo and the audiencia in their letters to Seville. He suggested the appointment of a vigorous viceroy to take the place of the aged Garibay; he suggested that a military leader be made governor of some nearby province, and that this governor be the designated successor of the new viceroy in case of accident; he recommended a title for Yermo and the regency of the audiencia for Aguirre; and he proposed that young creoles be sent to Spain for education and indoctrination in order to strengthen Mexican loyalties. His principal recommendation, however, was that the existing cabildo, which he called "the head or chief" of the independence movement, should be abolished and replaced by a new cabildo of twelve members, half European and half creole, appointed by the viceroy. In 1811 the audiencia repeated that same recommendation in a dispute over management of municipal finances.[57]

The audiencia, in a summary report written in April, 1809, claimed that the cabildo had attempted to gain the determining power over national affairs and that Iturrigaray had merely been its pawn. Having rethought the whole question of the viceroy's personal culpability, it concluded that he had not been a conscious traitor, for he believed that Spain's conquest by the French and the king's captivity were irreparable. It was, rather, the cabildo that sought to take advantage of a moment of great confusion and that was guilty of outright treason. This was Alamán's final conclusion as well.[58] The audiencia now assessed Iturrigaray's chief failing more accurately: "One minute he was a friend of Godoy, then of Ferdinand VII. One minute he wanted to hold his command from Charles IV, then from his august son, then from Mexico City alone, and finally from all the cities. . . . He was only consistent in not subjecting himself to anyone's advice."[59] In short, what Iturrigaray wanted was to stay in office in order to protect the millions of pesos he had acquired by fraud. That was motive enough.

The 1808 coup, therefore, is not properly understood if interpreted simply as a blow against Iturrigaray. Its other targets were the cabildo and the autonomists. The conservatives temporarily neutralized or preempted the cabildo's ability to influence political decisions. But autonomists continued to look to the cabildo for leadership since, no matter how great its defects, it was all they had. It is no wonder contemporaries and historians alike have had difficulty defining who was a royalist after 1808, for, as Villoro said, the very definition of loyalty was arrived at by extralegal action.[60] Creole and peninsular members of the elite who aspired to autonomy within the royal context were now classified as rebels, while all the elite and bourgeoisie alike would soon have real rebels to worry about.

The conservatives now had the upper hand in New Spain. Their violent preemption of options for future development destroyed the tenuous alliance of elite and bourgeoisie that had been in the making and divided creole and gachupine once again. The coup served to reinforce a regime that might have gone the way of the royal governments in Buenos Aires and Caracas. To be sure, some regularization of New Spain's relations with the government at home was still necessary. Strong viceregal leadership needed to be provided in order to restore the badly tarnished image of the office, a tarnish that was hardly checked by the ineffectual Garibay. For the next two years New Spain lacked a strong viceroy—it would not have one until Venegas's appointment in 1810—but for the time-being an effective holding action had been achieved. Given the circumstances, that was the best the conservatives could hope for until Spain itself had a functioning national government. Creole domination had been avoided, even if the price was further outrage among some creoles. The Mexican government remained badly imbalanced—loyal but not really royal, in the sense that the Crown had nothing to do with the change of viceroys—but at least the peninsulars felt they had control of it.

During the next two years no less than three governments existed in New Spain. It was a period of constantly growing insurrectionary ferment, as the legitimate complaints of most Mexicans were utterly ignored by two startlingly myopic viceroys and the audiencia. However one views the government of Pedro Garibay (September 16, 1808–July 19, 1809), of Archbishop Francisco Javier Lizana y Beaumont (July 19, 1809–May 8, 1810), and of the audiencia (May 8–September 12, 1810) the conclusion is that, while they were not necessarily any worse than some previous governments, they failed to provide the strong leadership needed at so critical a moment.

Garibay pursued a sufficiently independent policy that he soon incurred the enmity of the conservative Spaniards. The Yermo faction frequently requested Spain to replace him with a stronger leader.[61] As a caretaker who lacked control over his own administration, Garibay drew the complaints of both conservatives and liberals. Conservatives felt that he was not sufficiently vigorous in overcoming insurrectionary rumors, and liberals felt that he was the tool of the merchants. Garibay was replaced in July, 1809, by the archbishop, who it was hoped would function as a peacemaker among the dangerously divided population.

Archbishop Lizana's leadership was no stronger than his predecessor's. He is mainly noted for his activities in defending New Spain against the easily perceived menace of French propaganda and for his suspicious attitudes toward the Yermo and audiencia factions. Meanwhile, the loyalty of Mexicans continued to erode. In countless proclamations the archbishop-viceroy spoke to the people of brotherhood, of the unity of one blood and one church, exhorting them to duty and obligation, reminding them in the tradition of his ecclesiastical training that it was the child's duty to obey his loving but severe father.[62] It seems that while he was aware there was something very wrong with the traditional paternal gachupine-creole relationship, he had not the slightest idea what the problem might be or how to cure it. When revolutionary broadsides were distributed in the city's churches and posted on the walls of the viceregal palace, Lizana created in September, 1809, a special Junta of Security and Public Order. Originally proposed by Garibay, its function was to search out manifestations of support for the French and to ferret out insurrectionary ferment in the capital.

Such vigilance did the archbishop-viceroy little good, because he seldom recognized his own enemies, much less those of the royal cause. He did not like Mexico and consequently did not try to understand it. He so publicly showed his distaste for creoles and mestizos that in 1810 he was trying to bring charges in Spain against a creole clergyman there who had reported to the Seville government that Lizana was a "declared enemy of Americans."[63] These charges of prejudice were widely believed by the creoles themselves. His most serious error was that he almost succeeded in wrecking that delicate coalition of peninsular merchants and royal judges upon which the very existence of his government depended. When he took the viceregal office, he handed the administration of the archdiocese over to his cousin, Inquisitor General Isidoro Saínz de Alfaro, who had great influence over the viceroy's political activities. Saínz suspected that a plot was hatching among the peninsulars, especially among the Yermo faction, to depose the archbishop. Haunted by the fate of Iturrigaray—in whose overthrow Alamán says the archbishop had pursued a policy that was nothing short of "pusillanimous"—Lizana embarked on a program of persecution of the Spanish party of Yermo and the oidor Aguirre. He requested the retirement of the oidor Ciriaco González Carvajal and sent Aguirre to Puebla to get him away from the affairs of the capital. The outcries of the Spanish party were so great that Aguirre shortly returned to the capital. In the same period Lizana deposed Juan López Cancelada as editor of the *Gazeta* because of Cancelada's public criticisms of him. Cancelada was sent to Spain for a hearing. Thus Lizana removed from office the most outspoken and clamorous enemy of Iturrigaray. The viceroy concluded this politically inept defense of his tenure by cordoning off the central district of the capital around his palace, fortifying it with artillery, and placing the district under martial law with a curfew of ten o'clock. Members of the Yermo faction, of the guilds and the Consulado, petitioned Spain for Lizana's removal.[64]

In Spain sweeping political changes were taking place. The various regional juntas were consolidated, by persuasion or by force, into the Junta Central of Spain and the Indies, recognized in Mexico City in January, 1810. The Junta later gave way to the Regency, recognized on May 7 in Mexico City amid great pomp. Miguel de Lardizábal y Uribe, a member of the Council of the Indies and native of Tlaxcala (though he lived all his life in Spain) represented New Spain on the Junta Central; he had been nominated for that position by the cabildos of the chief cities of the country. He then became a member of the Regency.[65] The Regency, which located itself in Cádiz after the French armies entered Andalucia, called in turn for a meeting of the Cortes, which would include American representatives. The cabildo of each provincial capital in New Spain, including Mexico City, elected provincial representatives to the Cortes. The Mexican cabildo chose José Beye Cisneros, professor of law at the university, a moderate, and brother of the canon of Guadalupe who was arrested in the overthrow of Iturrigaray.[66] By the time the Cortes opened on September 24, 1810, in Cádiz (still lacking most of its American delegates), Viceroy Lizana had been removed from office by order of the Regency. Dated February 22, 1810, and received in Mexico in early May, the Regency's order was apparently influenced by the protestations of the Cádiz merchants, who were responding to the grievances against Lizana of their friends, the Mexico City merchants.

The audiencia governed during the next four months, divided by internal disagreements and unable to provide the quick policy decisions needed in a country in constant crisis. Only two days after Lizana left office, Manuel Abad y Queipo, bishop-elect of Valladolid de Michoacán and a major commentator and observer of the War of Independence, warned the Regency that a general insurrection was at hand.[67] He should know, for he presided over the diocese in which creole and caste grievances against the regime had already begun to produce insurrectionary conspiracies.

On August 15, 1810, the new viceroy appointed by the Regency, Lieutenant General Francisco Javier Venegas, touched on Mexican soil at Veracruz. A determined and experienced officer, he was the man the royalists had prayed for. He also was well disposed toward the merchants, for he came directly from his post as governor of Cádiz. A month later he made his formal entry into Mexico City, where a reception was provided for him at the city council's expense. Typically, although the audiencia ordered the cabildo to restrict its expenses to 3,000 pesos because of its chronic shortage of funds, it spent 9,500 pesos.[68] Venegas was the last viceroy provided with such a reception; the next elaborate reception was to be for the triumphal entry of Iturbide, O'Donojú, and the Trigarante Army in September, 1821.

Venegas soon proved his mettle. A poem caricaturing his informal dress and general style appeared within a few days on the palace wall; in response, he ordered an answering pasquinade to be tacked up next to it, advising one and all that treasonous pronouncements would not be tolerated in his capital.[69] At the end of the ceremonies marking his arrival, he called for a new round of special donations to help the war effort in Spain, most of which was expected to come voluntarily from the monopolists, the nobility, and the corporations. To sweeten the pot, he carried a list of promotions and titles from the Council of the Regency, all reflecting the extent to which Cádiz recognized its debt to major land owners, merchants, and peninsulars in Mexico City. Titles of nobility were offered to Gabriel de Yermo, José Mariano Fagoaga, Diego de Agreda, and Sebastian de las Heras Soto. The first two declined the titles, perhaps because of the costs involved.[70]

Soon the new viceroy was confronted with his greatest challenge. In the early hours of September 16, 1810, the second day of Venegas's sojourn in the capital, the parish priest of the small town of Dolores in the intendancy of Guanajuato, Miguel Hidalgo y Costilla, called for an end to viceroys forever and issued his famous *Grito de Dolores*—the cry that initiated the War of Independence. The viceregal regime, imbalanced and weakened by the turmoil of the last two years, was jolted out of its confusion and apathy as the nation faced a threat so grave that it united all factions and overcame all divisions. Land owners, clergy, monopolists, autonomists, and bourgeoisie joined together in self-defense. The main motion of autonomy took second place in the struggle for survival that followed. Tragically, the Hidalgo uprising and other uprisings may have served to prevent the early achievement of autonomy in the period when it was still possible, that is, before Ferdinand's restoration.

Chapter 3

The Second Threat: Armed Insurrection

FROM 1810 UNTIL 1815, the royal regime in New Spain was threatened chiefly by armed insurrection in the countryside. The Hidalgo phase of the uprising was a significant threat, to be followed by even greater danger from 1812 to 1814, when the regime was faced with the better-organized Morelos movement, occurring simultaneously with establishment of the Constitution, which encouraged a resurgence of white and upper-class activism.

The greatest strength of the Hidalgo uprising was the rapidity with which it swept central Mexico, spreading terror and shock. The movement's greatest weakness, and the reason for its failure, was that it did not have the support of either creole bourgeoisie or domestic plutocrats, without which none of the alternatives to royal power could hope to succeed. The royal government's greatest strength was its skilled leadership, combined with the fact that it continued to provide a rallying point for the whites of the nation who recognized that the Hidalgo insurrection had them as its intended victims. The government's greatest weakness was that it was caught without preparation—despite the frequent warning it had received—and it took some months to recover from the surprise and organize a coherent counterinsurrectionary program.[1]

Hidalgo's uprising of untrained and virtually unarmed Indians directed itself against the towns and cities of central New

64

Spain because it was in the cities that the greatest damage could be inflicted and the largest booty captured. Mexico City, as the ultimate attraction, was in danger from the first moment. In only a month and a half Hidalgo's horde stood outside the capital, threatening it with its first attack in three hundred years. In less than two months the insurrection overran the greater portion of the diocese of Michoacán, a large part of the archdiocese of Mexico, and the diocese of Guadalajara. Bishop Abad y Queipo remarked that the sedition began in Dolores with scarcely two hundred men but exceeded 20,000 when it reached Guanajuato, one of its first targets. By the time the Hidalgo uprising was over, more than two million inhabitants had been drawn into it. The rebels slaughtered most of the Spaniards they could capture. Abad y Queipo estimated that 2,000 gachupines (out of a total for all of New Spain of only 15,000) were put to death in the Hidalgo revolt.[2] Many creoles died too, for in the Indians' minds all whites comprised the ruling class.

The immediate reaction of Mexico City to the uprising was confusion and horror. Although Hidalgo and his two captains, Ignacio Allende and Juan de Aldama, proclaimed the destruction of the viceregal government as their purpose, the capital's whites viewed the insurrection merely as an Indian revolt—that rising of the oppressed classes they had so long feared. This was a danger that overcame all internal rivalries, and creole and peninsular alike rallied to the viceregal government. From his prison cell, Juan Francisco Azcárate, the only survivor of the men who led the drive for creole autonomy in 1808, wrote a public manifesto condemning the revolt. At its first regularly scheduled meeting following Hidalgo's *Grito*, the cabildo could not muster a quorum, as its members were busy trying to do what they could for the security of their haciendas and rural clients. When the cabildo met again on September 24, it offered the superior government its fullest support and aid. As Hamill has said, "There were creoles who responded favorably to the *Grito*, but their numbers were infinitesimal compared to those who did not. A few lawyers, ranchers, and lower clergy supported, led, and died for the insurgent cause, but a million other creoles in New Spain failed to follow."[3]

Bishop Abad y Queipo wrote the Regency, "The desire for independence is almost general in all the sons of the country."[4]

This statement was perhaps an exaggeration, but Viceroy Venegas could afford to take no chances. His greatest worry at the outbreak of Hidalgo's revolt was whether the army, consisting of 22,000 local militia and 10,000 veteran troops, could be depended upon. The militia, composed chiefly of creoles and mestizos and officered by wealthy creoles who purchased their positions, was suspect in its loyalties. Too many of the militia corps were subject to the suggestion of their private or corporate sponsors. In the capital, for example, the corps created by the Consulado and by individual guilds, with their uniforms and arms often paid for by private donors, functioned as a part of the system of clientage of their patrons. Had not Gabriel de Yermo been supported in the 1808 coup by militiamen of the Commercial Regiment? There was, in addition, some question as to the dependability of the veteran troops at the outset of the insurrection. One major problem was that the veteran troop units, which had been concentrated in Mexico City and Jalapa in 1808, had been scattered about the country by Garibay in order to avoid their becoming centers of discontent or threats to his administration. Now, two years later, Venegas found the capital itself defended by only a few token forces, while he could not be certain of the extent to which provincial discontent had infected his troops. More critically, the majority of the regular army was now Mexican. Christon Archer has shown, for example, that by 1804 the Regiment of New Spain consisted of 95.6 percent Mexican-born troops, while the regular army of New Spain as a whole that year was about 95 percent Mexican.[5]

No matter how suspicious the Spaniards may have been of creole militia, Viceroy Venegas faced the possible threat of an Indian attack against an undefended capital. Consequently, he hastily created yet another militia in October to help defend Mexico City. He called for the organization of citizens' battalions to be called the Distinguished Patriotic Battalions of Ferdinand VII, and to be composed of the peninsular and creole elite. All men from the age of sixteen who were not already enrolled in a military unit and who could provide their own maintenance and uniforms were ordered to present themselves for "volunteer" service.[6]

Meanwhile, internal security against treason was the job of the Junta of Security, which was first created by Viceroy Lizana and served as the government's major tool against subversion in Mexico City until its abolition by order of the Cortes in 1813. During the two years before Hidalgo's *Grito*, a number of minor or suspected conspiracies had been uncovered in the capital. Citizens sent to Spain for trial included the brothers Luis and Ignacio Rodríguez Alconedo, jewellers suspected but found innocent of a conspiracy to raise the Indians of the two districts of Santiago Tlaltelolco and San Juan Tenochtitlán; Mariano Paredes, a musician at the Basilica of Guadalupe; Manuel Palacio, a presbyter from a church near the city; Antonio Calleja, a bureaucrat; Manuel Peimbert, a conspirator with Palacio; and several soldiers.[7] Most of these were acquitted, although some, like Antonio Calleja, joined the rebels in the field after their return to New Spain.

After the *Grito de Dolores*, the goverment was more actively on guard against sedition. The night guards arrested numbers of persons as handbills in favor of the rebels appeared everywhere. The administrator of the royal customs was anonymously, and incorrectly, accused of treason. And for the first time, distinguished citizens, both creole and peninsular, came under open suspicion. Guards were dispatched to watch over the houses of the marqués de San Miguel de Aguayo, the mariscal de Castilla, the conde de Bassoco, José María Fagoaga, and the merchants Pedro Noriega and Francisco Chavarrí.[8] Dossiers on these people were compiled.

The most important reply of the royal government and its supporters to the Hidalgo revolt was the propaganda campaign immediately launched against the rebels. This campaign illustrates the breadth of opposition to Hidalgo, as well as the speed with which the regime could respond to danger. The effort was a necessary one, for, as Hamill pointed out, the majority of the population was uncommitted in the great struggle and both sides tried to sway the majority by force of argumentation or reasoned apologias.[9] The royalists had the upper hand over the rebels in propaganda activities because they controlled the nation's printing presses, paper supply, and pulpits.

Mexico City was barraged by printed tracts urging defense of the nation and adherence to the principles of Hispanism— monarch, religion, and order. On September 24, Bishop Abad y Queipo excommunicated Hidalgo and the other leaders of the conspiracy, including Allende, Aldama, and Mariano Abasolo, and in October Archbishop Lizana confirmed the excommunications. The Inquisition joined in and on October 13 published an edict falsely charging that Hidalgo had been found guilty of heresy and apostasy in the brief assembled against him by the Holy Tribunal in the years 1800 to 1809. In September the creole royalist-propagandist José Mariano Beristain de Sousa began to publish a series of dialogues against the rebels. The deputies elected to the Cortes of Cádiz issued an exhortation against the insurgents. Appeals to and from both major Marian cults in the capital—the Virgins of Guadalupe and Los Remedios—appeared constantly as the royalists attempted to counter the rebels' use of the Virgin of Guadalupe as their protectress. There were countless other proclamations and admonitions published by private, governmental, and religious groups.[10]

Viceroy Venegas fought the rebels on both the military and psychological fronts. His proclamations were a mixture of calls for confidence and warnings to the rebels and all who should support them. After the rebels captured Celaya, he offered a reward of 10,000 pesos for the capture of each of the chief leaders. The viceroy called upon Brigadier Félix María Calleja to serve as commander of the newly-created Army of the Center, making him the highest ranking royalist field officer. Calleja was a Spaniard who had lived in Mexico since 1789, owned an hacienda at San Luis Potosí, and was married to a creole. Although he was not particularly close to Venegas personally and later quarreled with him, Calleja brought to the task at hand a unique combination of skills that soon catapulted him into the viceregal office. As a long-time resident of San Luis Potosí, he was able to call upon a network of personal and family contacts among northern creoles that enabled him not only to field an effective army but also to call upon local militia at need. Although leader of the militarists in New Spain, he also commanded considerable loyalty among the frightened creoles, and this unusual position was a chief source of his success. In another astute political decision, Venegas made Manuel de Flon, conde de la Cadena (who was serving as intendant of Puebla) second in command of the Army of the Center. Flon, who was killed shortly thereafter at the Battle of Calderón, was

previously thought to have been an advocate of independence.[11] As a means of retaining the allegiance of the rural
masses, the viceroy published a decree on October 5 abolishing
the tribute for Indians and castes. This was a unilateral action
that would later be superseded by a decree of the Spanish
Cortes.

An important result of the government's propaganda campaign was that it pointed out to the residents of the capital the
unspeakable horrors being perpetrated by the uncontrolled
Indians. Many people got their news of the revolt only from
strongly worded government or other royalist pronouncements.
The emphasis was upon the dangers posed to all elements of the
population, not just the property owners. As a result, when
Hidalgo entered the Valley of Mexico, he received little aid from
the Indians and castes, much less from the creoles. There was
no spontaneous uprising of the lower classes in the vicinity of
the capital either before Hidalgo drew near or after. The government naturally claimed this as proof of the loyalty of the capital
and its environs. It is more probable that the population,
whether creole or Indian or caste, simply chose not to become
swept up in the Hidalgo maelstrom. Hamill thinks this was the
chief explanation for Hidalgo's failure in the central region
around the capital. "In those areas of maximum royalist influence," he says, "the advancing insurgents were contemplated
by the lower orders with revulsion bordering on panic as if they
formed another wave of barbarians from beyond the Chichimec
frontier."[12] The successful royal propaganda campaign was
another indication of the strength of the regime.[13]

All of these actions were taken within a month and a half of
the *Grito de Dolores*. On October 28, 1810, the dreaded threat
became a reality, as Hidalgo and his army, estimated at 80,000,
reached Ixtlahuaca, thirty miles from Mexico City.[14] Hidalgo was
obviously bound for the capital, and in the city Venegas had at
his disposal no more than 7,000 men, of whom only 2,000 were
trained veteran troops. On only one other occasion—in February, 1812, as the army of Morelos lay at Cuautla Amilpas
planning to move forward to Mexico City—was the capital to be
threatened with attack, and in 1810 the danger was far more
imminent.

Determined to prevent an attack on the city if possible, Venegas sent out a force, estimated at 1,300 to 2,500 men, under command of his personal friend Colonel Torcuato Trujillo.[15] Under no illusions, Venegas told Trujillo in a private letter that three hundred years of Spanish power were at stake. At the same time, he ordered Brigadier Calleja, commander of the Army of the Center, then in San Luis Potosí, to march to the defense of the capital. The time factor was crucial, since it would take them several days to arrive and the rebels were at hand. Meanwhile, the cabildo issued a proclamation reminding the populace that the city was sworn to uphold the title of "most loyal" bestowed upon it by the sovereign. Venegas had the city's streets barricaded and distributed arms among the citizens.[16]

On October 30, Trujillo's forces took up a position in the hills of Las Cruces at a pass in the mountains that protected the capital, and there he awaited Hidalgo. In uneven and undisciplined ranks, the insurgent forces drew within distance and joined battle. After dark, Trujillo's forces staggered into a retreat. On October 31, the capital's residents watched in dismay as Trujillo returned with but two hundred men, the only survivors of the famous Battle of Las Cruces.

Trujillo claimed to have won a massive victory—and in a sense, he had—but the city's residents panicked at the sight of the few haggard survivors. Trujillo remained at Chapultepec rather than show himself in the city, while Venegas decided not to publish an account of the engagement so as not to intensify the panic. Trujillo had lost nearly all his men and all his field artillery. He estimated the number of insurgents killed and wounded at 2,000. Another author said that on both sides more than 4,000 were killed. Diego García Conde, a royalist officer captured by Hidalgo, estimated that the losses to the insurgents in killed, wounded, and desertions were more than 40,000, reducing the rebel army by half. For the first time since the beginning of their bloody rampage, the Indians were met in open combat by a disciplined royal-army unit. The Indians possessed only about 1,000 firearms and were untrained in their use. Indian ranks were thus decimated by the continuous fire of a small number of opponents. The uprising lost much of its attraction for them at Las Cruces.[17]

The residents of Mexico City did not know that. The next day, October 31, Hidalgo moved his forces forward to the village of Quajimalpa, within five leagues of the city. In the capital people scurried to hide their valuables and barricade their houses. The viceroy stationed forces on the causeway of La Piedad and on the Paseo de Bucareli, the two main entrances to the city from the Toluca road down which the insurgents would move. He planted cannon at Chapultepec and sent out cavalry to watch the enemy's movement. The outer perimeters of the city would be guarded by the veteran troops, while the interior would be defended by local and provincial regiments.

Since the image of the Virgin of Los Remedios lay in the path of the advancing rebels, the viceroy ordered it transferred from its shrine to the cathedral. He also attempted to transfer the image of Guadalupe from its Basilica, but the canons of Guadalupe saw no reason to move their Virgin. Los Remedios thus became associated with the royalist defense of the capital through an accident of geography. On October 31, Viceroy Venegas came to pray before the statue of Los Remedios in the cathedral and placed the baton of his office at its feet. The Virgin was proclaimed generalíssima and captain general of the royal army, protector and guide of Spain's military forces in Mexico. The crowd was virtually hysterical with emotion.[18] A private citizen distributed 5,930 medals of the Virgin to the officers and soldiers. A corps of 2,500 ladies organized themselves into a group called the Patriotas Marianas to sew banners of Los Remedios and keep watch over the statue in the cathedral. Soon there appeared a proclamation pretending to be from the Virgin herself to her people. A second proclamation responded to the Virgin's statement. On November 1, the Day of the Dead, thousands of people again gathered in the cathedral to pray to the image.

Throughout the day of November 1, the second day of Hidalgo's encampment outside the city, rumors ran through the city that the rebels were about to attack. Various small detachments of insurgents entered the suburbs of San Angel, Coyoacán, and Tlalpan, spreading alarm. The rebels were awaiting a general uprising, and the elite of the city cast their thoughts toward the huge population of léperos. No one knew what their response might be.[19] Early in the afternoon, the viceroy turned away a coach carrying Hidalgo's representatives, who came to negotiate the surrender. After that everyone was convinced that the attack was only a matter of time.

On the third day, November 2, the anxious population awaited the inevitable. Suddenly, late in the day, Venegas's scouts brought the incredible news that Hidalgo was turning his troops about and retreating from the environs.[20] Moving up the road to Querétaro, Hidalgo encountered the army of Calleja on its forced march toward the capital, and on November 7, at Aculco, sustained a disastrous defeat.

Why did Hidalgo not attack? Carlos María Bustamante, the prorebel journalist and historian, advanced the thesis that Hidalgo withdrew out of a wish not to submit the capital to destruction. Hamill dismisses this explanation by pointing out that the rebel leader had not hesitated to attack Guanajuato and would not hesitate again in Valladolid and Guadalajara.[21] Another factor in the retreat was the interception of copies of Venegas's orders to Calleja to come to the capital's aid. The leaders feared being caught between the capital's defenders and Calleja's army. Hidalgo himself explained the retreat as a result of the catastrophe at Las Cruces. He told his friend José María Landa that his army retired in order to replenish its artillery.[22]

The most cogent reason for the retreat was the one that the royalists themselves recognized: Hidalgo's presence failed to provoke an uprising in the capital or its vicinity. His messengers were captured, and one was hanged. On the first anniversary of the city's deliverance, the cabildo itself stated that Hidalgo had withdrawn because the rebels were "terrified of the punishment they had received [at Las Cruces], fearful of suffering even greater [punishment], and disillusioned by the constant and stainless fidelity of the inhabitants of this capital."[23] All of Mexico City rejected the Hidalgo formula.

As a result of Hidalgo's refusal to press the attack, his lieutenants, notably Allende and Aldama, lost faith in him as a military leader and shortly removed him from effective control over the armed insurgents. In only a month and a half, their illusions of a quick and easy victory crushed, the insurgents lost their greatest opportunity to win independence, and among the leaders a feud began that led to the downfall of Hidalgo. At

Aculco on November 7, the Indians ran in blind panic before a well-trained and well-commanded army—this time largely creole, mestizo, and caste militiamen under command of Calleja and Flon. H. G. Ward has pointed out that the flight of the Indians from the field at Aculco determined the creole militiamen in their opposition to lower-class insurrection. In the next few weeks, the Hidalgo forces slaughtered hundreds of Europeans in cold blood, making it clear that Hidalgo not only had failed to control his horde, but had actually condoned, and in some cases ordered, the massacre of gachupines. When Calleja retook Guanajuato on November 24, he exacted retribution, as did the royalist brigadier José de la Cruz among the villages near Querétaro.[24]

Mexico City gave full honors to the defenders of Las Cruces. Antonio Bringas, a royal officer who died in the battle, was interred by the viceroy's orders in a splendid public ceremony. The Tres Villas regiment, which contributed a majority of the soldiers in the battle, was given the honor of using as its battle cry the refrain "el monte de las Cruces!" The city of Veracruz struck a medal honoring the defenders, and Mexico City solemnly celebrated the first anniversary of the battle the following year. As a result of exemplary action in the battle, a young creole officer named Agustín de Iturbide, future liberator and emperor of Mexico, received promotion to captain.[25]

Hidalgo's failure to capture Mexico City in 1810 prolonged the armed insurrection until 1816, when the final defeat of the various rebel forces occurred. Control of Mexico City was absolutely necessary for the achievement of independence. Because of its position as the most populous city of the kingdom, as the center of wealth, commerce, and intellectual activity, and as the seat of the royal government, the capital alone could prevent the realization, or at least the effectiveness, of independence.

Obviously Mexico City did not function in a vacuum in its confrontation with the Hidalgo revolt or with successive revolts. Quite the contrary, most of the military resistance to the rebellions was headquartered in and derived from regional centers of royal power such as Guadalajara, Veracruz, Valladolid, Oaxaca, Zacatecas, San Luis Potosí, Puebla, and Guanajuato (these were the capitals of intendancies that possessed

commandants, *comandantes generales*); Sonora, Durango and
Mérida, each with a commandant or captain general, commanded the military forces of the Internal Provinces and of Yucatán. In addition, there were militia brigades established at Tabasco, Isla del Carmen, and Acapulco. Operating on the assumption
that, as Calleja wrote later, "the Empire of Spain is a giant . . .
whose conservation depends on physical force," Venegas and,
especially, Calleja set out to guarantee that, without dispatching
central armies, the royal regime could be defended locally in
each region. Every town and large hacienda was ordered to raise
its own corps of armed residents, each under the command of
an officer named by the regional commandant. This program was
worked out by Calleja in June, 1811, in a fourteen-point *Reglamento*. It was partially accepted by Viceroy Venegas and
further implemented when Calleja became viceroy. Although
never stated, it seems always to have been assumed that the real
fighting would occur in places other than the capital—as it did.
Even when the capital itself faced the threat of attack, the
front-line troops that defended it were drawn from regional
centers. By the time Calleja retired as viceroy of New Spain in
1816, he had built up in these regional centers, according to his
own testimony, an army of 39,436 veteran and provincial troops
(the standing army) and 44,098 royalist or urban troops (the
urban and other militia corps that would be called out in time of
need).[26] Each of the nine capitals of intendancies had a commandant. In some of these capitals—as in Guadalajara and San
Luis Potosí—the officer was also a captain general. The Internal
Provinces of the East and West had commandants at Sonora and
Durango, while Yucatán had a captain general at Mérida. At
Tabasco, Isla del Carmen, and Acapulco there were militia
commanders who did not have the status of commandant. In
Mexico City the viceroy himself was a captain general.

This multiplicity of semiautonomous military commands
could make for some confusion, especially when there were
personality disputes between regional commanders and the
viceroy and, more than ever, when the Constitution intervened
in 1812 to confuse the situation hopelessly by separating military
command from civil command. However, the system also made
for a widespread network of regional centers that fought and
won the war. The secret, as Calleja pointed out, was that these

armies were "accustomed to war, and maintained at the expense of the people they defend."[27] The system reflected the reality of a huge country that possessed regional centers not only of political and military power, but of economic influence as well.[28] Calleja's own attitude toward this multiplicity of command appears at first glance to have been confused. He frequently complained of the independence of the most important of the regional commanders, especially in the Internal Provinces and New Galicia. Yet, in 1818 he advocated placing all regional commands in the hands of peninsular generals so that all would be equal under the supreme command of the viceroy. What he advocated was not inconsistent. He wanted powerful regional commanders, but he wanted them to be subservient to the orders of the viceroy (or the superior political chief under the Constitution). It was regional independence he objected to, not regional power centers. He repeatedly urged full integration of the Internal Provinces into the viceroyalty, from which they had previously been separated. He felt strongly that this division of command caused much harm, although, strangely, he never objected to the existence of a separate captaincy general in Yucatán.

This network of regional command centers made possible the stopping or slowing down of uprisings at their place of origin. The armies were chiefly composed of creoles and castes from the provinces, and were under the supreme command of Calleja, who was intimately connected with and highly regarded by the regional creole elite of north-central New Spain. Viceroys Venegas and Calleja based the preservation of royalist power upon the broad and strong shoulders of the provincial creole who, in addition to fighting to defend his own home or region, had always actively sought army appointment as a means of advancement and social distinction. At least half the officers and nearly all the men of the royal army that defeated Hidalgo were Mexicans.[29] Not the least of the regime's achievements is that it was able to use Mexican manpower in what might be interpreted as a struggle to maintain foreign rule over Mexicans. Iturbide's final campaign for independence in 1820 and 1821 was predicated upon this regional defense network, for he deliberately directed his campaign at winning over the various regional capitals before he approached Mexico City. In effect

Iturbide won over the creole army first, then directed his attention against the royalist center of strength, which he knew could not resist without its regional armies.

The Hidalgo revolt swept on quickly to its final destruction. On January 17, 1811, the rebels met the army of Calleja and Flon at the bridge of Calderón, eleven leagues east of Guadalajara. The rebels were routed, losing 1,200 men and all their artillery, and Hidalgo and the other leaders fled. The royalist dead amounted to no more than fifty, of whom Flon was one. Royal armies regained control of most of the cities in central Mexico by March. On March 21, Hidalgo was captured in Coahuila; five months later, on July 30, 1811, he was shot. The heads of Hidalgo and three other rebel leaders were displayed for the next decade on the four corners of the Alhóndiga at Guanajuato, site of the first and greatest rebel massacre of gachupines.

Hidalgo accomplished nothing. The memory of the bloody depredations of his horde remained after his death to prevent potential supporters from joining the rebellion.[30] Hidalgo's colleagues, notably José María Morelos and Ignacio Rayón, remained in the field as leaders of the rebellion. Morelos created a superbly organized and effective army, providing the chief military threat to the royalists until his capture and execution in 1815. Morelos provided a clear set of political and social objectives for the rebellion—a clear alternative to royalism. His program consisted of independence (declared in 1813), social reforms of the most sweeping kind—including permanent abolition of tribute, of the caste system, and of legal barriers to lower-class advancement—income tax, and a congressional form of government.[31] Among other insurgent leaders who emerged were Mariano Matamoros, the Bravo family, the Galeano brothers, Guadalupe Victoria, and Vicente Guerrero. Some were merely bandit chiefs, some were dedicated patriots. Armed insurrection thus remained a threat to royal hegemony for the next few years, but Venegas and his successor, Calleja, never faltered in their task of providing effective and, if necessary, brutal opposition.

On the civilian side as well, the royalists launched an effective campaign of counterinsurrection. In April, 1811, after receipt of the news of Hidalgo's capture in Coahuila, a group of sympathizers in the capital plotted an attack against Viceroy Venegas, planning to kidnap him and force him to order Hidalgo's release. The leader of the plot was Mariana Rodríguez de Lazarín, recently married to Manuel Lazarín, a miner from Guanajuato. The conspirators met in the Lazarín house, where they made their plans and set a date for the attack. The night before the attack was to occur, José María Gallardo, one of the conspirators, confessed their plans to a priest at the convent of La Merced. The priest immediately informed the viceroy, and Gallardo, captured in a few hours, disclosed the names of the other conspirators. Because of the vague nature of their plot, none of the conspirators was executed. Mariana Rodríguez and her husband were imprisoned until December, 1820.[32]

One of the conspirators, however, was found to be in possession of a document that entirely altered the nature of the case. José María Espinosa, a businessman, possessed a list of persons involved in the conspiracy and a list of prominent individuals chosen by the conspirators for appointment to a National Junta that would assume the government after Venegas's capture. The list presented momentous problems for the government, for among the persons implicated were several score of Mexico City's leading creoles. Even though most of these men did not know their names were on the list, the government found it an excellent guide to suspicious individuals. The conspirators planned to appoint as members of the National Junta the liberal José María Fagoaga, Tomás Murphy (the business agent of an English firm) and Carlos María Bustamante (the liberal publicist who would soon become an outright rebel). Among those to be named to the new audiencia was the oidor Jacobo de Villaurrutia, whom the viceroy had long suspected. Cited as accomplices to the plot were the marqués de Rayas, the conde de Santiago, the conde de Regla, the conde de Medina, the marqués de San Miguel de Aguayo, the marqués de Guardiola, the regidor Manuel de Gamboa, José María Belaunzarán (later bishop of Monterrey), several officers, and the entire religious communities of the capital's convents of San Francisco, Santiago, Santo Domingo, La Merced, and San Agustín.

The government launched an immediate secret investigation, which lasted for a year and a half. Finally, in December, 1813, the official in charge of the investigation, Vicente Ruiz, reported that sixty-seven persons had been arrested and imprisoned in connection with the plot, but not one of the prominent men had been arrested. Ruiz decided to suspend further prosecution of the case, with the agreement of other authorities, because the investigation of so many important people "would cause consternation among an enormous mass of personages."[33] Nevertheless, suspicions were planted, and several of those same creole gentlemen were later arrested on other charges.

In the midst of the first investigations of the April plot, a second and far more serious conspiracy was uncovered in August, 1811, adding considerable substance to the viceroy's suspicions of at least one religious order in the capital. Almost the entire Augustinian convent was implicated. The plot, given away on its eve by one of the conspirators, Cristóbal Morante, was to kidnap Venegas on August 3 as he took his customary after-dinner drive in the Paseo de la Viga. The conspirators argued that the viceroy would be too drunk at that time to resist capture. He was to be handed over to Ignacio Rayón, who was then at Zitácuaro. Other rebels, supposedly hiding in the suburbs, would raise the city while Rayón's forces captured the government.[34] Venegas, as soon as he became aware of the plot, moved rapidly to suppress it. Late on the night of August 2, he ordered extra troops and heavy artillery to the palace and in a secret letter informed the cabildo of his actions.[35] The cabildo replied by sending a deputation to offer him its services, congratulating him on his escape. On the morning of August 3, viceregal authorities took twelve conspirators into custody. The leader seems to have been Antonio Rodríguez Dongo, in whose house the conspirators met. Others included Antonio Ferrer, a lawyer; Ignacio Catano and José Mariano Ayala, subalterns in the Commercial Regiment; Félix Pineda; José Mariano González; and three Augustinian friars, Juan Nepomuceno de Castro, Vicente Negreiros, and Manuel Rosendi. In a public proclamation, the viceroy promised they would be punished with dispatch.[36] Six of the prisoners were condemned to death and, on August 29, less than a month after the discovery of the plot, were executed in the small square of Mixcalco. Soldiers faced the populace, with orders to fire on the crowd watching the executions if there were any movement to rescue the condemned.

The fate of the three Augustinian friars was far more problematic, as they possessed the ecclesiastical fuero—the privilege of being tried only by a clerical court. The Sala del Crímen of the audiencia insisted on its right to try their case and demanded the death penalty for them.[37] Nancy Farriss has shown that by this time the Juntas of Security in the rural regions of New Spain had begun to try ecclesiastics for treason but were required to have one clerical member voting in such cases.[38] The archdiocesan court, however, refused to allow the Augustinians to be tried by civil processes and refused to degrade them from the priesthood. A stalemate was reached, which was broken only by the intervention of Viceroy Venegas, who had no desire to witness the spectacle of the first execution of clerics in Mexico City since the Conquest. He sent all three to exile in Havana. Castro died on the way there in the prison at Veracruz.

Several other friars of the Augustinian convent in the capital were tried at a future date for implication in the conspiracy, for failing to denounce the storage of weapons in the convent and for suspicious activities and seditious sermons. All of them were also sentenced to exile or prison without prior degradation from the priesthood.[39]

The protracted legal quarrel over whether the friars could be tried by civil courts was but one of several such disputes involving clergy accused of treason. The clear complicity of a considerable portion of the nation's clergy in the rebellion induced Viceroy Venegas on June 25, 1812, to publish his famous "blood and fire" order abolishing all special fueros for ecclesiastics guilty of treason. Declaring that "these monsters neither deserve immunity nor will be spared any consideration because of it," he authorized royal military commanders in the field to try all clerical insurgents without any intervention from ecclesiastical courts and to execute them without prior degradation from the priesthood. This order, which the Council of the Indies a few years later termed "the most inhuman, illegal, and pernicious document to appear in this unhappy epoch," was not applied to either Mexico City or Guadalajara, though it was extensively implemented in the field. Farriss thinks that viceregal concern for arousing public opinion explains Venegas's exemption of Mexico City.[40] Clearly the capital, seat of the hierarchy, was not a suitable location for such harsh treatment of ecclesiastics, and none was ever put to death in Mexico City. Although Morelos, who was a priest, was formally degraded by the ecclesiastical authorities there in November, 1815, he was executed outside the city at the nearby town of San Cristóbal Ecatepec.

The August conspiracy appeared to have a disproportionately unsettling impact on the government. Given the fact that the April plot received no public notice, it is all the more striking that Venegas played up the August one for all it was worth. The fullest public discussion was given to every aspect of the plot. The viceroy announced it in the dead of night to a hastily assembled cabildo, he released full details in the *Gazeta*, the trials of the civilian defendants were conducted with constant news releases, and the executions were witnessed by many. Even the complicated negotiations with the Church over the fate of the friars was allowed to become public knowledge. Venegas was apparently using the plot as propaganda, and in this regard it served a most useful purpose. It reminded inhabitants that traitors could wage their struggle not only on the battlefield but also by subversion. It also reflected very favorably upon the viceroy's bravery, determination, and constancy in the face of personal danger. A public outcry filled the pages of the *Gazeta*, as corporations and groups of every description, both military and civilian, announced their loyalty to the viceroy. Altogether, Venegas used the conspiracy brilliantly. Most importantly, it gave him an excuse to impose a type of martial law in Mexico City.

In February, 1811, Venegas had created a system of internal passports for the region of Mexico City. Decreed in February, the system was scheduled to go into effect in August. Appointed to direct the passport system and to hear cases involving it were José Juan Fagoaga, former alcalde of the cabildo and police judge, and Pedro de la Puente, the alcalde del crímen of the audiencia.[41]

The August conspiracy, discovered just as the passports were supposed to go into effect, gave Venegas the excuse he needed to create an even more sophisticated technique for domestic surveillance and control. He immediately created a new agency called the Junta of Police and Public Security, which superseded and absorbed the existing passport system and, more importantly, the Mexico City Junta of Security, which had existed since 1809. Pedro de la Puente became superintendent of this Junta of Police, while José Juan Fagoaga became deputy superintendent and treasurer. Reflecting popular alarm over the recent assassination plot, a public drive for funds quickly produced the startling sum of 52,703 pesos.[42] It takes a very strong government to create a repressive police network by popular subscription, but that is precisely what Venegas did.

The Junta of Police and Public Security was composed of the superintendent, the deputy superintendent, and sixteen deputies appointed by the viceroy from the cabildo and nobility.[43] Each deputy had supervision over two of the thirty-two districts of the capital. Members of the junta served without pay and were assisted by secretaries and porters; each deputy had under his orders four paid police corporals whom he appointed himself. Their function was to assure the peace, collect and issue passports, search suspicious houses, inspect places of public amusement, make nightly inspections of the city, and arrest drunkards, troublemakers, and vagrants—all while keeping a sharp lookout for signs of treason. The superintendent was empowered to hear cases and impose penalties in his own court. Each of the sixteen deputies built a shelter, or precinct house, which included dormitory rooms for the guards. The new system was not supposed to usurp any of the traditional peacekeeping powers and responsibilities of the city council or the alcaldes de barrio, but the cabildo later objected that it did just that.

The passport system was quite sophisticated. Each of the deputies was ordered to form a census of the inhabitants of his two districts. Once counted, no person could change his residence without signed permission from the deputy. No one could admit new dependents, servants, guests, or strangers to his house without notifying and explaining the reasons to the deputy. Innkeepers submitted daily accountings of their guests. No person could spend more than two nights outside his house without advising the deputy in the district he was visiting. In addition, the census lists could be, and were, used to determine forced contributions and troop conscription.

The police could refuse to issue passports to anyone they suspected. Regular passports were good for only one trip outside the city and were collected upon their bearer's return. For the accommodation of persons who left the city regularly— including the peons who worked in outlying farms—"perpetual passports" were issued. This made it possible to distinguish between casual and regular travelers. A stranger visiting the city received surety papers to keep on his person at all times, and without them he was subject to arrest. A report prepared at the end of the first six months showed that over 6,000 persons entered Mexico City every day using the permanent passports and approximately 200 entered every day on regular passports.[44]

The aspect of martial law was further heightened by the use of four soldiers at each police station for the first months. Superintendent Puente at first kept himself busy simply establishing the system and getting it to work. He prepared six different decrees in the first months clarifying procedures and regulations.

Both police and passport aspects of the system soon caused loud complaints. A large number of arrests resulted from nonpossession of passports. In the first months, from eight to forty-five persons, usually Indian porters and workers, were arrested each week on this charge. The cabildo soon began to complain about the takeover of its police powers. On the grounds that it was losing its traditional jurisdiction in these matters, it sent a long and outspoken petition to Venegas asking for abolition of the Junta of Police. It claimed that the network did not prohibit rebel infiltration but merely caused popular reaction. The cabildo especially criticized the Junta on the grounds that it kept Indian carriers from supplying the markets, that it was used in troop levies, and that it bore too close a resemblance to the repressive controls enacted in Madrid by the French conquerors. The viceroy refused to act on these complaints. Consequently, the cabildo repeated the charges in an even stronger representation to Spain, accusing Venegas of taking the law into his own hands and of imposing tyranny.[45]

In reply to these complaints, the Junta of Police in January, 1812, published a long statement in its own defense, reviewing its services in defending against rebel infiltration. Puente denied all the cabildo's charges and accused it in turn of being unable to keep the peace. He said that Indian porters were never fined for not having a passport but were put to work on beneficial public projects instead. In reply to the charge that the police were involved in conscription, he accused the cabildo of obstructionism and concluded that "the interest of public defense justifies any rigor."[46]

A succession of Spanish metropolitan governments agreed with the cabildo's sentiments concerning the dangers of viceregal initiative in so central a question. On several occasions in 1810 and 1811, the peninsular authorities had ordered the abolition of the earlier Juntas of Security that had been established throughout New Spain. These orders were ignored by Viceroys Lizana, Venegas, and, later, Calleja. After creation of the Constitution, the Cortes informed Viceroy Calleja that the Junta of Police was unconstitutional. (That controversy will be considered in the next chapter.) The Junta of Police remained in existence in Mexico City, despite direct orders for its abolition, until 1813.

The passports remained in use until independence, except for a brief period from August, 1820, to March, 1821. Venegas's successors renewed his 1811 decree on several occasions. When the Constitution was reestablished in 1820, Viceroy Apodaca abolished the passports, but in March, 1821, after the outbreak of Iturbide's revolt, he reestablished them. The complaints also continued. In July, 1820, the cabildo again charged that the passports caused the virtual collapse of city markets by obstructing free entry of goods into the city.[47]

Opposition to the police system became so bitter that in February, 1813, Pedro de la Puente resigned the superintendency, claiming he was the object of such public hatred as to be "in imminent danger of assassination."[48] The deepest bitterness was undoubtedly provoked by the viceroy's use of police censuses for military levies.

The maintenance and expansion of royal military strength was the regime's first priority in its counterinsurrectionary campaign. The total military force of New Spain before the war was about 32,000 men; by 1820 it had grown to over 85,000 men. Veteran troops numbered only 10,620 at the outset, and an additional 8,448 men came to New Spain in several expeditionary forces sent from the peninsula between 1812 and 1817. The remainder of the army was composed of militia. Nearly 22,000 men belonged to the various provincial militia, while the city militia forces throughout the country numbered 44,000 men. For its part, Mexico City was required to support not only a wide array of local picket corps, but also the Provincial Regiment of Mexico—whose officers were chosen by the cabildo with the viceroy's advice—plus the Patriotic Battalions of Ferdinand VII. By the first months of 1811, the Patriotic Battalions had grown in number to four and, like the rest of the army, had ceased to be voluntary.[49]

On April 6, 1811, Viceroy Venegas sent a circular to all tribunals, offices, and colleges in the capital saying that although three of the Patriotic Battalions were complete, the turnout of volunteers was inadequate to fill the fourth. He ordered all corporations to submit a list of their members or employees and the battalion to which each belonged and to make a special note of any man who had not yet volunteered for armed service. Although such haphazard conscription had been employed in Mexico City as early as 1796, it now extended to both upper and lower classes. Its effects were soon felt in the government itself, as well as in every college, tribunal, and guild. The city treasurer, for example, wrote the cabildo that all his employees were drafted and he could not operate his office without them. In this particular case, the viceroy allowed two of the treasury employees to return to their jobs, although they remained on call with their battalions.[50]

One of the first and most lamentable casualties of conscription was the Royal and Pontifical University of Mexico, whose students, despite their claim of traditional exemption, were enrolled in the Patriotic Battalions. Furthermore, in October, 1810, Venegas ordered that the first regiment of the Patriots should be housed in the university's main building. In order to prevent possible clashes between students and soldiers, classes in most of the faculties were thereupon disbanded, the rector's office was transferred to the College of San Ildefonso, and the library was permanently closed and barred to prevent damage to its collection. This effectively brought about the dissolution of the university, although it was still expected to make financial contributions as a corporate entity. Without a student enrollment, however, it was unable to meet these demands, and in turn the government suspected its loyalty. Quietly, almost without notice, one of the most venerable institutions of higher learning in the New World ceased to function.[51]

After the defeat of the rebel horde at the bridge of Calderón in January, 1811, and Hidalgo's capture in March, it appeared for a time that the revolution might be over. But the ever-vigilant General Calleja knew better. He wrote the viceroy, "The insurrection is far from calm; it returns like the hydra in proportion to the number of times its head is cut off."[52] Calleja frequently urged Venegas not to let down his guard against the rebels even though royalist victories were constantly being achieved. He accused the peninsulars living in New Spain of a lack of patriotism and cowardice on the grounds that they were shirking their duty to take up arms, and he proposed that Venegas order a general mobilization of Europeans. The viceroy, though he refused to order a mobilization specifically of Europeans, could not refuse Calleja's pressure for more troops. As a result, on July 31, 1811, he ordered the cabildo to produce within eight days enough men to fill the ranks of the Provincial Infantry to the level of 1,000 men and to put the Provincial Cavalry on a war footing.[53]

The only way to fill the regiments, particularly the Patriotic Battalions, was by direct levies, and Venegas turned to the police system to provide them. Among the papers of Pedro de la Puente is evidence of the use to which the police censuses were put; the military commander of Mexico City wrote on August 28, 1811, to the commandants of the Patriotic Battalions, "I am sending you the lists of individuals useful for service as Patriots, which the Superintendent of Police has just now delivered into my hands."[54] This rapid expansion of the capital's garrison led to the publication of orders for the confiscation of private weapons and, subsequently, for the confiscation of privately owned horses.[55]

For the remainder of the war the viceregal government made periodic, haphazard levies of soldiers and army laborers in the capital. José Joaquín Elizalde, a police official commissioned to take conscripts, reported that in a two-month period in 1813 he took over 1,000 men in the capital, of whom he found 349 to be "useful" and sent them to various corps.[56] The only recognized grounds for exemption were being the only support for a widowed mother and family, and being physically unfit. Early in the war, skilled artisans and food suppliers were supposed to be exempt, but many farmers, bakers, charcoal sellers, and artisans were taken. Eventually, the government even rounded up léperos for army labor details. There was a long tradition of conscripting vagabonds in Mexico City. It had been employed in 1796 under Viceroy Branciforte and in 1801 by Viceroy Marquina. In 1799 Viceroy Azanza conscripted guild apprentices. Archer concludes that "the pressures for recruits opened the way to abuse of the common people," and he points out that even tributary Indians, previously exempt from armed service, were being drafted as early as 1805 in the Intendancy of Mexico for use in the capital's garrison.[57] Since the need for manpower increased after 1810, the conscription of Indians probably continued.

In January and February, 1812, the capital was threatened for a second time with direct military assault when Morelos's troops advanced as far as Taxco, only twenty-five leagues away. By mid-February, the advance guard under Nicolás Bravo had pushed to Chalco and had outposts at San Agustín de las Cuevas, only three leagues from the city's gates. Rebel bands intercepted mail and provisions destined for the capital, and the royalists feared they would block the roads to Texcoco and Toluca. For a second time, Viceroy Venegas summoned General Calleja and his Army of the Center to the capital. Calleja arrived in February, fresh from his victory over the rebels at Zitácuaro, a battle in which the city's own grenadiers participated and in reward for which the cabildo sent them the silver coins specially minted in 1808 in honor of Ferdinand's accession. The city council informed Spain that Calleja and his army of "liberators" were welcomed by thousands of delirious citizens.[58]

After his triumphal return from Zitácuaro, General Calleja was immensely popular with the ultraroyalists. He quarreled publicly with Venegas over military policy and promotions, and he offered to resign a number of times. The two men cordially disliked each other, the viceroy viewing Calleja as a potential rival. A temporary respite in their quarrel occurred when Calleja led his army out of the capital to besiege Morelos for two months at the little town of Cuautla Amilpas, where the rebels made their general headquarters in preparation for the planned attack upon Mexico City. The siege, which according to Bustamante cost the government a staggering 564,000 pesos, resulted in only a limited royalist success, since Morelos was able to escape. In May, Calleja returned to the capital to a distinctly muted reception. The feud between the viceroy and general now became so intense that royalists began taking sides. In order to dispel an army that Venegas judged personally loyal to Calleja rather than to himself, the viceroy disbanded the Army of the Center on May 17.[59] Calleja thereupon took up residence in the capital, where he became the leader of a coterie composed both of royalists unhappy with the Venegas government and of creole liberals unsuccessfully bidding for his support. Ladd lists among the members of Calleja's coterie many of the men who had been close to him in San Luis Potosí, such as the marqués de Jaral, the marqués de Guadalupe, the conde del Valle Orizaba, Anastasio Bustamante, Manuel Gómez Pedraza, Miguel Barragán, and Manuel de la Soto Riva. Also included were Canon José Mariano Beristain, city councilor Francisco Manuel Sánchez de Tagle, and auditor of war José Antonio Cristo y Conde.[60]

When Morelos captured the important southern city of Oaxaca, the viceroy became aware that royalist hard-liners in the capital strongly favored Calleja. Venegas therefore appointed him military governor of Mexico City in December, 1812. Calleja's partisans, meanwhile, successfully petitioned the peninsula to have the general appointed viceroy.

General Calleja—the Spanish Tamerlaine, as Bustamante called him—exacted the greatest sacrifices from the inhabitants of Mexico City in support of the army, just as he required the greatest financial contributions.[61] For the first year of his administration he kept for himself the office of military governor of the capital, finally relinquishing it in April, 1814, to Brigadier Juan José de Olazabal, chairman of the Junta de Guerra. Calleja, the victor of Aculco, Guanajuato, Calderón, Zitácuaro, and

Cuautla, was New Spain's most brilliant officer, a remarkably skilled politician, a dedicated royalist, and the most capable of the last viceroys. Alamán called him "one of the most notable men Spain has produced." In only three years he crushed the revolts. After he left office he was granted, on the petition of the city council, the title conde de Calderón in recognition of his achievements at that decisive battle against Hidalgo.[62]

Calleja was not only the leader of the militarists in New Spain—a role in which he was ably seconded by the fierce commandant of New Galicia and president of Guadalajara, José de la Cruz—but later functioned as one of the chief militarists in Spain. After his return to Spain in 1816, he was one of a group of officers who, under the direction of Ferdinand VII's minister of war, Francisco Eguia, advocated a military rather than a negotiated settlement, or "pacification," of America. Several commanders who had returned from military service in America or who were still in the field were key figures in the group. Among them were Pablo Morillo, commander in chief of the expeditionary army sent to pacify Venezuela, Juan Sámano, viceroy of New Granada, and Pascual de Enrile, former naval commander of the blockade of the coast of New Granada. Juan Friede has dubbed them the "militarist party."[63]

In 1819 Calleja received the appointment that might well have made him the new, and greater, Morillo; he was chosen to replace the disgraced Enrique O'Donnell as commander in chief of the huge expeditionary force that was then being gathered in Cádiz to be dispatched to Buenos Aires. This would have been the largest expeditionary force sent to America in the War of Independence period, and the decision to form the army constituted a clear victory for the militarists in their campaign to urge a military settlement upon the king. Its object was to seize Montevideo from the Portuguese, who were then holding it; from that base to recapture Buenos Aires, ending its ten years of independence; and thence to launch a massive pincers movement against the Buenos Aires rebels in Upper Peru, consolidating the security of the viceroyalty of Peru and perhaps even reconquering Chile. The uprising of the troops at Cádiz on January 1, 1820, brought these dreams of military conquest to an end.

Like Morillo, Calleja frequently advocated the replacement of civilian authority by military authority as the chief means of ending the revolts in America. In 1818 he submitted to the Spanish government a blunt request that in all the nine intendancies of New Spain and in the Internal Provinces of the East and West a Spanish general should be appointed to hold not only the military command of the district, but the intendancy as well. There was some merit to the proposal, for one of Calleja's chief complaints during his term as viceroy had involved the multiplication of authority and its consequent confusion, caused by the existence in the intendancies of a military commander and a civilian intendant. In fact, the situation was even more confused than that. In several of New Spain's intendancies, the civilian and military command had already been joined, while in others they remained separate. José de la Cruz, for example, was both president of the audiencia of Guadalajara and commander in chief of New Galicia, while for a period he also held the intendancy. In 1817 he asked for the appointment of a civilian intendant, but in 1819 he complained that the intendant should be strictly limited to control over the hacienda and the royal accòunts. In Yucatán, Captain General Miguel de Castro Araoz took over the intendancy in November, 1818, when the incumbent died. In Spain, the Contaduría General offered the opinion that Calleja's proposal and Araoz's assumption of the intendancy should not be permitted, accusing the officers of mixed motives in their desire to gain control of the civilian government. The peninsular Council of War, however, recommended strongly in favor of Calleja's proposal. The matter was still pending when the change of government in 1820 suppressed the question and, in turn, brought further confusion to the lines of authority in America.[64]

Levies became more frequent after Calleja's appointment as viceroy. Intensely aware of the need to keep the army well supplied and paid, Calleja claimed that he needed an additional two million pesos a year to clothe and feed the troops.[65] Gradually, but quite consciously, he converted the royal regime into a military regime.

In October, 1813, Viceroy Calleja ordered the enlistment of all eligible men over the age of sixteen in Mexico City. They were given eight days to present themselves for service in the Patriotic Battalions. Not even members of the cabildo were exempted. Several of them held commissions in the Patriots and were ordered to come to arms. The cabildo strongly protested, claiming it was an insult to the corporate inviolability of the council. As a result of its protests, the viceroy excused councilors José Garay, José Ignacio Adalid, Juan Ignacio Orellana, and Juan Cervantes y Padilla in 1813. When the regidor Mariano Icaza voluntarily agreed to serve as captain of the first battalion of Patriots in 1814, the cabildo pointedly reminded him that "just because he was taking up military service, he did not cease to be a regidor," and had to fulfill his various commissions on the council. Consequently, Icaza also asked to be excused from service, and the viceroy agreed. Not until 1821, however, was the cabildo granted its request for an exemption of all regidors.[66]

The desertion and draft-evasion rate was so high that conscription remained necessary throughout the remaining years of the war. In 1815 Calleja ordered the judges of the eight major quarters of the city to begin rounding up léperos and vagrants for use in army labor gangs. This was necessary, he said, because the general levies could not provide enough men. One year later, the commander of the Provincial Regiment asked the viceroy for more men, and Calleja again ordered new levies. Again in 1817 the commander complained of a shortage, and Viceroy Apodaca ordered a levy of léperos, declaring that "since the desertions never cease . . . the corps do not have enough people to carry out their duties."[67] Yet, in August, 1817, the Provincial Regiment was still short 216 men.

The cabildo made only half-hearted attempts to protect inhabitants from these forced levies. In March, 1814, it complained that the army's methods were harsh and that "the soldiers charged with the levy have mistreated many people and have committed outrages." When it complained officially to the viceroy, however, no action was taken.[68]

The soldiers were blamed for the general increase in crimes in the city during these years, though the increase may well have been a result of the social fragmentation of the war. In October, 1813, for example, the city council complained to the viceroy about "the many excesses committed by the troops," particularly with regard to allegations that they were forcing Indian carriers to work for them or were stealing produce destined for the markets. The viceroy responded with an order forbidding soldiers from abusing the Indians and mestizos, and forbidding civilians from insulting soldiers. The cabildo wanted a general prohibition against soldiers' carrying arms while off duty, but, failing that, settled for ordering the night guard increased by forty men. In 1814, the council discussed the possibility of declaring the Alameda park off limits to the soldiers, who were accused of destroying the park's stone statues and benches, but nothing came of the debate.[69]

Mexico City was spared only one significant burden related to New Spain's rapid militarization. In 1814 the capital was specifically exempted from a viceregal order requiring all the nation's cities and towns to garrison troops at public expense and to house them in private homes if necessary.[70] No doubt the capital was exempted because it offered so many public and semipublic buildings—schools, factories, institutions—in which soldiers were quartered, and because most members of the capital's militia were residents of the city. Periodic orders for the confiscation of private arms and horses, however, remained an annoyance to the inhabitants.

By the end of the first six months of Viceroy Calleja's administration, the burden of supporting New Spain's rapid militarization was becoming noticeably painful for individual inhabitants of the capital. The archive of the Real Hacienda preserves a remarkable collection of private letters from lower-class residents of Mexico City to viceregal authorities requesting various favors. These letters indicate that the exemptions from conscription that supposedly existed were sometimes ignored. They also suggest that the ordinary men and women of the city were being called upon to pay a very heavy price for royal military preparedness. Viceroy Calleja's handling of these complaints shows him to be a fair man, but overwhelmingly dedicated to military discipline.

The stories told in these letters run the gamut of human tragedy. Juliana Zamudio wrote that her two sons were in service, and the oldest was killed by rebels while serving in the escort that traveled with Viceroy Venegas to Veracruz when he left the country. She asked for the release of her other son since she had no one to support her and her daughters. The viceroy ordered the young man's officers to decide the case. Mariana Manrrí, whose husband and two sons were members of Colonel Iturbide's battalion, said that her husband had deserted her, and she asked for his back salary to support herself and her five other children. Calleja ordered her to take the matter up with Iturbide. María Manuela Fernández wrote that her brother had deserted in order to attend her in the city while she was sick in the epidemic of 1813. Military police captured him, and he was given fifty lashes and three months in jail. As he was only eighteen, she asked for his release from prison. Calleja ordered the man returned to his regiment. María Ignacia Zúñiga, widow and mother of two sons, wrote the virreina that one of her sons was imprisoned for some infraction and about to be sent to military service. Since he suffered from epilepsy, she begged that he not be conscripted. No answer was forthcoming. María Vicente Flores complained that the "Patriots . . . entered her house one night and took in levy her husband José Antonio Lagunas," who was the only support of herself and her children, and she asked for his release. No decision was noted. The presbyter Matheo Ocampo, chaplain to the regiment of Tlaxcala for nineteen years, asked for a pension of thirty pesos a month, as he could not find a new chaplaincy in the capital. The viceroy refused. The widow Ana María Hernández asked for her son's release from the Mexico City regiment, in which he had already served two and a half years, because he was the family's only support. Calleja granted her request. María Hipólita de Campos asked for the four months of back salary for her husband, who had overstayed his leave visiting relatives in Veracruz. His baggage had been stolen on the convoy. The viceroy ordered the salary be paid only after the man returned to his regiment. Viviano Suarez, a police guard of the capital, was condemned to six years service in the Regiment of Veracruz for wounding another police guard in his company. He asked to be allowed to remain on the police force instead, in order to support his widowed mother and sister in the capital. The viceroy refused.

Joaquina Diaz said that she and her children and her husband's mother were all sick in the 1813 epidemic, and she requested her husband's transfer to the Urban Commercial Regiment so he could be near them in the capital. Calleja refused. A grenadier, José Zuleta, injured at Zitácuaro, asked to be released from service on the grounds that he had seen action at Las Cruces and sixteen other battles, during which he had killed six of the enemy and taken one enemy cannon. The viceroy refused. Francisco Fernández, a veteran of five years, asked to be forgiven for deserting, which he said was owing to illness and the severe punishments handed out by his commander, "who tied soldiers nude to a tree trunk, and in this shameful state gave them fifty lashes, so that many died." The viceroy referred the case to the man's commander.

Perhaps the saddest case was that of María Rita Camacho, who had lost three of her four sons in battle. She asked for the release from service of her fourth and only surviving son, who had been condemned to the Dragoons for refusing to marry a girl he seduced. The viceroy called on the family's parish priest, who testified that, although it was true the other three sons were killed in battle, the fourth was not worthy of clemency, for he had held no job for five years and had seduced an Indian girl, Màría Guadalupe, under promise to marry her. This matter came twice to Calleja's attention, and both times he refused to grant the mother's plea. Although so many pleas were refused, it seems that some special privileges were granted to sons of government servants. José de Rozas, commander of the city's guard, asked that his young son be transferred to a different regiment, as the one he belonged to was about to leave the city for active duty in the field. The viceroy agreed to transfer the boy as soon as possible.[71]

These letters reveal much about military service, Viceroy Calleja's view of discipline, and the harshness of life for the poor. The conscription of men who were the sole support of their families created further hardships for the poor. No remission of terms of service was granted, even for extraordinary heroism and being wounded in action. Military discipline in the field was very severe, and service in the capital was obviously considered much easier. The fact that men were condemned to military service for criminal offenses is further proof that the military life was not an easy one. No special or unusual financial favors or pensions were granted under any circumstances for ordinary people. Appeals to the virreina—a creole aristocrat thought by the common people to be more concerned with their welfare than her husband—were definitely frowned upon and received no action of any kind. Calleja himself often referred decisions back to regimental commanders. Desertion, on any grounds, was harshly dealt with.

No wonder the royal authorities were kept constantly busy in the arrest and punishment of what appeared to them to be crimes of disloyalty. Throughout 1811 and 1812 the viceregal government received weekly reports from Police Superintendent Puente concerning the numbers of persons arrested in the capital on charges of treason, plotting against the government, and making insulting remarks about the government. In the week of September 23, 1811, forty-one men and seven women were arrested on such charges. The next week sixteen men and four women were arrested; the first week of October, twenty-one men and one woman; the third week of October, eight men; the next, four men. Separate reports kept by the police on the numbers of men arrested for desertion in Mexico City reveal that from one to four were apprehended each week on this charge. From August 26 to December 24, 1811, the police apprehended 1,631 people in Mexico City alone; 345 of these were tried by the Junta of Security on suspicion of treason, and 1,024 were tried by the Sala del Crímen. In the nation as a whole, according to N. M. Farriss, the Juntas of Security heard nearly 45,000 cases in the years 1810 to 1812. The Constitution of 1812 established many judicial reforms, but the crimes of treason, spying, and contribution to the desertion of soldiers were specifically exempted by decree from constitutional protections.[72]

One aspect of the viceregal regime's counterinsurrectionary campaign in the capital was less than successful. After many years of discussion, the government initiated a project to dig a giant ditch (*zanja cuadrada*) around the city to prevent the infiltration of rebels, to provide a first-defense works, and to guard against contraband. The idea had been initiated under Viceroy Iturrigaray, who accepted a plan put forth by an architect to dig a vast canal, 32,000 meters in length, at a cost of 600,000 pesos, directly through the city to Lake Texcoco in order to control the periodic flooding of the valley. Iturrigaray obtained a loan of 200,000 pesos from the Mining Tribunal on behalf of the audiencia to begin the project. In response to a public invitation for bids for construction of the canal, Pascual Ignacio Apecechea, a gold and silver smelter, proposed an alternate plan for the construction of a great ditch around, not through, the city, which would act as a spillway. After the outbreak of the insurrections, this plan gained preference, as it seemed suitable for the defense of the unwalled city. A general subscription to collect funds for the work produced only a few hundred pesos. Nevertheless, the government proceeded to invite laborers to sign up, clearly implying that this was meant to be a "make-work project" to provide jobs for some of the countless unemployed. Fear of working in the disease-infested swamps near Lake Texcoco prevented most laborers from volunteering and the use of insurgent prisoners was briefly contemplated. The real blow to the project came when Apecechea's brother submitted an estimate that it would cost 1,600,000 pesos. The audiencia was not even able to pay the Mining Tribunal the 45,000 pesos of interest on its earlier loan. Despite these difficulties, Viceroy Apodaca later reported that Venegas and Calleja had completed the digging of 23,000 varas of the ditch before 1816. Apodaca wanted to continue the project, even though the sides of the ditch collapsed as rapidly as the ditch was dug, and he admitted it provided no protection from rebel infiltration. Plans were also drawn up to wall the city, but nothing ever came of them.[73]

By the end of 1811, the Venegas government had launched a remarkably effective campaign of counterinsurgency. Though the *Grito de Dolores* had at first caught the royal regime unprepared, by the time of the Battle of Zitácuaro it had been able to organize a multifaceted response to the threat of military insurrection. As Hamill says, the royalists proved by the end of 1811 "that the revolution could be contained."[74] The royalists had denied Hidalgo an effective foothold in the region of Mexico City, they had driven his Indian horde back until it dissipated of its own internal weaknesses, they had strengthened intellectual and emotional ties to the motherland through a propaganda campaign, they had unearthed, as shall be seen, new methods of raising revenues, they had erected a system of internal surveillance and trial for suspected traitors, and they had replied to rebel terrorism with terrorism of their own. For his efforts Venegas was granted the title marqués de la Reunión de Nueva España. Calleja's administration, in response to the even more dangerous Morelos phase of the rebellion, would intensify this campaign of counteroffensive and would smash the rebellion utterly. None of this would come without cost, of course. Gradually, almost imperceptibly, the royal regime was converting itself from a system based on self-interest and Mexican respect for the mother country into a regime based on force, and many people were beginning to suffer from its effects. This would have extraordinary consequences, but, for the moment, the important thing was that the royalists prevailed over the threat of armed insurrection and would continue to do so. Armed insurrection alone could not, and did not, destroy Spain's right to govern.

Only Spain could destroy its own right to sovereignty, because sovereignty is based on the recognized right of the government to exercise power, to command its subjects; this right, in turn, is based on the capacity for "reasoned elaboration" as Carl Friedrich calls it, the ability to convince.[75] In Mexico, Spain's sovereignty was based on three hundred years of legitimacy, reinforced by a clearly recognized and widely accepted ethos of monarch, Church, law, and order. The enemy, the rebel, could not single-handedly deprive Spain of this legitimacy. Spain itself would have to falter badly before her enemies would even be heard. Hidalgo and Morelos accomplished only the presentation of alternatives to Spanish imperial control. Hidalgo's consisted of Indian insurrection and received short-shrift because of it. Morelos's consisted of a program of radical social reform, which was equally unattractive to the elite who aspired to just the opposite—less royal control over the use of Indian and caste labor. As long as Spanish policy remained fairly consistent, as long as Spain did nothing to weaken further the authority of its representatives in America, defense of the viceregal regime against armed threats remained possible.

Spain's antagonists had now seen three alternatives to status-quo royal government: limited, elite-dominated, creole-oriented autonomy, which was untimely squelched by a handful of reactionaries in 1808; Indian uprising, which was met by massive resistance from many quarters of the nation and many classes; and mestizo-dominated, radical social reform, which was also unacceptable to the policy-making governmental and civilian elites. Meanwhile, the royal regime had also changed. From the chaos of 1808, through two make-shift viceroys, it emerged to Venegas and, later, Calleja, two immensely competent leaders who helped organize a unified resistance to rebellion. They restored the prestige of the viceregal office, so badly tarnished by Iturrigaray's corruption and the incompetence of Garibay and Lizana, and they reestablished a true royal government that was no longer dominated by a handful of local merchants (though those merchants continued to be a privileged group whose advice was always listened to). Most importantly, Venegas and Calleja were able to reach the real depth of support for the royal regime in New Spain. After all, the 15,000 gachupines living in the country in 1810—of whom 2,000 were slaughtered in a matter of months—could not, and did not, defeat the rebels by themselves. Vast segments of the native-born population, whether creole, or mestizo, or Indian, or caste, must have helped. This was the heart of the regime's success.

At the same time, Venegas and Calleja were beginning to convert the rather easy-going, perhaps even benevolent, regime that heretofore existed, into a regime dominated by hard-line imperialists and militarists, a regime in which not only rebellion was firmly resisted, but also reform. The contradictions began to multiply. To counter the undoubted threat of armed insurrection, the viceroys were mobilizing the nation to a do-or-die struggle to restore absolutism. In this they were taking a terrible and unforeseen risk. Suppose the motherland, Spain—the source of their authority, the parent whose child they were now attempting to discipline—were to change the ground rules. Suppose Spain abandoned absolutism. What would happen then? That is exactly the problem Venegas and Calleja faced upon the implementation of the Constitution in 1812.

Chapter 4

The Third Threat:
The Cortes and the Constitution

THE CORTES, which assumed sovereign power over the empire in 1810, and the Constitution, which was promulgated in 1812 and lasted until 1814, did not so much threaten the continued existence of Spanish power in New Spain as they threatened the existence of the absolutist government that Viceroys Venegas and Calleja were attempting with such effort to rebuild and strengthen. Consequently, the highest ranking figures of the viceregal regime viewed these radical changes of government, especially the Constitution, as a dire threat to the restoration of loyalty. The viceregal leaders tolerated the Cortes because they had little choice. It solved the legitimacy crisis provoked by the capture of the king and, in spite of its radicalism, it derived from the deepest traditions of Castilian history. The tradition of calling the Cortes in times of crisis, though little used in the past three centuries, predated the creation of the unified monarchy under the house of Austria. The Constitution however, was a different thing. New Spain's rulers viewed it as heresy incarnate, convinced that it would give victory to the insurgents.[1]

Their fears were not ungrounded. The radical reforms initiated by the Cortes and Constitution provided a new impetus to the desire for autonomy among Mexico City's domestic elite and creole bourgeoisie. The autonomist urge had been suppressed in 1808 and superseded by armed insurrection in 1810. Now the cabildo, as the leading focus of creole political discontent, had a second chance to be heard. New Spain was being presented with yet another alternative to status-quo royal government.

This resurgence of autonomism occurred simultaneously with the Morelos revolt, which itself strained viceregal resources to the limit. For two years, 1812 to 1814, the absolutists had to counter the radical armed insurrection, which in 1813 declared independence as its object, and they had to fight the threat of autonomist subversion, which royalists equally termed "independence." To do this, they had to resist those aspects of the Constitution that they perceived as inimical to royal authority. They received their reward in 1814 when Ferdinand VII restored absolutism, but, in achieving their goal, they had disobeyed the supreme law of the empire. This created another weakness in Spain's armor of legitimacy, another of those contradictions that began to prove to Mexicans the invalidity of imperial authority. The viceroys were fighting for something that Spain itself had supposedly abandoned. The Mexican domestic elite and bourgeoisie, having rejected the alternative of radical insurrection, found the Constitution's limited reforms entirely reasonable.

While New Spain was undergoing the Hidalgo insurrection, Spain itself was experiencing no less traumatic political upheavals. The tremendous ferment of the uprising of the Spanish people against Napoleon and the French conquerors, beginning in 1808 and lasting until the Spanish victory in 1814, produced a new era in the history of Spain. The many rival juntas formed by the patriots to fight the French eventually resulted in the election of a Central Junta, which located itself first in Seville. It was then forced to flee to the island of León in the marshes off Cádiz. The Central Junta called for the meeting of a Cortes but, under heavy criticism for its management of the war, dissolved itself before any further action could be taken. A five-man Regency replaced the unfortunate Central Junta and proceeded, though slowly and reluctantly, to call a meeting of the Cortes to take place in September, 1810. The capital of each province in America was to elect and send a deputy to the meeting.[2]

Here was a political revolution of the first order, and the Mexico City cabildo responded enthusiastically. It selected as its

delegate Dr. José Beye Cisneros, professor emeritus of law at the
university, and celebrated the convocation of the Cortes with
three days of illuminations, special theatrical performances, and
a ball in the municipal chambers. There was cause for celebra-
tion, for the election of the Cortes deputy once again gave the
city council a voice in national, even imperial, policy-making and
a tool for the advancement of creole power. It thus constituted
an obvious threat to the peninsular elite who had moved so
quickly to withdraw Mexico City from a position of influence in
1808. In spite of its chronic revenue shortages, therefore, the
cabildo gladly paid out a total of 12,640 pesos over the next year
for Cisneros's expenses in Spain. When the Cortes dispatched
its new oath of loyalty—in which citizens swore to obey as the
sovereign powers the Cortes and the Constitution it was then
writing—the cabildo took the oath with its chamber door open
so that the public could witness it. Before long the Cortes
transferred its location to Cádiz.[3]

The American Cortes delegates, including Dr. Cisneros, made
no secret of the colonial elite's aspiration to autonomy. Cisneros
thought of himself as the deputy of Mexico City. The city council
called him "our representative." He wrote directly to the cabildo
to inform it of the completion of the Constitution, although he
was under no statutory obligation to do so.[4] It is all the more
significant, therefore, that he participated in two important
representations to the Cortes that set forth in clear terms the
political aspirations of creoles. Both proposed American autonomy as the solution to the insurrections then raging throughout
the empire.

The first was a unanimous statement from all the American
delegates and was read to both the Cortes and the Subcommit-
tee on Overseas Affairs. Dated August 1, 1811, it was not known
in Mexico until its publication there in 1820. This document was
the American delegates' assessment of the causes of the wars
underway in all the colonies and their suggestions for remedies.
It was in fact a suggestion for the establishment of an empire of
autonomous states. The Americans saw this as the only way to
end the wars. They said that a small minority of the overseas
population really wanted independence but that nearly all of
them were dissatisfied with the current state of government.

They thought Hidalgo's insurrection was caused by the over-throw of Iturrigaray by a nonrepresentative faction of Euro-peans, which was then rewarded by Viceroy Venegas two years later. In every instance, the pretext for the commencement of insurrections in America had been the desire of Americans to protect themselves from the supposed threat of the French, but since the wars began, the kingdoms had all come to fear the French less and to turn their desires toward the goal of equality with the peninsula. Each colony wanted to be a separate kingdom but to remain under the king's suzerainty. The Ameri-can delegates said that government by Europeans was illegiti-mate; what they were really fighting for was not independence, but the right to form their own governments under the king.[5]

In a separate representation, Cisneros set forth his views of Mexico City's political objectives. His statement was secret but was filed in the cabildo's archives, indicating that he sent it a copy. He said quite simply that "under the best laws, the inhabitants of America suffer a weightier yoke than that of any other nation." An overstatement, to be sure, but this was a list of grievances. Cisneros said that the insurrections of Hidalgo and Morelos resulted from the high-handed tactics by which the Europeans overthrew Iturrigaray, from the stupid mistakes of Garibay, and from the stagnation of the audiencia government. He was especially bitter about the overthrow of Iturrigaray and dwelt at some length on the persons arrested and mistreated in the coup, one of whom was his brother. He accused Venegas of favoritism toward Europeans and prejudice against Americans. He especially singled out intendant-corregidor Mazo for criti-cism, protesting that the Regency should not allow one man to possess both offices simultaneously. In all, he summarized, the principal cause of the insurrection in New Spain was lack of confidence in the regime.

To end the insurrection Cisneros proposed the same auton-omist reforms as all the American delegates. The first point in his plan was "to erect Provincial Juntas in every viceroyalty and superior government in America, composed of subjects named by their own peoples." The provincial juntas would be the supreme power in their territories, recognizing no other sov-ereign above them except the Cortes, and the audiencias would be reduced to mere courts of law. The juntas would have the power to prosecute the wars in any manner they saw fit. Finally, Cisneros proposed that the American territories, in order to repair their chaotic finances, be freed from the economic control of Spain in trade and commerce and in the negotiation of foreign loans and contracts. Further, they would no longer be required to contribute a large portion of their revenue to the peninsula.[6]

These two representations make it clear that, in the view of the American delegates, the overseas kingdoms aspired to autonomy. Their proposals constitute only a slight refinement over the cabildo's 1808 aspirations. Autonomy, free trade, tax revenues spent at home, and locally elected provincial juntas were the delegates' solutions to the insurrections. Their plan did not mean independence, though the absolutist viceregal authorities interpreted it as such. Cisneros's proposal fell far short of the objectives of the proletarian insurrections of Hidalgo and Morelos, which had already been rejected by elite and bourgeoisie alike. This autonomist regime would be controlled by the elite, and its reforms would be limited principally to political and economic, not social, affairs. This dedication to limited reform and autonomy is the one constant that runs through the whole War of Independence.

Not surprisingly, the Cortes, for all its liberalism, was hardly willing to act on such suggestions, for the peninsula depended upon American contributions in its struggle against the French. Peninsular delegates, who held a majority in the Cortes, were no less imperialists for being liberals. Although the Cortes did decree, in October, 1810, that the Spanish territories formed one nation and that each overseas province was equal to the peninsula, equality remained manifestly a myth. The Cortes also abolished the ancient ceremony of the royal pendant by which each year Mexico City commemorated the Conquest and renewed its subservience to the throne. In addition, generous pardons and amnesties were granted to rebels who would acknowledge Spain's sovereign power, and this leniency was practiced periodically in New Spain until independence.[7]

Meanwhile, the royalists who controlled the Mexican government recognized that the Cortes was a new threat to their power, not only because its decrees whittled away at absolutism, but also because its mere existence encouraged independent action among the creoles and even the lower classes. What would be the royalists' response to this nonmilitary threat to their power? As royal authorities over the centuries had done, they simply ignored individual decrees of the superior government, while protesting grateful loyalty to it. Since the Cortes was the only legitimate government that could speak for the absent king, Venegas was bound to respect it and appear publicly to conform to its orders. He adopted the policy of *Obedezco pero no cumplo*—I obey but I do not comply.

The clearest example of this policy was Venegas's reaction to the Cortes's decree of freedom of the press, one of its first and most important reforms. Convinced that only an informed citizenry could continue to maintain its exertions against the French tyrant, the Cortes issued the decree on November 10, 1810. The decree, received and read in the Mexico City cabildo on January 21, 1811, declared that, subject to certain restrictions, "all bodies, and private persons of whatever status or condition, have liberty to write, print, and publish their political ideas, without the necessity of a licence, revision, or approval."[8] It abolished the press censors who formerly had charge of reviewing all writings before publication. Only religious works remained subject to prior censorship. To supervise the free press, the Cortes provided for the establishment of a Supreme Censorship Board composed of nine members to reside in Spain; smaller boards of five members each, including two ecclesiastics, were to be organized in each province. These boards had the duty of examining works denounced to them by executive or judicial powers, and if the publications were found to be objectionable, they were to be confiscated. However, the boards were not allowed to censor works prior to publication. Furthermore, the author might demand a copy of the objections brought against his work so he could defend it before the provincial board, and he had the right of appeal to the Supreme Censorship Board in Spain.

The Supreme Board submitted its list of proposed members for the Mexico City board to the Cortes, which approved it on December 12, 1810. Those named were Canon José Mariano Beristain de Sousa, royalist publicist and author of *Biblioteca hispanoamericana setentrional*; José María Fagoaga, who at that time was an honorary member of the audiencia; Agustín Pomposo Fernández de San Salvador, rector of the university, royalist publicist, and uncle of the heroine of Mexican independence Leona Vicario; Pedro José de Fonte, canon of the cathedral and future archbishop; and Guillermo de Aguirre, regent of the audiencia, who died before the censorship board could be installed.

The new law would provide undreamed of freedom of publication and potentially gave the insurgents an open public voice. Viceroy Venegas, therefore, simply refused to implement it. Only two days after receipt of the decree, he showed his contempt for it by ordering the rounding up of some "seditious papers" that had entered the capital from Hidalgo's forces. He had no intention, in the current situation, of permitting the publication of rebel manifestoes, decrees, or essays. He persisted in this throughout the next two years, although his position aroused great bitterness among the creoles and moderates. He made no public statement or decree concerning the law; he simply ignored it. The death of the Regent Aguirre and the failure of the Cortes to name a successor to the Censorship Board provided his excuse. He sought the advice of the ecclesiastical hierarchy and political chiefs, and the majority of them, including Archbishop Lizana, advised against implementation of the law. One of the few bishops who favored the free press was Antonio Bergosa y Jordán of Oaxaca, who was appointed by the Regency to succeed Lizana upon the archbishop's death.[9]

What could advocates of a free press do in the face of the viceroy's disobedience? The Mexican delegates to the Cortes challenged his actions. Under the leadership of José Miguel Ramos Arizpe, delegate for Coahuila, Nuevo León, Tamaulipas, and Texas, they called the attention of the Cortes to the viceroy's procrastination and asked for a direct order to him for implementation. On March 21, 1811, Venegas wrote the Regency vaguely offering to accept and implement the law but not indicating that he had done so. Ramos Arizpe insisted the viceroy be ordered to obey. The Cortes resolved to do so and ordered the Supreme Censorship Board to appoint a fifth censor for Mexico City. It thereupon appointed Pedro de la Puente, member of the audiencia who was serving as superintendent of the Junta of Police. On February 6, 1812, the Regency ordered Venegas to proclaim the press law in New Spain.[10] The viceroy's reaction? He ignored the order.

Meanwhile, Venegas continued to decree the collection and destruction of what little rebel propaganda slipped into the capital. In November, 1811, he issued a proclamation prohibiting the circulation of manuscripts that might foment rivalry between peninsulars and creoles. As late as April, 1812, he ordered the collection and public burning of seditious manuscripts dispatched to the capital by the rebels José María Cos and Francisco Velasco. The papers claimed that all creoles supported the rebellion.[11]

The cabildo now entered the fray by complaining to the Cortes of Venegas's procrastination. In its clearest statement of support for the Cortes and the new reforms, it declared its complete agreement with the necessity and value of a free press and reviewed the viceroy's delaying tactics, calling his actions despotic. It ascribed this despotism to the excessive and unchecked power he and the other royal officials possessed, to the fact that he had not as yet consciously recognized the Cortes's authority, and to the "ascendancy that some individuals have over the government"—referring to the deep-seated creole complaint that the reactionary merchants, prelates, and oidors held disproportionate influence over viceregal decisions. It warned the lawmakers that the viceroy would suspend other Cortes decrees at will if he found them undesirable.[12]

There the matter rested until September, 1812, when the Constitution was proclaimed in Mexico City. The viceroy had demonstrated his power in the face even of intense pressure from local and imperial authorities alike. For two years he ignored the free press decree, never explaining his actions, never defending himself. This technique of viceregal disobedience to Cortes decrees would be employed in other instances by both Venegas and his successor, Calleja. Viceregal obstructionism, with the fullest support of the audiencia and other peninsular authorities, was the chief means of limiting reform.

On March 19, 1812, the Cortes promulgated the long-promised "Political Constitution of the Spanish Monarchy," which included among its many reforms all those already passed by the Cortes. It was one of the most profound political revolutions in Spanish history, and it threatened to alter the balance of power that the ultraroyalists had forged in Mexico City. On May 10, 1812, an order for the Constitution's adoption was sent to a very reluctant Viceroy Venegas. An authorized copy arrived at Veracruz on September 6, 1812. On September 11, Venegas forwarded to the city council the several decrees accompanying it, and a week later he sent a copy of the Constitution along with the affirmative vote of the royal accord and his official confirmation of its applicability to New Spain. He could not avoid putting it into effect, though he did fail to enact key portions of it, as shall be seen.[13]

Composed of ten titles and 384 articles, the Constitution was not a model of brevity or clarity. Almost every article swept away some ancient usage and practice of the empire or created a new administrative function. It made Spain a limited hereditary monarchy, with the king reduced to the status of chief executive charged with the execution of laws. The Cortes and king together constituted the sovereign. The Cortes reserved to itself the right of taxation and said that, if the king should return from his captivity in France, he would be required to accept the new law before he could resume the throne. The Constitution put the king and royal family on a yearly pension. It reduced the viceroy to the position of superior political chief (*Jefe político superior*). He, too, was meant to be merely the chief executive, though the precise extent of his powers remained a subject of much dispute. The captains general were also made superior political chiefs of their territories. The viceroy was thus deprived of jurisdiction over those portions of the kingdom—the Eastern and Western Interior Provinces, Nueva Galicia, Yucatán, and San Luis Potosí—that already had their own captains general. Venegas's hostility to the new system of government is understandable. The audiencia was reduced from its position as a semilegislative privy council to a mere court of law.[14]

On the provincial level the Constitution made further sweeping reforms. In keeping with the desire of its authors, especially the American delegates, to limit the extent of absolutism on the local level, the Constitution created Provincial Deputations. The

Mexican delegate Ramos Arizpe was the chief advocate of this type of local autonomy.[15] Another Mexican delegate, José Miguel Guridi y Alcocer, representing Tlaxcala, had advocated that the Provincial Deputations be local legislatures having powers derived from the people and representing the interests of its province. This was identical to the 1811 proposals for autonomous provincial juntas. The Cortes was unwilling to accept the proposal, which would effectively have converted the empire into a federation of autonomous provinces. As finally constituted, therefore, the Provincial Deputations were administrative councils with advisory capacities but no independent legislative function. As with so much else in the Constitution, the extent of their power in policy-making would depend on how aggressive their members were and, more importantly, on how aggressively the superior political chief defended his own administrative prerogatives. Venegas and Calleja defended theirs by simply refusing to be bound by decisions of the Deputation for the province of Mexico.

Members of the Provincial Deputations, and Cortes delegates, were to be chosen by a complicated formula of indirect election. Months before the final selection of the Provincial Deputation and Cortes delegates, voters were to meet in their home parishes to choose a list of electors. These electors then met at a scheduled time in each province to select that province's junta of electors. The junta of electors—consisting of one member from each partido—then met to choose the Cortes delegates and Provincial Deputation members. The number of Cortes delegates was proportional to the province's population. Mexico province was allotted fourteen, with four alternates. The other provinces of the adumbrated New Spain received the following number of Cortes delegates: Puebla, 7; Oaxaca, 6; Guanajuato, 5; Michoacán, 3; Veracruz and San Luis Potosí, 2 each; and Tlaxcala and Querétaro, 1 each. This structure of provincial political chiefs, deputations, and Cortes delegates was the fundamental precedent for the federal system created in Mexico by the Constitution of 1824.[16]

Just as important as the creation of Provincial Deputations, the Constitution made massive reforms in municipal government. Ramos Arizpe had been the leading advocate of this reform as well. In debates concerning draft articles of the Constitution, he and other American delegates argued that Spanish tradition based municipal power in the citizens, not in an appointed Spanish official administering a town or city. More conservative Spanish delegates argued the opposite—that municipalities derived their only power from the king and Cortes—and that is the point of view that prevailed. Thus the cities were denied total autonomy, for the political chief of each city was ordered to preside over the city council. Nonetheless, proprietary chairs were abolished and the ayuntamientos made elective. Mexico City's delegate, Cisneros, had presented a complaint from the proprietary regidors claiming that the abolition of their chairs was a violation of their contract with the Crown. The elections for city council members were simpler than the provincial elections and were entirely separate from them. Each parish in Mexico City would choose a number of electors proportionate to its size, and the electors would then elect regidors, alcaldes, and syndics.[17]

The creoles of Mexico City greeted the Constitution with enthusiasm, believing it heralded the coming of a new dawn in the nation's affairs, for now it seemed that the representative functions of government were given dominance over the absolutist. Except that autonomy was withheld, the Constitution created a political structure remarkably like the one proposed in 1808 by Primo Verdad and Azcárate.

The Constitution was introduced in Mexico City in lengthy and elaborate ceremonies. It was formally proclaimed and published in a splendid pageant on September 30, 1812. A few days later the formal oaths of allegiance to it were administered, again with great pomp. First the viceroy took the oath, then, on October 5, the cabildo. On the following Sunday, the oath was administered to the public in all the parishes. Afterwards the city sponsored a free gala performance in the theater.[18]

The viceroy's position, meanwhile, was one of watchful waiting. From September, when the Constitution was proclaimed, until November, when the parish elections were held in Mexico City, he took no overtly hostile action toward it. No doubt he was waiting to assess its full implications. By December, however, he had become convinced of the Constitution's danger, and he swept down upon it with a fury. After the first parish elections, it became clear to him that not only had the Constitution abolished the office of viceroy itself, it had removed from his hands effective control over the political affairs of his own capital. Consequently, a full-scale contest for control of the kingdom between the viceregal power and the constitutionalists developed.

Freedom of the press, which Venegas had successfully prevented from implementation for two years, automatically came into effect with Article 371 of the Constitution. As part of the supreme law of the empire, he could no longer obstruct it. The five members of the Mexico City Censorship Board were sworn into office. Immediately, a number of liberal publications appeared, but, although they were critical of the regime, they were hardly the wholesale threat the audiencia later described them as being. Among those journalists who appeared in print legally were Carlos María Bustamante and José Joaquín Fernández de Lizardi, who was called "El Pensador Mejicano" after the journal he published. Both men were strong critics of colonial society and viceregal government. The audiencia later accused Bustamante's journal, *El Juguetillo*, of criticizing the Juntas of Security in several issues, of writing approvingly of Azcárate and his actions in 1808, of approving everything the radical cabildo did, and of criticizing Spanish treatment of the Indians and Spain's restrictive trade policies. The audiencia reminded the peninsula of the saying of one rebel publication that "as long as the birdshots continue [that is, the plumes of the writers' pens], so will Morelos's shots."[19] Neither Lizardi nor Bustamante was yet a declared rebel. Indeed, Lizardi did not declare himself until 1821, while Bustamante joined the rebels openly only after the viceregal crackdown of December, 1812.[20] The usually sedate *Diario de México* during this period printed such items as the complete freedom of the press law, the Constitution of the United States with its Bill of Rights, and the Manifesto of the revolutionary government of Buenos Aires—all very suggestive to the Mexican who was simultaneously preparing to vote for the first time.

The cabildo meanwhile prepared for the election of the new city council. On October 23, Venegas ordered the cabildo to complete its plans for the parish elections scheduled for late November. Immediate confusion appeared on all sides. The proprietary aldermen were concerned with the problem of how they would be compensated for the prices they had paid for their seats and what their prerogatives would be after they left office. The cabildo decided on a formula by which they would be paid annually out of income on city property, 5 percent of the purchase price of their seats a year (this plan may never have been implemented). The problem of prerogatives was eventually solved by a decree of the Cortes in March, 1813, that all dispossessed proprietary regidors should continue to enjoy for life all the public honors owing to them, including the right to be addressed as "excellency" and to wear the uniform of the office of regidor.[21]

In spite of the warnings of the regidor Francisco Maniau that the proprietary cabildo should not become involved in planning the election, the cabildo proceeded to proportion the number of electors to be chosen by each of the capital's fourteen parishes and to detail regidors to supervise the voting. Intendant-corregidor Mazo, in his role as political chief of the city under the Constitution, pointed out to the viceroy some of the problems likely to be encountered in the parish elections. The giant Sagrario parish, for example, had over 80,000 parishioners, of whom 8,000 were eligible to vote—too many, he thought, to be manageable. He therefore suggested that an age limit for voters be set at 18 or 20 years of age (the Constitution had failed to set an age limit) and that ballots be distributed to the Sagrario voters beforehand. These two problems—the absence of a clear definition of who was eligible to vote, and the distribution of Sagrario ballots beforehand—formed the basis of the irregularities that Viceroy Venegas later claimed occurred in the voting.[22]

The audiencia's attorneys, after criticizing the cabildo for its inability to decide the proper voting age, concluded that a citizen with the right to vote was any white male head of a household able to administer his own property; this, they thought, implied a competent age. Nevertheless, they also failed to establish a definite age, for they could not decide if they preferred 21 or 25. It was clear, however, that according to Cortes directions, women, children, mulattoes, and domestic

servants were barred from voting. The constitutional requirement of literacy for voters was not to become effective until
1830.[23]

The final statement on the issue, which came from the intendant-corregidor, only served to confuse things more. Mazo
sent letters to the city's parish priests instructing them to preach
to their parishioners on Sunday, November 22, concerning the
arrangements that had been made for voting. He decreed that
the requirement for eligibility was that the voter be a house-
holder or head of a family and at least 25 years old. Only a few
days later, however, he had to send a second directive to the
priests saying he had made a mistake and that no one had yet
decided on a definite voting age. The curate, therefore, was to
try to get in touch with as many parishioners as possible—there
were no more Sundays before the election—and was to tell them
"whatever you think is prudent" concerning the voting eligibility. Mazo thus ended up placing on the shoulders of the
parish priests the burden of explaining voting procedures to a
populace that had never voted before. The secular clergy
themselves, though permitted to vote, were barred from being
chosen as regidors.[24]

The parish elections occurred on November 29, and everyone
was acutely aware of their importance. If a slate of Europeans or
conservatives were chosen, the viceregal regime would receive a
popular endorsement. If creoles and liberals were elected, and if
the various constitutional institutions and guarantees were fully
implemented, viceregal power would be sharply diminished.
The answer was crystal clear. Of the twenty-five men chosen as
electors on November 29, every one was a creole.[25]

The audiencia, in a famous letter of November 18, 1813,
criticizing the entire constitutional system, testified that the
victory of the creoles in this first Mexico City election was
interpreted by the rebels as the winning of the capital for their
side. Among the electors chosen were such well-known pro-
ponents of autonomy as José María Alcalá, a canon of the
cathedral, Jacobo de Villaurrutia, the oidor suspected by viceroy
and audiencia alike, and Carlos María Bustamante. Many electors
were directly implicated, in the royalists' view, in treasonous
activities. Alexo Norzagaray was imprisoned for complicity in the

August, 1811, plot to assassinate the viceroy, as was the elector José Manuel Sartorio. Another elector, Juan de Dios Martínez, had been arrested for communicating with the rebel chieftain Villagrán. The elector José Victorio Texo was intimate with a convicted traitor.[26] The audiencia damned them one and all by charging that all were adherents of independence, or had refused to contribute money to the war in Spain, or had been confidants of Iturrigaray in 1808. Eleven of the electors were priests, and the royalists suspected their loyalty as well. Though none of the electors could themselves be chosen for the city council, the viceroy had substantive grounds for fearing that they would elect men of their own persuasion.

Everyone else assumed the same. On the night of November 29 the creoles gave themselves over to such a public demonstration that Viceroy Venegas, General Calleja, and the audiencia all described it in their reports to Spain as a riot. They spoke of unrestrained mobs assaulting the cathedral and palace, shouting revolutionary slogans, and even plotting assassinations. All of it was overstated, for there was no damage or personal injury that night, and even the ringing of the cathedral bells that the demonstrators demanded was prescribed by law.[27]

Most damning of all, the rebels in the field were delighted. Venegas reported that in districts controlled by insurgents the outcome of the voting was celebrated with thanksgiving masses and salvoes of artillery. In the capital itself a secret insurgent group called Los Guadalupes, which was in constant contact with Morelos and other rebel leaders in the field, took the election as a sign of victory for their cause. These partisans wrote to Morelos in early December:

In the fourteen parishes of this capital our electors came out with 28,000 to 30,000 votes, which astounded all the Europeans, because until that day they had not known the disposition of Mexico City or how much it abhorred them. For all Americans this day was one of joy; for the gachupines, one of sadness and desperation. They were so alarmed . . . that the government, and the Yermos, the Batallers and others began to intrigue with their accustomed deceit.[28]

Although they suspected the Spaniards were plotting some sort of intervention, the Guadalupes declared to Morelos, "This week our plans will be fulfilled and a new cabildo will be elected, for we have worked for this without a moment's rest, and we will have a cabildo of confidence."

For his part, Viceroy Venegas had seen enough. In two remarkable acts of outright insubordination to the Constitution, he moved to restore viceregal dominance. On December 5 he suspended Article 371 of the Constitution—the free press—with a consultative vote from the audiencia. Then on December 14, claiming that irregularities had occurred in the voting, he annulled the election and ordered the hereditary cabildo to remain in office. In essence, Venegas and the audiencia simply agreed to ignore the Constitution in so far as possible. It was a viceregal coup d'état, to which no reply was possible except recourse to arms. Mexico City was not prepared to pursue such a course, and the viceroy knew it.[29]

The irregularities in the election of which the royal authorities complained were that many minors and castes had voted, that in some parishes more votes were cast than there were eligible voters, that some persons voted in more than one parish, that premarked ballots were distributed beforehand to the illiterate, that there was clear collusion to get certain men chosen as electors, and that léperos were paid to vote. Nettie Lee Benson has convincingly shown that these allegations were largely false, and that the annulment was motivated by purely political considerations. She concludes that, although there were many problems in the first election, nearly all of them owing to inconsistency or obscurity in the Cortes's instructions, the voting took place remarkably peacefully for a people who had never voted before.[30]

The Guadalupes wrote Morelos that Venegas and Mazo, "working with their accustomed despotism," had declared the old cabildo reelected for another year. The viceroy began to move against a few leading suspects. The oidor Villaurrutia was ordered to Puebla in preparation for a journey to Veracruz and then to Spain; the elector Juan Martínez was indicted on charges of corresponding with the insurgents; a price was put on the head of Carlos María Bustamante; and José Joaquín Fernández de Lizardi went to jail. General Calleja was made military governor of the city to enforce viceregal security. The Guadalupes informed Morelos that most Europeans in the capital openly wished Calleja to become viceroy.[31]

Creole insurgent sympathizers in Mexico City were furious. Francisco Galicia, governor of one of the Indian districts (later elected to the constitutional cabildo when it was finally chosen) wrote to the rebel chieftain Ignacio Rayón that the authorities had struck down the electors because they knew no Europeans would be chosen for the cabildo. He concluded, "Our every desire is to throw off the tyrannical yoke that now deprives us even of breath. We remain in the resolution to be free or to die in the attempt. This is the spirit that moves all my sons and that inflames all the inhabitants of this city."[32]

From the short-term point of view, Venegas's coup was timely, limited, and successful. Its object was to restore viceregal control of governmental mechanisms in the face of insurrection. The rebels were active in the center of the country and had closed the road between Mexico City and Veracruz. The coup did not solve the problem of the viceroy's loss of control over the provinces that had their own superior political chief. It did make it clear that Venegas and his administration would pay only token lip service to constitutional niceties. He and Calleja would ignore the Constitution where it affected their ability to govern; they would obey but not comply.

For the first months of 1813, the road to Veracruz was closed by rebel action, so Venegas was in no danger of being embarrassed by further Cortes pronouncements. Not even the new archbishop-elect of Mexico City, Antonio Bergosa y Jordán, could get from Veracruz to the capital to claim his see. The road was reopened on March 1, 1813, and along with the flood of directives and personages that arrived in the capital came an order from the Regency replacing Venegas as viceroy. General Calleja quietly took office on March 4, with only limited formal ceremonies.[33]

Venegas had prepared the way for Calleja's accession. Venegas was the buffer, the viceroy who first met and checked the insurrection. Now Calleja, the reconqueror, took power. The Guadalupes, who had recently been involved in informal negotiations with Calleja, wrote Morelos of the new viceroy's accession and paid Calleja the supreme compliment of recognizing him as the most dangerous of all possible enemies. They affirmed that he was a more brilliant politician than Venegas, that he had much greater military knowledge, and that he had a much larger following among the conservatives, notably including many creoles. They explained to Morelos that there were then three factions dividing political opinion in the capital. The Americans or lesser creoles, whom they called "insurgents," were very weak. The gachupines, whom they called "chaquetas," were disproportionately powerful. The third group, whom they called "Callejistas," included both creoles and peninsulars, but mainly creoles, and was now represented by the new viceroy.[34] Having family connections in San Luis Potosí, Calleja was in the unusual position for a Spanish viceroy of actually possessing a pre-existing creole following. Thus Calleja came to office not only with determination and skill behind him, but also with his own partisans—conservatives, law-and-order advocates, royalists, and, chiefly, creoles. These partisans represented the backlash from the violence and radicalism of Hidalgo's and Morelos's insurrection.

Although Viceroy Calleja was no friend of constitutionalism, he was, as the Guadalupes pointed out, the most astute of politicians. He therefore pursued a program of apparent acquiescence in the constitutional reforms while studiously neglecting the constitutional agencies themselves. In this way he achieved the same results as Venegas without needlessly provoking moderates and liberals.

Calleja ordered the aborted city council election to be carried out. The electors chosen in November, 1812, met on April 4, 1813, and elected the new cabildo. The conde de Medina y Torres and Antonio Velasco y Torre were elected alcaldes. Regidors chosen were Juan Ignacio González Guerra, the conde de Valenciana, José Garay, Dr. Tomás Salgado, Francisco Manuel Sánchez de Tagle, the conde de la Presa de Xalpa, Juan de Antepara, José Ignacio Adalid, Francisco Galicia, the marqués de Valleameno, Juan Vicente Gómez Pedroso, Francisco Villanueva, Manuel Santos Vargas Machuca, Juan de Orellana, José María Prieto Bonilla, and Juan Pérez Juárez. Syndics chosen were José Rafael Marques and José Antonio López Salazar. The conde de Valenciana declined election because of age and ill health. All were creoles, and the viceroy and audiencia later claimed that three-quarters of the twenty men chosen were rebel sympathizers. Calleja reported that "the enmity against the Europeans was so strong that . . . when they installed the new ayuntamiento there was not a single European on it." The audiencia wrote in stronger terms: "Among two alcaldes, two syndics and sixteen regidors there was not one single individual of proven patriotism."[35]

Elections for the Provincial Deputation and Cortes followed more slowly, as Calleja first required a new voter list for Mexico City to be drawn up.[36] In the final vote, on July 18, 1813, only creoles were chosen as parish electors, and only creoles or persons associated with their point of view were chosen for the Cortes and Provincial Deputation. Because of the six-month delay in the election, however, the Cortes deputies were unable to get to Spain in time for the opening of the 1813 session, and few of them managed to attend at all.

Calleja permitted completion of the elections—because of their visibility he could not avoid them—yet he pursued Venegas's policy of selective disobedience of the Constitution. In his first proclamation to the people on March 26, 1813, he declared that the entire Constitution would be put into effect. "I am going . . . to put you in entire possession of all the rights contained in the Constitution," he said, "and I will be the first to observe its precepts scrupulously."[37] Despite such unequivocal statements, meant for domestic and peninsular consumption, he refused to allow the free-press article to be implemented. Indeed, he remained silent on the matter for over a year. Finally, on June 23, 1814, he published a manifesto in which he said he had thought it necessary to maintain the free press in suspension in order to prevent the insurrection from spreading. He admitted that his early hopes that the Constitution would end the rebellion were misplaced.[38]

In the face of such viceregal determination, no power could prevail. The American delegates to the Cortes continued to demand enforcement of the free press article, but no clear order to that effect was dispatched by the Regency. In September, 1813, the constitutional city council complained once again to the Regency "about this new disobedience to the royal order that the liberty of the press should be put in effect."[39] The viceroy remained determined; as long as armed insurrection existed, he could not allow a free press.

Calleja's hostility toward the Constitution, which he made clear in letters after the king's restoration, was chiefly based on his fear that the Constitution would limit his authority to such an extent that he would be unable to defeat the insurrection. That he found it necessary to explain his absolutist use of authority to his own advisers as well as to Spain on a number of occasions suggests that his actions met with some resistance. His authority was frequently questioned by the other political chiefs of the nation with whom he now shared political power. On July 24, 1813, the Regency approved Calleja's actions as captain general of New Spain, and a Cortes committee actually recommended that a military regime be established in Mexico.[40] At that point, however, Calleja had effectively created his own military regime without any outside authorization.

The constitutional cabildo, as might be imagined, remained a favorite target of viceregal suspicion. Only two months after the cabildo took office, Calleja sent the Spanish government a detailed description of the complicity of its members in the insurrection. He warned that the regidors and other supporters of independence inside the capital were planning to take control of the city and turn it over to the armies of Morelos or Rayón as soon as they should draw near. Nor were these mere allegations, for Calleja possessed captured rebel documents, especially letters from persons within the city to the rebel chieftain Berdusco, clearly suggesting the complicity of some councilors. One alcalde, the conde de Medina, was under suspicion because his slave Ignacio Salazar was a rebel chieftain. The other alcalde, Antonio Velasco, was known to have been in communication with the rebels and to have given them money and shelter in his hacienda. The regidor Juan Santos Vargas Machuca was under suspicion for having put the Indians to work making arms for the rebels while he was governor of the Indian district of Santiago. Another former governor of an Indian barrio, the regidor Francisco Galicia, had offered the aid of his Indians to Ignacio Rayón. Regidor José Ignacio Adalid was known to be giving aid to rebels in his haciendas. And one of the new syndics, José Rafael Marques, was implicated by his intimacy with José María Fagoaga. Fagoaga himself, elected a Cortes deputy in 1813 but prohibited by the viceroy from attending, was so widely suspected that all his dependents, servants, friends, and relatives were under suspicion.[41]

The audiencia, in its hundred-page letter of November, 1813, compared the situation in mid-1813 with the Directorate in France. It said the city council was composed "of men disposed to increase the number of conspiracies under any pretext, in order both internally and externally to foment revolutionary movements that threaten the capital."[42]

In June, 1813, Viceroy Calleja confronted the cabildo with his suspicions against its members by ordering it to submit a list specifying "the principal subjects of this capital, in whose number may be comprised various electors and constitutional regidors, who are sympathizers of the revolutionary movement." The cabildo virtually confirmed Calleja's allegations by reporting the matter to the Regency and refusing to submit the list on the grounds that to do so "would severely weaken the effectiveness of this ayuntamiento."[43]

Calleja's suspicions of the councilors' loyalty, heightened by his personal acquaintance with members of Los Guadalupes, was fully confirmed when this group's entire correspondence with Morelos fell into royal hands at Tlacotepec in 1814. These partisans dispatched regular reports to Morelos and Rayón on military affairs in the capital, social relations, government orders, convoy movements, and anything else that might be useful. In addition, they helped recruit new rebels, induced royal forces to desert, gave passage to rebels and their families, helped supply the rebels with a printing press, and tried to influence the constitutional elections in 1812 and 1813. In all there were thirty-two letters, to Morelos and Rayón, dating from September 15, 1812, to January 15, 1814, and a diary listing day by day events in the capital from October 28, 1813, to January 12, 1814.[44]

In late 1812, when Viceroy Venegas and General Calleja were quarreling over war policy, the Guadalupes tried to induce Calleja to join the rebel camp. They chose two of their members, the regidor Francisco Manuel Sánchez de Tagle and José Antonio Cristo y Conde, the auditor of war arrested in the 1808 Iturrigaray coup, to negotiate with him. The negotiators, unfortunately and unknowingly, came to confer with Calleja on the day after he received the announcement of his appointment as viceroy. When they arrived before him, he greeted them with the words, "If you were not my friends, I would have you shot. You are speaking to the new viceroy of New Spain." Apparently, at a later point, Calleja made attempts to negotiate with Morelos for the cessation of hostilities, using the Guadalupes as his communication link. It is likely that this was a ruse to draw the Guadalupes into the open so they could be identified. By mid-1814 the viceroy had the entire correspondence of the society in his hands and was able to patch together much information on its membership and its activities.[45]

The membership included many prominent creoles. Lawyers were chief among them, and Juan Bautista Raz y Guzmán apparently was the central figure. Other lawyers included Nicolás Becerra, Manuel Díaz, José Ignacio Espinosa, José María Falcón, José Benito Guerra, José María Llave, José Matoso, Juan Nazario Peimbert, and Antonio del Río. From the city council or commercial class were Francisco de Arce, Juan Wenceslao Barquera, Manuel Cortázar, José Antonio Cristo y Conde, Agustín Gallegos, Francisco Manuel Sánchez de Tagle, Félix López de Vargara, Ignacio Velarde, and Anastasio Zerecero. Among the several women included were the wives of Raz y Guzmán, Río, Guerra, and Díaz, and Margarita Peimbert, who later married Espinosa. Other prominent individuals referred to by the Guadalupes as their friends included Carlos María Bustamante, José Joaquín Fernández de Lizardi, Andrés Quintana Roo (the scholar-statesman of the republic), and the Mexican folk heroine Leona Vicario, niece of Raz y Guzmán and later wife of Quintana Roo. Constitutional regidors Ignacio Adalid and Francisco Galicia, José María Alcalá (canon of the cathedral and delegate-elect to the Cortes), and José María Fagoaga (former regidor and Cortes delegate-elect) were also closely connected with the group.

There can be no doubt that these rebel sympathizers looked to the newly elected city council to extend their influence in the

capital and that some constitutional regidors were rebel sympathizers. Calleja's defense, therefore, consisted chiefly of keeping
a sharp watch on the cabildo's political activities, intervening
personally whenever necessary, and simultaneously ignoring its
pretensions to speak on behalf of the nation as a whole. The
office of regidor endowed its possessors with a certain personal
inviolability which, although it was not an absolute fuero, made
Calleja hesitant to arrest sitting councilors. When the cabildo
was newly seated and the city was enthusiastic about its implied
reforms, such direct intervention by the viceroy would also have
provoked adverse public reaction. Calleja therefore insisted that
Intendant-corregidor Mazo should serve as president of the city
council. This was required by the Constitution, but the cabildo
protested that Mazo, who simultaneously presided over the
Provincial Deputation, should not have ex-oficio powers in both
bodies. Calleja, when asked for a ruling, said that Mazo was the
appropriate person to be chairman of the cabildo. The regidor
Sánchez de Tagle complained bitterly against this ruling, saying
that the viceroy was acting arbitrarily. Several other councilors
threatened to resign, insisting that Mazo's presence meant that
city employees would take orders from him rather than from
them. Calleja was adamant and informed the Spanish government that it was absolutely necessary that someone of Mazo's
political persuasion remain as head of the cabildo, in order
"incessantly to invigilate the ayuntamiento because of the type
of men who compose it, and because the spirit of independence
here animates all such bodies." Mazo was also, of course, the
only European in the cabildo.[46]

There was no end of rhetoric issuing from the cabildo, no limit
to the implied promises of reform. After considerable discussion, the cabildo reorganized the supervision of municipal
affairs along the lines indicated in the Constitution's article
listing city-government jurisdiction and responsibilities. A Plan
of Commissions was instituted to unify all the diverse duties of
the municipal government under a simple group of nine commissions. One of the commissions was to begin drawing up new
municipal ordinances for eventual approval by the Cortes,
which would effectively bypass viceregal intervention. Table 2
compares this more rational structure of municipal authority

with the ad hoc system that the proprietary cabildo had developed over the years. Only two duties—to form new municipal ordinances and to promote agriculture, industry, and commerce—constituted an expansion of cabildo jurisdiction, but nothing substantive was accomplished in either area. Nor was the constitutional cabildo any more skilled in financial management than the proprietary, for in two years it dissipated all of the surplus of 40,384 pesos that it inherited when it took office.[47]

The relationship and distribution of powers between the constitutional cabildo and the Provincial Deputation was clarified in a Cortes decree of June 23, 1813, the *Instrucción para el govierno económico-político de las provincias*. The cabildos were ordered to submit annual statements of accounts to the Provincial Deputations and to give yearly reports on general municipal affairs to the provincial *Jefe político*. Provincial Deputations were charged with provincial public works, but their jurisdiction did not extend to the cities. Evidently they did not have substantial revenues, since the Cortes had to grant them new funds. The Deputations were to supervise municipal responsibilities over public education and report to the Cortes on municipal abuses of power.[48]

In the particular case of Mexico City, unlike that of other cabildos in other parts of the country, this law constituted largely unnecessary repetition and did not effectively guide either the city council or the viceroy. The inherited traditions of three centuries provided a much better guide to their respective powers. The city council, for example, never submitted its accounts to the smaller and—in its view—less prestigious Provincial Deputation, nor was it necessary to submit yearly reports to the viceroy, who supervised municipal affairs on a daily basis. The Law of June 23, nonetheless, did specifically enumerate the city council's powers (some of which the Mexican council had always possessed): to care for roads and public works, to create Juntas of Health in times of disease (this had previously been a viceregal power), to take censuses, to supervise markets and prices, to supervise hospitals and welfare agencies, to supervise granaries, to protect the lives and property of the people, to manage municipal finances with the supervision of the provincial *Jefe político*, to solicit new funds for necessary

TABLE 2

DISTRIBUTION OF MUNICIPAL DUTIES

PROPRIETARY CABILDO, 1812 OFFICES AND EMPLOYMENTS IN THE CITY ADMINISTRATION	CONSTITUTIONAL CABILDO, 1813 PLAN OF COMMISSIONS
(Note: Most of these duties were given to employees. Those marked by an asterisk were held on a rotating basis by regidors and syndics.)	(Note: The nine commissions were each composed of regidors. Employees of the city would be responsible to the appropriate commissioner.)

* Alferez real	1. La policía de salubridad y comodidad
* Procurador general	
* Junta de Propios, Abastos, Gremios, Elecciones y Pobres	Teatros, paseos, y diversiones publicas — One regidor
* Juez de Informaciones de Maestros de Escuela	Aseo de la ciudad — One regidor
* Tribunal de Fiel Executoria	Alumbrado — One regidor
* Junta del Pósito y Alhóndiga	Mercados y alimentos — One regidor
* Junta de Policía	Coches de alquiler — One regidor
* Comicionado asistente para la Real Lotería	Buen arreglo de los edificios — One regidor
* Juez administrador del Fiel-contraste	Desembarazo de calles — One regidor
* Juez de Plazas	Fiestas de concurencia — One syndic, in turn
* Juez de Arquerias, Canerias y Aguas	
* Juez de Ríos, Calzadas, y Caminos	2. Auxiliar el alcalde en todo lo que pertenesca a la seguridad de las personas y bienes de los vecinos
Obrero Mayor	
Archivero	Rondas ordinarias y extraordinarias — Four regidors
* Alcalde de la Alameda y Juez de Paseos	Revisión de pesos y medidas — One regidor
* Alcalde del Rastro, y Veedor de la Piedad	
Comisario de Milicias	3. La administración o inversión de los caudales de Proprios y arbitrios
Secretaria de Cartas	
Contador	Revisar y examinar a todos — Three regidors and one syndic
Mayordomo Tesorero	
Capellán de la Nov. Ciudad	4. Hacer el repartimiento y recaudación de las contribuciones
Capellán del Santuario de Los Remedios	
Portero	Lo que especifica — Three regidors and one syndic
Porteros Segundos	
Porteros supernumerarios	5. Cuidar de todas las escuelas de primeras letras
Escribano de Diputación	
Escribano de Alhóndiga	Lo que especifica — Two regidors
Abodagos de Ciudad	
Maestros mayores de Arquitectura	6. Cuidar de los hospitales, hospicios, casas de expositos y demas establecimientos de
Alcalde de la Alhóndiga Mayor, y Mayordomo del Pósito	
Alcalde de la Alhóndiga de S. Antonio Abad	
Alcalde del Puente de Tezontlale	
Veedor de Matadero	

(Table 2 con't.)

Proprietary Cabildo, 1812 Offices and employments in the city administration	Constitutional Cabildo, 1813 Plan of commissions
Fieles de la Carnicería Mayor	beneficencia
Fieles de los Barrios	Lo que especifica Four regidors
Administrador de Plaza	7. Cuidar de la construcción y
Teniente de la Villa de Guadalupe	reparación de los caminos,
Teniente del Pueblo de Popolla	calzadas, puentes, y carce-
Procuradores de esta Audiencia	les, de los montes y plantíos
Ordinario	del común, y de todas las
Interprete	obras publicas
Médico y Cirujano de la Cárcel	Aqueductos One regidor
Boticario de la Cárcel	Calzadas y caminos One regidor
Guarda Mayor del Alumbrado	Puentes y obras
Zeladores del Ramo de Policía	publicas One regidor
Alguacil de la Junta de Propios	Montes y plantíos One regidor
Alguacil de Gremios	Carceles The alcaldes
Alguacil de Policía	8. Formar las ordenanzas
Alguacil de Fiel Executoria	municipales del pueblo, y
Guarda de Rios	presentarlos a las Cortes
	Lo que One regidor and
	especifica both syndics
	9. Promover la agricultura, la
	industria, y el comercio
	Lo que especifica Three regidors

Source: A. Ex-A., Actas de Cabildo, vol. 131, January 1, 1812; "Plan de comisiones de esta N.C.," April 21, 1813, A. Ex-A., Ayuntamiento-Comisiones, vol. 406, no. 10.

public works, to take taxes, to supervise public primary education and private schools, to discipline its own members, to appoint its own secretary, to supervise parish elections, to make special efforts to provision the troops, and "to take care of all the other things that they are empowered by law to do."

It was the viceroy who suffered the greatest change in duties and responsibilities. The Law of June 23, for example, specifically removed military command from the *Jefe político superior* except in territories engaged in warfare, where he was allowed to keep military command "temporarily"—which Calleja did.

This necessitated a direct grant to Calleja of the powers of captain general so that he could continue to exercise command. The intendant was made legal successor in case of Calleja's death or disability. These restrictions were largely ignored by Calleja, for he surrendered only one power—that of viceroy. He lost control over provinces that had their own superior political chiefs, but beyond that he never went. The question of whether the Law of June 23 was applicable to the superior political chief was never clarified.

Having securely checked the pretensions of the constitutional cabildo, Viceroy Calleja had no objections to the completion of regularly scheduled elections in December, 1813. On January 1, 1814, therefore, the second elected council was seated. The mariscal de Castilla and the conde de Regla were chosen as alcaldes. Incumbent members reelected as regidors were Juan Ignacio González Guerra, José Garay, Tomás Salgado, Francisco Manuel Sánchez de Tagle, and Juan de Antepara. New regidors were Ignacio García Illueca, Mariano Ycaza, José María Valdivielso, Pedro Extolinque Patiño, Manuel Arechaga, Pedro Prieto, and Manuel Terán. Syndics were José Rafael Marques, who was reelected, and Manuel de la Peña y Peña.[49]

Constitutional government made no advances during the remaining months that it existed in Mexico. Calleja continued to refuse to put into effect any constitutional requirements he considered inimical to his effort to quash the rebellion. Freedom of the press was not reinstituted, most of the newly elected Cortes delegates never got to Spain, the viceroy monopolized all aspects of government not delegated to other authorities, and the constitutional cabildo exerted only minimal influence over the kingdom as a whole.

The enthusiasm for the new political order that swept the city in November, 1812, turned to coolness as residents saw that the elected council had become embroiled in jurisdictional disputes, empty ceremonials, and financial mismanagement, just as its predecessor had. By 1814 the council had lost the support of the population, according to the regidor Sánchez de Tagle, who presented a report concluding, ''I lament . . . the lack of public agreement with our worrisome task; the lack of knowledge they have of it; and the lack of interest our fellow citizens have in protecting us and helping us."[50] Thus the constitutional system ground forward to its demise, producing no lasting reforms.

The royalist authorities of Mexico City presented a united front against implementing any more of the Constitution than was absolutely unavoidable. The constitutional system was for them a nightmare that threatened at any moment to bring about independence because of the restrictions it imposed upon viceregal power and the confusion of authority it entailed. A revealing summary of royalist fears appears in an audiencia letter of November 18, 1813. The oidors frankly admitted that "in these moments of calamity, the great Charter of the Spanish people . . . is not, and cannot be, carried into effect in New Spain," because "if the will of the people, corrupted as it now is, prevails, the independence of the country will be established, for the great majority of the natives is undoubtedly in favor of it." While they admitted that many creoles were still loyal to the Crown, they believed "it is nonetheless true that the majority of the people, and almost all the towns, are in favor of the rebellion." They accused the Mexico City cabildo of actively encouraging independence in 1808 and 1810. Now that the Constitution permitted the cabildo to reflect the interests of local citizens more directly, its effects were even more pernicious, for Mexico City always provided the example for other cities of the kingdom. The breakdown of authority since the overthrow of Iturrigaray had taught the people "that in Mexico City they might attempt everything with impunity," while the Constitution provided the rebels a shield behind which to hide. The result was the total collapse of governmental authority, so that now the rebellion was within Mexico City itself. "The sentinels in Mexico are fired at in the very center of town, nor can a soldier leave the gates without being lassoed." How was the rebellion to be ended? The audiencia bravely suggested that the only solution was revocation of the Constitution.[51]

The royalists' greatest fear was that constitutional guarantees of civil liberties made it impossible to suppress the subversive activities of the dissidents, especially socially prominent ones such as the Guadalupes, city councilors, and ecclesiastics. Ever since taking office, Viceroy Calleja had chafed at the constitutional obstructions that prohibited him from attacking the problem as he desired. He frequently complained of the tortuous legal system that obstructed his prosecution of alleged traitors and of the fact that public opinion and tradition prohibited civil prosecution of clerics in Mexico City. In December, 1812, Police Superintendent Pedro de la Puente wrote a long and pessimistic letter to the Spanish government declaring that the steps thus far taken by the regime to discover secret partisans of the insurrection were insufficient, especially since "no one can now deny that the clerics were the principle authors of this rebellion." Puente wanted an immediate crackdown on suspected partisans in the capital, as did most other hard-line gachupines.[52]

But Calleja's hands were tied by the Constitution and by the burdensome processes of Spanish law. After capture of the correspondence of the Guadalupes, for example, he had clear evidence of the complicity of the marqués de Rayas and the constitutional elector José Manuel Sartorio, but he could not get convictions. Referring to Sartorio, he wrote, "There are about him many strong suspicions, yet our complicated judicial system . . . makes them useless." Concerning Rayas, he reported, "The cleverness of the criminal and the tortuous methods of our civil tribunals . . . have seen to it that nothing can be proven."[53]

The problem became even more acute when the Cortes informed Calleja in 1813 that the Junta of Police established in Mexico City was unconstitutional. Calleja, in a strong defense of the junta, accused the cabildo of wanting to have police powers returned to itself because so many of its members were supporters of the insurrection. The rebels' object, he said, was simply to wear down the resistance of the royal government by subversion until the city should fall, and the elected cabildo played a major role in this plan.[54]

The Junta of Police, however, had provoked fierce public opposition. The reaction against the police was so intense that in February, 1813, Pedro de la Puente resigned the superintendency on the grounds that he was in danger of assassination. He admitted to the viceroy that the police had not stopped rebel activities and declared that even stronger measures were needed, for "the pacification [of New Spain] can no longer be the work of magistrates." José Juan Fagoaga succeeded him as police superintendent.[55]

In the latter half of 1813, the small peninsular population of New Spain gave itself over to panic, and apparently many of them attempted to flee the country. This rush of Europeans to leave Mexico was so widespread that in October, 1813, Calleja prohibited the issuance of licenses for travel to Spain "in order to avoid a general emigration, now already underway." The object of the order, which remained in effect until July, 1814, was to prevent the wealthier Europeans from leaving behind "those who are not so favored by fortune," thus exposing them to the "hatred and proscriptions sworn against all good Spaniards by the insurgents."[56]

The peninsular government, however, was even more convinced by these events that the viceregal police force was endangering Spanish control of the colony. Consequently, in September, 1813, it again ordered abolition of the police, this time in the strongest terms. Calleja had no choice but to obey. In December both the audiencia and the viceroy announced to Spain that the order had been carried out and the viceregal police system in Mexico City was abolished.[57]

As the royalists in Mexico City contemplated the spectacle of a Spanish parliamentary government at home striking down the viceroy's every effort to crush the rebellion in New Spain, their panic increased. Miguel Bataller, the oidor who played a leading role in the 1808 coup, asked permission to take his wife and eight children to Spain. He stated that, although he himself would die for the king, he could no longer expose his family "to the hatred of their countrymen who have long wanted to see them dead." The senior member of the audiencia, Ambrosio Sagarzurrieta, also asked to retire from his post and return to Spain.[58]

Where formal civil processes and the Junta of Police had failed, Calleja had to intervene personally. Over a period of several years Calleja swept down upon the suspected rebels among the capital's elite in a stunning series of arrests that, although they rarely resulted in conviction, had the desired effect of removing various suspects from the city. In late 1813 he gave the final order to send the oidor Jacobo de Villaurrutia to Spain. Villaurrutia's transfer had been ordered in 1812, but he had been allowed to linger on in the capital to deal with family affairs. Calleja said of him, "His continuous association with the partisans of independence, and the confidence, the respect, and the estimation with which the rebels view him . . . proves him to be one of the leaders of the insurrection." Guilt by association was, to the viceroy, proof aplenty.[59]

Even when no wrongdoing could be proved, the viceroy sometimes acted to remove an individual from the city. In 1814, for example, he turned against the fiscal Ramón Osés, who had pleaded before the audiencia the case of the secular members of the August, 1811 conspiracy. Although the viceroy was unable to prove anything against Osés, he ordered him transferred to Cuba, declaring that the fact that the cabildo had made a special plea to keep Osés in Mexico was proof enough. Calleja said, "The only motive the ayuntamiento had for making its recommendation . . . is the excessively liberal principles of Osés."[60]

In mid-1814 the royalist authorities restated their defiance of the Constitution in the strongest terms yet. On July 31, 1814, Viceroy Calleja wrote the Spanish government that, since he was still confused as to his own duties under the Constitution, he and the audiencia had agreed that he should continue operating as viceroy, not merely superior political chief, over those regions of the country where his jurisdiction prevailed. The royal accord agreed that he was the personal representative of the monarch and that, in the spirit in which he was first appointed, he would continue to function as viceroy. The audiencia's resolve was strengthened by the fact that in this period, as its letters testify, the viceroy was very ill. It pointed out that as long as the Constitution remained, he was the only man who could uphold Spanish power. In case he should die, the pretensions of the cabildo to national leadership would be unrestrained, while the intendant-corregidor would constitutionally inherit the executive. Their only salvation was to adhere to absolutism and await the coming of a brighter day.[61]

Even as the viceroy and audiencia worried over these problems and resolved to hold firm to absolutism, their brighter day was dawning. The rule of Napoleon in Spain was fast coming to an end. The Battle of Vitoria in late 1813 broke his military dominance. In March, 1814, Ferdinand VII, "the desired one," was released by Napoleon and crossed the Spanish border. On May 4, after becoming aware of the extent of plebeian loyalty and army support he still possessed after so long an absence, he issued a long manifesto at Valencia annulling the Constitution and all its provisions.[62]

Viceroy Calleja received news of the king's return and invalidation of the Constitution on August 5. He reacted, as he wrote himself, with "unspeakable joy." He desired to withhold announcement of the happy event in order to take the constitutionalists by surprise, but his hand was forced early when merchants arriving at Veracruz made the news public. On August 10 he called the leading personages of the city together at the cathedral for a *Te Deum*, during the course of which Dr. José Mariano Beristain announced from the pulpit the fall of the Constitution. On August 12, Calleja warned the constitutional cabildo that its days were numbered.[63]

There followed a remarkable exchange of letters. The city council replied to Calleja's announcement of the king's restoration in a pro-forma letter of only two paragraphs, in which it expressed its support of the king but showed little enthusiasm or obeisance. On August 21, Calleja informed the cabildo that its reply did not indicate proper subservience to either himself or the king and that it was "vaguely cold." He therefore ordered it to reply within four hours whether it was "disposed to guard, obey, and execute everything that was touched upon in the Royal Decree of May 4 . . . including the nullification of the Cortes and Constitution." Calleja took the cabildo's first letter as proof of the "bad faith of the constitutional body and of all those like it." Thus constitutional government in Mexico City ended.[64]

The elected council continued in office for another five months, but its only purpose was to plan and execute the series of bull fights and fiestas by which the king's restoration was celebrated. The audiencia gloated over its own return to power and dispatched letters pointing out the duplicity and treason of the cabildo. A succession of royal decrees quickly returned the affairs of government to their former state. Even the Inquisition, abolished by the Cortes in 1813, was reestablished. On December 15, Calleja published a decree returning all governmental bodies to the former methods of administration and to the persons who possessed office as of the king's fall on March 18, 1808.[65]

The ninth article of Calleja's decree ordered the restoration of the proprietary cabildos. The elected city council had only one day of warning. On December 16, it was formally dissolved and the perpetual cabildo, consisting of the surviving members of the 1808 body, took office. Proprietary members returned to their seats were José Juan Fagoaga, José Sánchez Hidalgo, Antonio Méndez Prieto, Ignacio Iglesias Pablo, Francisco José de Urrutia, León Ignacio Pico, and Augustín del Rivero.

The proprietary regidors went immediately to work cancelling all the projects begun by the elected council, firing its appointees, changing any salaries it had granted, and abolishing its commissions. Since the viceroy agreed that the honorary regidors of 1808 should return to their seats (with the exception of Francisco Azcárate, who was still deprived of his right to hold office), the cabildo elected six honorary members. Those elected, all of them military officers, were Manuel del Cerro, Joaquín Cortina González, Juan Antonio Cobian, Juan José de Acha, José Miguel de Ozta y Cortera, and Nicolás Galindo de la Rivera. The first three were to serve a one-year term; the second, three-year terms. Shortly after they were seated, Calleja permitted Azcárate to take his old seat as honorary regidor. The cabildo thus began 1815 with a full complement of members, the majority of whom were conservatives.[66]

Now that the Constitution was gone, Calleja was free to act against suspected rebel partisans in the capital. In 1815 he arrested four former regidors—Francisco Galicia, Ignacio Adalid, José María Fagoaga, and José Juan de Arechaga. Shortly thereafter he arrested the oidor José Ignacio Ortiz Salinas, the audiencia attorney Antonio López Matoso, and the canon and former Cortes deputy-elect José María Alcalá. In January, 1816, he arrested the marqués de Rayas. It is no coincidence that these suspected partisans were also among the leading constitutionalists.[67]

The cases against the ex-regidors are examples of the types and disposition of cases the government brought against alleged partisans. All four men were held incommunicado in the viceregal prison—a serious breach of the highly prized rights of former regidors. The cabildo requested their transfer to the municipal jail, but the viceroy ignored the request. The cabildo made no effort to defend these men, largely because it did not know the charges against them, but it appealed to the viceroy for clemency on the grounds of their family connections and records of service. The cabildo drafted a letter to the king urging royal favor in the case of Fagoaga.[68]

The case of Francisco Galicia is the most tragic. Clearly a partisan of the rebels, he was condemned in Mexico to eight years in a presidio in the Mariana Islands. The viceroy reduced the sentence but ordered it carried out. Galicia died in prison in Acapulco while awaiting embarkation for his Pacific exile. He was thus the second regidor, after José Primo Verdad, to die in viceregal custody. Ignacio Adalid was accused of giving aid to the rebel leader Eugenio Montaño at his hacienda of Ometusco in 1813 and of helping to smuggle Montaño's wife out of the capital to the hacienda, but he was found innocent in Spain in 1817 for lack of evidence. José María Fagoaga, the man Calleja was most anxious to convict, was also found innocent. The viceroy called Fagoaga "one of the principal partisans of independence" and based his case on his belief that there was a plot during the first constitutional elections in 1812—led by the known rebel sympathizer José María Alcalá, the fiscal Antonio López Matoso, the regidor Sánchez de Tagle, and the known Guadalupes Raz y Guzmán and Cortazar—to have Fagoaga elected to the Cortes. He was elected but never took his seat. When confronted with the case against him in 1815, Fagoaga defended himself by pointing out that there was only hearsay evidence to connect him with the rebels. He said the royalists thought he was a rebel because the insurgents did, while the insurgents thought him a rebel because the royalists did. And so the Council of the Indies agreed when it released him from all charges.[69]

The arrest and removal from the scene of men like Fagoaga, Adalid, Galicia, Arechaga, Matoso, and Alcalá accomplished what the viceroy hoped it would. By mid-1815 the government was no longer preoccupied by the threat of internal subversion in the capital, a fear that had troubled it for five years. The cabildo, until 1821, was again entirely subservient to viceregal authority. The defeat of the Morelos movement in 1815 brought the insurrection in the countryside nearly to an end. However, the Spanish government's granting of amnesties and its failure to convict such men as Fagoaga meant that many of these men had returned to the scene by 1821, and they became politically important again.

What was the impact of the two-year experiment in constitutional government? The audiencia and Calleja both insisted it had been immensely destructive of royal authority. The audiencia declared it had produced among the inhabitants of New Spain the same effect that "spiritous liquors cause among savages." The remarkably perceptive Calleja, in a letter written only days after receipt of the May 4 royal manifesto, assessed the damage fully. First of all, the Constitution occurred at a time of insurgent aggression, when royal resources were strained to their limit. Calleja was intensely pessimistic. He told the royal government that "the mines are abandoned; all our resources exhausted; the troops wearied out; the loyal discouraged; the rich in dismay; in short, misery increases daily, and the state is in danger." Economic and social disruption were causing a crisis of confidence in the royal regime, "for even if the arms of the rebels prove unsuccessful . . . still misery, and a growing consumption will do that which neither force nor intrigue may be able to effect." Proving he was more than a militarist, Calleja pointed out that the very process of royal resistance endangered the security of the regime, for the longer the war continued, the greater would be the misery and disruption resulting from it, and the greater thereby the possibility of independence. To destroy the rebel army would bring the royal cause "gradually to death's door," for as long as there was hope of the Spanish being defeated, whether by war or by the gradual wearing away of their will to resist, the rebellion would continue. Calleja recognized that authority was more than military power, and that it was the royal regime's ability to continue providing "good government"—to continue feeding and housing the populace—

that was at stake.[70] (See chapter 5 for a full discussion of the economic situation.)

"The rebellion has increased fearfully," Calleja said, "in consequence of the road opened by the Constitution for the execution of its criminal projects." The Constitution paralyzed his power to fight the rebels, while protecting suspected traitors with judicial niceties. "This is the reason for the attachment the Americans have displayed toward the new institutions. They have discovered that under their safeguard they advanced rapidly toward the great object of their wishes, the independence of the country, and the proscription of the Europeans, whom they detest." Mexico City was the focus of this subversion. "Notwithstanding our victories, little has been done against the spirit of the rebellion, the focus of which is in the great towns, *and especially in this capital.*" Despite this doleful exposition, Calleja promised not to let New Spain escape from the king; if necessary, the viceroy would march at the head of the whole army across the country, laying it waste with fire and sword.

Calleja also recognized the damage the Constitution had done to authority, or, more precisely, to the authority of Spain's agents. Nor would the mere restoration of political institutions to the norms of 1808 suffice to undo the damage: "The mere reestablishment of the old laws will no longer suffice. There was a time when they were sufficient to keep up the ancient illusions of these people with regard to their chiefs and magistrates. . . . But now—decried, discredited, and even turned to ridicule by the Constitution—they have lost their *prestige*, and even their respectability."

These qualities of observation are what made Calleja, in the cabildo's words, "the Reconqueror of New Spain" and "our Liberator" and, in Alamán's words, "the second Cortés." No other royalist recognized so clearly the legitimacy vacuum that was beginning to develop and that could undo all the military victories he had won. Calleja understood that the regime's authority, its very right to exist, was based on "ancient illusion"—myths. These included the illusion of divine-right monarchy, the illusion of the viceroy sharing and reflecting that authority, the illusion of one nation on either side of the

Atlantic, the illusion of the imperial ethos itself. These were all weakened, they had lost their respectability. The audiencia said that Spain had lost its "moral force."[71]

One essential fact, however, escaped the viceroy: the Constitution itself was not necessarily the source of the corrosion of royal authority. It might as easily have provided the foundation for new interoceanic links of affection and regard for Spain. Its full implementation might have reaffirmed the Crown's prestige, rather than weakening it. The Mexican elite sought limited reform, and the Constitution could have provided it. The fact that in 1821 the Mexican policymakers supported the Plan of Iguala suggests that they still preferred limited reform. Until the king's restoration of absolutism in 1814, Spain possessed the ideal opportunity for fulfilling these legitimate aspirations. Venegas and Calleja, however, refused to do so. They converted their regime into a government opposed not only to insurrection, but even to change; liberals like José María Fagoaga or the regidors Galicia and Adalid or the canon Alcalá were dubbed traitors because they sought to implement constitutional reform.[72]

What was the point of mobilizing the nation to fight for the maintenance of Spanish authority if the agents of that authority refused to adhere to the law? Viceroys Venegas and Calleja, the personifications of Spanish legalism, disobeyed the supreme law of the empire, scorned it, and openly defied it. Surely this was an anomaly too vast for even the most obtuse Mexican observer to ignore. The king, in his decree of May 4 abolishing the Constitution, affirmed that he was not a tyrant, nor were any of his predecessors, because by definition the king, as the ultimate focus of his peoples' aspirations, could never be a tyrant. The difference between the absolutist and the tyrant was that the first was divinely endowed to possess total authority while the second ruled in disobedience to both natural and man-made law. In New Spain the viceroys governed by fiat, disobeying the man-made legal code; they became tyrants. This is what weakened the Mexicans' "ancient illusions" about their magistrates, for the viceroy was the foremost of those magistrates. The regime disobeyed the law, which made it despotic, and it did not meet the needs of the people, which made it "bad government."

By 1814 it was clear that an extraordinary chain of events had discredited the Crown beyond recovery. The disasters of the ministry of Godoy, the fall of Charles IV, the forced exile of Ferdinand VII, the radicalism of the Cortes of Cádiz, had all brought an end, in Spain itself as well as in America, to the sanctity of the throne. Ferdinand might be powerful enough to abolish the Constitution—chiefly because he had not yet exhibited his true colors—but he could not reestablish the prestige of the Crown, which was dead beyond recall. As Richard Herr pointed out, Ferdinand's attempt to restore the eighteenth-century form of government only gave the Crown "a partisan role in the new political life, hardly different from other interest groups."[73]

During the period of Ferdinand's restoration, Spain had perhaps its greatest opportunity to enact substantive reforms to salvage the empire. Yet, the king remained adamant in his refusal to accept reform. A full explanation of Ferdinand VII's government requires (and deserves) a full-length study. Briefly, the chief problem was its combination of instability and intransigence. For a king who sought stability with almost pathological fervor, Ferdinand's record was abominable. The constant change in ministers is typical. During the nineteen years of his actual reign (1814–1833) Ferdinand had 33 ministers of state, 25 ministers of government, 20 ministers of grace and justice, 17 ministers of marine, 28 ministers of finance, and an incredible 44 ministers of war. Compare this to the record of his father, Charles IV, who, in a reign of twenty years (1788–1808), had only 7 ministers of state, 7 ministers of grace and justice, 5 ministers of finance, and 7 ministers of war and marine. Ferdinand, who in Stanley Payne's words was "cowardly, selfish, grasping, suspicious and vengeful," governed through a palace camarilla. Like the despot he was, he made and unmade governments at will, but he was unable to control the seething conflict between liberals and conservatives that continued tearing Spain apart. As Miguel Artola said, between 1810 and 1840 Spain lived in a state of permanent civil war. Ferdinand's greatest personal failure, as Carr implies, was not that he was a despot, but that he was too unsure, too timid, too much of a "trimmer" to be a successful despot.[74]

Ferdinand VII was intransigent when it came to considering reform in any of the fundamental institutions of the overseas empire. He was presented with a multitude of memorials and representations from both America and Spain suggesting methods of settling the American uprisings, but his conviction that change was revolution caused him to reject them all. A special Junta of Pacification was created, by royal order of December 3, 1815, to augment the Ministry and Council of State in their task of finding a political solution.[75] Another royal order of June 17, 1814, called upon the former Cortes deputies of the American territories to report to the Crown any solutions they might have. The order elicited a large number of long and detailed reports of extraordinary importance, asking for everything from autonomy and free trade to more audiencias and universities.[76] From 1815 to 1818 (when it was suppressed) the Junta of Pacification occupied itself with a discussion of whether to allow America free trade with all nations. Every councilor of state and every viceroy or commander returning from service in America was asked his opinions.[77] In an astonishingly outspoken representation, the councilor of state José Baquíjano, conde de Vistaflorida (a creole and former Lima oidor), ascribed the American rebellions to Spain's "anti-political" policies of the past and warned Spain to bring its actions more in line with its professed tenets of government or else it would lose the colonies. In 1817 the minister of state, José García de León y Pizarro, openly proposed free trade in America, admitting that "by the year 1817 I had no doubt of the loss [of America], and decided it was time to think of getting what advantages [we could] from the now inevitable separation." But the ultrareactionary party of Minister of War Francisco Eguía and Minister of Grace and Justice Juan Esteban Lozano de Torres "gave a shout of zealous opposition at the mere mention of 'free commerce.'" Even General Calleja, now commander in chief of the Expeditionary Army being gathered for the reconquest of Buenos Aires, pointed out in 1819 the impossibility of provisioning his army once it reached America if it were not permitted free trade with the foreign merchant fleets that now controlled all coastal waters. And the king's intimate advisor, the Lima-born duque de San Carlos, companion of Ferdinand in his captivity in France and long-time ambassador to London thereafter, proposed dividing the American territories up among the Great Powers of the Holy Alliance as a means at least of preserving them from the threat of republicanism. None of these proposals, whether they were wise or scatter-brained, was accepted. The Spanish Crown dedicated itself to an unyielding and disastrous policy of utter intransigence. It was not until 1822, after most of America was already independent, that the government of the radical Cortes appeared willing to grant even minimal concessions to the universal American aspiration for free trade and institutional reform, and the Cortes never implemented the kind of reforms Americans clamored for.[78]

Spanish imperial policy at its highest level was bankrupt. The imagination, courage, and spirit of Venegas, Calleja, or the Peruvian viceroy Abascal were not equalled in the penurious, mournful councils of power at Aranjuez or the Palacio Real in Madrid. Too frightened about their own tenure of office, a succession of ministers toadied to a paranoid king who himself gave more attention to the question of how to get Spain's representative included in the meetings of the Holy Allies than he gave to methods of preserving the vast patrimony of his forebears. When individual ministers of peculiar courage and patriotism did venture to present the king with the real facts of empire, they were deposed and exiled from court—as in September, 1818, when Pizarro (State), José Vazquez Figueroa (Marine) and Martín Garay (Finance) were overthrown in the wake of the scandal of Ferdinand's purchase of a water-logged, worm-eaten Russian fleet. Pizarro, referring to his enemies in other ministries, asked, "a country where such vermin live and thrive wants to prosper? No, it is not possible, it will not be."[79]

If these contradictions within the royal regime were at work by 1815, sounding the death knells of Spanish imperialism in Mexico, why did the regime last until 1821? Why, indeed, did Calleja retire in 1816 leaving behind him a New Spain internally secure, on the road to recovery, with only a few insurrectionary guerrillas left in the field? Why, most of all, did the royal regime in Mexico City survive the terrible year of 1813?

The first reason for the survival of the regime was that the insurrections were too weak and were improperly based; they were founded upon the wrong classes and aspired to unacceptably extreme social reforms. As early as 1811, Calleja recognized that the only thing needed for the insurrection to succeed was for it to clarify and limit its objectives. He had written, "This vast kingdom weighs too heavily upon an insubstantial metropolis; its natives and even the Europeans themselves are convinced of the advantages that would result from an independent government; and if the absurd insurrection of Hidalgo had been built upon this base, it seems to me as I now look at it, that it would have met with little opposition."[80] H. G. Ward, first British minister to independent Mexico, made similar comments some years later, pointing out that, until Iturbide, the insurrections were threatening to too large a portion of the population. When people's lives and security are at stake, he said, they must fight to defend them. But when the question is reduced to one of right between two governments, in which security is not endangered, then a change of even the oldest regime becomes possible. After independence many Mexicans, including José Joaquín Fernández de Lizardi and Manuel de la Bárcena, noted the same thing, criticizing the anarchy, disorder and destructiveness of the first stage of the rebellion in comparison with the moderation of the Iturbide phase.[81]

The second reason for the survival of the regime was that, as Friedrich says, authority once corroded cannot be reestablished, but it may be maintained for an indefinite period of time by the use of force.[82] Viceroys Venegas and Calleja made no secret of their increasing dependence on force.

Calleja made his thinking clear in an exchange of letters with the liberal bishop of Puebla, Dr. Antonio Joaquín Pérez. The bishop wrote the viceroy in April, 1816, complaining about the cruelty of royal troops and the destructiveness of the war in general. Calleja in his reply did not deny the excesses of his troops, but justified them by citing the excesses of the rebels. Pérez said farms and factories of those suspected of treason were needlessly destroyed; Calleja said the government had been too soft. Pérez accused royal troops of demanding excessive supplies; Calleja replied it was the duty of the countryside to supply a marching army. Pérez complained that the army was guilty of capricious and unwarranted bloodletting when capturing rebel towns; Calleja replied that he could not restrain successful and victorious troops, that the laws of war permitted every excess. Pérez alleged the royal government published false accounts of battles; Calleja said lies were justified by political expediency.[83] In all the history of New Spain, after the initial Conquest phase, there is hardly another instance of so unashamed a dedication to naked force.

Royal authority had never been based on force before. Rather, it was based, as the Liberator of South America, Simón Bolívar, said in his "Letter from Jamaica," on various ties that bound Americans to the motherland. In his words these were "the habit of obedience; a community of interest, of understanding, of religion; mutual goodwill; a tender regard for the birthplace and good name of our forefathers." All that had disappeared, and in 1815 Spain had become, in Bolívar's words, "an aged serpent, bent only on satisfying its venomous rage."[84] Having lost the true pillars of authority, Spain had only force to depend upon.

Thus the essential paradox of New Spain during the War of Independence was this: viceregal armies swept to victory after victory, the threat of constitutional reform was overcome, the regime triumphed over its enemies, and all the while royal legitimacy slowly declined—evidence that power and authority are not the same thing. There were two wars going on. One was the struggle for territory; the second, the struggle for men's minds. The Spaniards were winning the first, but losing the second, as Calleja himself perceived.

Viceroy Calleja, having lived in New Spain since 1789, was still essentially a soldier in the service of a late eighteenth-century absolute monarchy. And it was in the job of soldiering that he was most comfortable and successful.[85] He was totally dedicated to the task of destroying every vestige of insurrection by the skillful use of force. He succeeded so well in this that the regime, though weakened at its very core, continued to prevail. It defeated the rebels and still possessed the power to survive the other threats that confronted it in the realm of revenue, supplies, and civilian services.

Chapter 5

The Fourth Threat: Supply and Revenue

PRIVATION AND economic collapse were as real a threat to the viceregal regime as military and political challenges. Mexico City, of course, had faced food shortages, breakdowns in civilian services, and disease before in its history, and financial difficulties were endemic. Never before, however, had it faced these problems in conjunction with insurrection and internal subversion. This combination of circumstances resulted in a veritable fire storm of trial and tribulation that would have destroyed many other governments. The fact that the royal regime survived these crises is clear evidence of its strength, but the costs were great. The poor suffered the ravages of starvation, the rich paid an increasing tax burden, and the viceregal and municipal governments hovered on the brink of financial collapse. The danger was ever present, as Calleja said, that "misery and a growing consumption will do that which neither force nor intrigue may be able to effect"—destroy the regime.

The questions of supply and revenue, and the viceregal regime's responses to crises in those areas, touch upon two related, but distinct, realms of activity. Since the viceregal government had effective control over tax collection and the creation of new sources of state income, it faced the challenge of revenue shortages with what can only be described as remarkable imaginativeness. As a result, it was more successful in that

140

area. In food and fuel supply, on the other hand, the regime—contrary to its claims—actually had very little say, because it could not effectively control production, distribution, or prices. There existed a great mass of legislation controlling markets and market practices, but, as Florescano has made abundantly clear, the producers, not the government, controlled the critical functions of production, pricing, and distribution. Some government control was made possible by the creation of city-controlled slaughterhouses and markets and the establishment of institutions to guarantee at least a minimum supply of grain (the Pósito and Alhóndiga) and meat (the *abestecedor*, or city supplier who was granted a half-year contract to supply a minimum quantity of fresh meat to city markets). However, the government had no effective jurisdiction over the operations of a free-market system that was dominated by great monopolists in the provision of both finished goods and food. Another weakness in the government's position was that, at the outbreak of the War of Independence, royal revenues were closely linked with supply, so that as war-related disruptions limited food supply, royal revenues also suffered. Because of the mass of existing legislation, royal authorities probably were not sufficiently aware—as historians, until recently, have not been—of this critical fact: the government could not effectively direct and control production and pricing. In time of internecine war, this was another fatal internal contradiction in the regime.

Florescano has shown that in the half century before the outbreak of insurrection the hacendados and food producers of New Spain had succeeded in gaining control of market pricing. From 1742 to 1810 New Spain's population nearly doubled, producing a need for large-scale suppliers. After the economic boom of the 1780s, furthermore, the great haciendas expanded in size, sometimes taking over the land of the small independent farmer and Indian. As a result, the two chief institutions designed to prevent famine in Mexico City—the Alhóndiga and Pósito (public granaries)—had ceased to function correctly. Both depended for their revenue on a tax on each load of maize and wheat brought into the city. Thus as Florescano says, ''The economic base of the institutions dedicated to combating 'the tyranny of the agriculturalists' was practically in their [the producers'] hands, because by only refusing to take their grain to the Alhóndiga they compromised its economic stability and reduced the funds of the Pósito to buy maize." The inhabitants were thus required to buy at the going market price rather than at a reasonable price controlled by the government. As John Tutino has shown in the case of the hacendados in the region of Chalco south of the capital, these provisioners made a common practice of withholding grain destined for sale in Mexico City until scarcity or drought drove prices to a peak. These estate agriculturalists, who lived in the capital and formed an important part of its elite, exploited the Mexico City market. During the War of Independence the Alhóndiga and Pósito ceased to function entirely. In 1814 the Alhóndiga reported it had on hand only ten loads of corn. In 1813, as the great epidemic raged through Mexico City, the cabildo confiscated the 8,000-peso balance on hand in the Pósito—the institution designed to purchase grain in times of shortage.[1]

Mexico City, like any other city, did not produce its own food supply, though some kitchen gardens existed, and it was entirely dependent on its markets. The fresh vegetables and fruits and some of the grain for these markets were supplied by haciendas in the Valley of Mexico. Meat and more grain came from a wider orbit, sometimes including the huge haciendas in the north of the country. As an organized market, the city was heavily dependent on organized producers, rather than small farmers, for only the wealthy hacendados had the wherewithal to dispatch great mule trains of products from outside the vicinity of the capital or to drive herds of cattle or sheep hundreds of miles overland from the north. Mexico City's dependence on a few great merchants and provisioners made it especially vulnerable to price manipulation. The city's chief provisioners were also active in other realms of the economy—including merchandising, importing, and mining—and possessed disproportionate influence over the government, as the cabildo sometimes complained. Yermo's first act after Iturrigaray's overthrow was to get the royal accord to agree to tax reductions or postponements on the very goods—cane alcohol, pulque, mutton—he and his coconspirators produced and for which the capital was a chief market. These same men controlled the

Consulado, where their power to set prices for imported neces-sities was extensive. Finally, though they did not necessarily control the Mining Tribunal, they were the suppliers and, more importantly, sometimes the financiers, of the great mines, or were linked by family ties to the mining aristocracy. On top of all that, they were also the chief financial contributors to special taxes and collections after the outbreak of insurrection. In the economic functions of late colonial New Spain, these were the real rulers of the country. The government not only could not control them, it was dependent on them.

This network of economic, financial, and agricultural relation-ships might cause high prices, but it did not necessarily cause starvation. The producers might be able to control prices, but they could not control climate, rainfall, temperature, and the other exigencies upon which production depended. As Flores-cano has shown, New Spain suffered throughout its last century from a series of drastic agricultural cycles in which sharp falls in production—whether the result of natural disaster or human intervention—led to skyrocketing prices. This in turn would set up a whole string of disastrous consequences: inability to buy grain for draft animals led to further agricultural underproduc-tion and to a drop in the output of mines, for mining depended on draft animals; unemployed miners and peons would then flock to the cities, causing an increase in crime, further price increases for what little grain was available, and the breakdown of welfare institutions such as granaries and hospitals; and this led ultimately to outbreaks of contagion and social unrest. No one understood the causes of these crises, and the country thus lay unprotected before their ravaging effects.

In the twenty years before the War of Independence there were two such periods of agricultural crisis and rising prices. Both caused widespread suffering among the poor. Shortages of maize from 1797 to 1803 caused the price in those years to jump from a yearly mean of thirteen reales per fanega to twenty-six in 1803. Again in the years from 1808 to 1813 the price rose from a previous high of nineteen reales to an incredible thirty-six, and in 1810 and 1811 it averaged thirty-six reales every month. This constituted price increases of up to 300 percent over previous years.[2]

There was a statistical correlation between the periodic cycles of price increases and the great epidemics and outbreaks of banditry that troubled New Spain. Of the ten major epidemics in Mexico City in the years 1709 to 1813, seven were directly attributable to cycles in agriculture. Six of the ten occurred in the years 1736 to 1813 and carried off nearly 124,000 people in Mexico City, a number equal to the 1813 population. In every one of the great agricultural crises, government authorities invariably blamed price increases on the hacendados, although the greater problem was the inability of viceregal government to control the nation's economy.

The insurrection intensified supply problems. The last viceroy of New Spain, Juan Ruiz de Apodaca, admitted in 1817 that "one of the evils of greatest importance that the rebellion has caused in these Dominions is the abandonment of the fields and the consequent shortage of produce, and the danger of a general famine."[3] The first and most violent phase of shortage during the war occurred in the years 1810 to 1815. The second phase occurred in the years 1820 to 1821. In both these periods, food shortages preceded the outbreak of insurrection. The first shortage had been underway since 1803, while the second actually began in 1819. During both periods armed insurrection swept the country, and fields and haciendas were attacked, disrupted, or closed off from their markets. In the first phase tens of thousands of refugees flocked to the capital for protection and housing, further straining the city's resources.

The effects on Mexico City of the scarcity of food and the decline in manufacturing and commerce can best be illustrated by statistics for the alcabala, or sales tax, collected there. A basic viceregal tax of 6 percent levied on all sales, it roughly indicates the amount of goods, including foodstuffs, being distributed within the city. Total sales tax collections for 1810 in Mexico City amounted to 698,000 pesos. In 1811 the total dropped drastically to 565,000 pesos as the war began to take its toll. It again dropped in 1812 to only 330,000 pesos, less than half the level of two years before. The income from the tax on pulque, the liquor of the masses, showed the same drastic decline, falling from 244,000 pesos in 1810 to 226,000 in 1811 and to 87,000 in 1812. These figures may not indicate that the total of goods and produce on sale in Mexico City declined by half during these years, since a variety of tax changes were implemented—exempting some goods from the alcabala, adding others—but in general these figures suggest a dangerous disruption in the market and a radical decline in government revenues. The figures for the later portion of the war, beginning with the calm in 1816, show the same general trend. The income from the alcabala dropped again from 670,000 pesos in 1816 to 520,000 in 1817 and to 500,000 in 1818. The year 1819 saw a slight recovery with an income from sales tax of 600,000 pesos, but the tax fell drastically again during the Iturbide revolt, dropping to 500,000 pesos in 1820 and to 380,000 in the last year of Spanish domination. The total of all taxes collected in the customs of Mexico City, which reflects the total volume of all business activity, showed a loss in 1811 of 55,000 pesos over the previous year and was followed by a further loss of 267,000 pesos in 1812.[4]

By the beginning of 1811 the ravages of the war and the shortage of maize had led to a shortage of meat as well. On January 5 and February 25 of that year, Viceroy Venegas temporarily repealed the city's customs duties on sheep and goats. In April he further extended the freedom of entry to all meats and permitted the sale of certain types of livestock that had previously been prohibited, including heifers and old oxen. Strict price levels were naturally decreed, but the machinery to enforce them was not functioning.[5]

In April, 1812, one year after the decree opening the markets to all meat suppliers, the viceregal government found the shortages even greater. By that time a civilian committee called the Junta of Supply, headed by Intendant-corregidor Mazo, had been organized to aid in the procurement of food and fuel. On April 7, the government sent this committee an urgent request to begin emergency measures for the collection of meats and grains from the valleys of Mexico and Toluca. Meanwhile, permanent patrols had to be posted along the Viga Canal, the principal canal by which Indian carriers brought supplies into the city, to defend against guerrilla harassment. These patrols remained on duty until 1819.[6]

On March 1, 1813, the viceroy took the unprecedented step of exempting all meats and grains from paying either the customs duty on entry into the city or the sales tax. This measure was supposed to help alleviate the shortages by permitting greatly

increased profits to producers—strong evidence of the producers' power. Nevertheless, the shortages continued. By August, 1814, the Alhóndiga had on hand only ten loads of corn for
the coming months. Many wealthy citizens who owned haciendas were asked to contribute to the government in kind rather
than in cash. Hoarding, speculation, and fraud became widespread. The exemption of grains and meats from the customs
duty and the alcabala remained in effect until 1819, although
new taxes were imposed in the same period on other foods such
as chiles and beans. In 1819 the king restored the customs duty
on meat and grain, largely at the repeated insistence of the city
council, which had experienced a crippling loss in the revenue it
usually derived from that source. But the alcabala for meat and
grain was not restored.[7]

Fuel prices were also a constant worry for the city's poor. In
1813, while Mexico City was suffering from the combined on-
slaughts of a food shortage and an epidemic, there was a serious
fuel crisis as well. The people came closer to rioting over fuel
than over food, and there was widespread panic. In July, 1813,
prices for charcoal—the basic fuel for cooking—skyrocketed. In
a report to the cabildo, Francisco Galicia, the councilor charged
with supervising the sale of charcoal, said some dealers were
asking prices as high as two pesos (16 reales) a load although the
city-operated markets charged only 12 reales a load. According
to a report by two other councilors, the cause of the high prices
was monopoly. They stated that many soldiers were going out
to the highways to intercept mule trains loaded with charcoal
and, after paying the price asked by the Indians, they resold the
shipment in the city at a higher price. Many retailers began to do
the same, and so did the government—in order to assure an
adequate supply for the Royal Mint. Most of the shipments,
however, were on consignment. Galicia was ordered to intercept all fuel entering the city and to see that it went to its
consignee.[8]

This policy resulted in several violent encounters in which the
city councilors, after confiscating charcoal at the gates, were
assaulted or threatened by citizens. On October 29 the cabildo
ordered the confiscation of reserves hoarded by retailers. In
November the viceroy ordered government troops to reinforce
city guards in all the major plazas and at the entry gates, where

all entering charcoal was intercepted and sent to five specified plazas for sale under city supervision. This decree remained in effect until January, 1814, when it was reported that there were bumper shipments of charcoal and an adequate supply at last on hand. The fuel crisis, which lasted six months, was caused by panic rather than by shortage. A viceregal official testified that there actually was no lack of charcoal and that, if the homeowners had only waited for their regular delivery instead of rushing out to the highways to intercept shipments, there would have been no crisis.[9]

Yet another fundamental problem related to the markets was the scarcity and inflexibility of the currency. Rebel assaults against silver shipments, interruptions in the supply of quicksilver, decline in mining production, and hoarding all led to a currency shortage, especially in denominations small enough for market use. On September 30, 1814, therefore, Viceroy Calleja ordered the creation of a new specie of copper coins of very low value, with an initial coinage worth 51,000 pesos. The coins were specifically designed to permit easier trade in commodities of small value "for the benefit of the poor." They would also alleviate the drain of silver, apparently a pressing problem.[10]

The net effect of these food and fuel shortages—which remained critical up to 1815 when royal armies overcame the insurrection—was insupportably high prices. A police report at the end of 1811 indicated that prices reached new heights in this period, and the report ascribed much of the popular discontent to that fact. In 1811, wheat sold for sixteen pesos a load; corn was eight pesos in August and six pesos in December; beans reached sixteen pesos a load in August; and peas sold for twelve pesos a load.[11] At six pesos a load, much less eight, maize had reached the same prices as those that set off the hunger riots of 1692 in Mexico City. Viceroy Calleja testified in a letter to Spain that the price of livestock had quadrupled by 1814. He complained that the special grant of 20,000 pesos a year he received to provide for the expenses of official entertaining was insufficient in light of such drastic increases.

In addition to the destruction of haciendas and the disruption of the labor force caused by the insurrection a major cause of the shortages and high prices in the capital was rebel capture of the highways. Under Morelos, and even after his fall, the rebels concentrated on holding the principal roads and preying upon highway traffic for supplies or plunder. The worst period was 1812 and 1813, when Mexico City itself was frequently cut off from supplies and communication. The road to Veracruz was the prime target, and the government expended extraordinary effort to keep it open. In the first half of 1812 the Veracruz road was closed for the first time, and a large expedition was sent out from the capital to reopen it. As soon as the royal army passed, however, the insurgents again took possession behind them. Consequently, the governor of Veracruz sent a second force to clear it. They were attacked and destroyed on August 20, 1812, by six hundred rebels under command of Nicolás Bravo, and the highway remained closed. In July, 1812, the Mexico City–Querétaro road was also closed by rebels.

In order to maintain even a trickle of commerce, the royalists came to depend on large and heavily escorted convoys. Even convoys were a risk, of course, because their getting through depended upon their being escorted by a larger force than the rebels could muster against them at any one point. After the arrival of a great convoy from Veracruz in March, 1813—the one carrying Calleja's appointment as viceroy—rebel activity became so intense that even convoys stopped. Calleja asked the Mexico City Consulado for recommendations on how to keep commerce with Veracruz open. It suggested the establishment of a military road maintained by a series of standing garrisons.[12]

The viceroy agreed to this massive undertaking, employing the contingent of 2,000 troops from the Regiments of Savoy and Extremadura that arrived at Veracruz in April, 1813. The troops traveled in a body from Veracruz to Jalapa, and then on to Puebla, clearing the highway, leaving the road to give chase to rebel bands, occupying and destroying rebel ranches and villages, and establishing permanent garrisons at various points. At the same time a force left Mexico City to meet the approaching troops. Convoys were exchanged at Puebla. Six locations along the road, in addition to the towns of Jalapa and Puebla, were garrisoned and fortified. The total force required to maintain these garrisons was 1,200 regular soldiers, not including the many local militia units that might be called upon to lend aid.

This was an extraordinarily large number and indicates the importance accorded the project. Construction of new outposts cost nearly 10,000 pesos, while salaries of the troops alone cost 6,000 pesos a month.[13]

In order to protect the mails, the government instituted a complex system of monthly convoys throughout New Spain to meet and transfer mails at intermediate points between major centers. The one originating in the capital went only as far as Perote, where it met another one coming from Veracruz and transferred cargoes. Similar convoys traveled from the capital to other cities north and south. The only weekly mail runs left were those in the immediate environs of the capital, going only as far as Toluca and Tula.

The mail convoy system apparently worked. The governor of Veracruz, however, complained that the escorts were too large and that he would not be able to continue supplying so many men. For example, the November, 1815, convoy from Veracruz had an escort of 1,100 men; it was escorted on the return trip by 600 men. This was one of the most extensive and expensive operations of the war. The safe arrival of the mail in the capital became a matter of such concern to the citizens that in 1817 the viceroy ordered that it be greeted with a fifteen-gun salute.[14]

The supply situation began to ease in 1816. Viceroy Apodaca reported then that trade and commerce were moving much more freely, and he optimistically announced that the insurrection was over. In October, 1816, he reported that the capital and its vicinity were quiet and well supplied with food. In November he reported he had begun weekly mails between Mexico City and Puebla, although monthly mails continued in use for most of the provinces. In December, 1816, he reported that all the area around the capital, from Puebla on the south to Querétaro on the north, was free of rebels and frequent mails and convoys traveled quietly with small escorts. However, not until June, 1819, after Veracruz province was finally cleared of rebels, did the government resume the prewar twice-weekly mail schedule with the port.[15]

These disruptions in trade and commerce inevitably had a disastrous effect on viceregal and municipal revenues, since taxes on commerce were one of the three major sources of royal revenue. The second major source of viceregal revenue was cut when the Cortes of Cádiz, as one of its first acts, abolished the tribute collected from Indians and some castes. Venegas had already abolished the tribute as a temporary expedient. This cost the regime an estimated one million pesos a year.[16] The government was soon faced with financial ruin, and it turned to private contributors—the third major source of revenue—to make up the difference. The elite and bourgeoisie were called upon to make new and extensive contributions to uphold the regime.

The tradition of large private contributions to the government in time of need was an old one. Indeed, the Mexican elite actually preferred this method to any other. Their opposition to the Cedula of Consolidation of 1804—by which pious funds were ordered confiscated to finance the peninsula—was based both on their dependence on the loans granted by the Church and on their desire to adhere to the time-tested formula of private donations. They infinitely preferred that to the option of losing a vital source of mortgage capital.[17] In addition, private direct contributions had advantages that indirect or disguised taxes lacked. Chiefly, they bought government influence and favor, which after the *Grito de Dolores* became even more important. Applicants for government appointments invariably listed their financial contributions to the state as one of their chief recommendations. Direct contributions also bought local status—contributors' names were always published in the *Gazeta*—and they allowed corporations to embellish their names, honor their members, and extend their influence as a group. The Consulado, as the chief civilian corporate donor, kept scrupulous accounts in order to present bills for services when in need of some government favor. The ecclesiastical cabildo of the cathedral was the chief clerical donor, and it also made sure the peninsula never lost track of the amount.

Many gentlemen who held disproportionate influence over the government did so because of their contributions. This was the price of their influence, and they were willing to pay, as long as they got the credit. Since their stake in the Spanish regime was the greatest, peninsulars were the chief private contributors, and the sums involved were staggering. For example, the conde de Bassoco loaned or granted the Crown more than two million pesos from 1772 until his death in 1814. Gabriel de

Yermo often gave in kind rather than in cash. In 1808 he gave 200,000 pounds of sugar; in 1809, 64,000 pesos and a contribution of 2,000 pesos to buy shoes for Spanish soldiers; in 1810, 100,000 pesos. He established a 4,000-peso fund to reward soldiers in the war against the insurgents. In 1810, in response to a demand from Spain for a loan of twenty million pesos, Yermo pledged 355,000 pesos in money and kind, the largest single private pledge recorded in this period. He also maintained a troop of five hundred men under arms, entirely at his own expense. The heirs of the conde de la Cortina claimed in later years that he gave a total of 1,712,000 pesos to the war effort. He organized a troop of soldiers from his estates who served until his death in 1813. He equipped, armed, and maintained another eight companies of royalists and claimed to have spent 79,000 pesos for that purpose. He held the contract for supply of all horses to the royal army in New Spain, and his heirs claimed he spent a great deal of his own fortune in that activity. In addition, he claimed to have been responsible for maintaining the loyalty of the 70,000 persons who lived on his ten estates. José María Fagoaga, arrested in 1815 for treason and accused of failure to respond to government demands for donations, had given 80,000 pesos to the government under Viceroy Lizana, and thereafter he assigned the product of some of his holdings to the government, which his defenders claimed produced the sum of 22,000 pesos a year.[18]

The increasingly desperate state of the kingdom's finances can be traced through the government's efforts to acquire funds. Until 1812, donations and loans were usually voluntary. In most cases, special contributions to military defense of either the peninsula or the colony were repaid with a lien, or *juro*, on future royal revenues.[19] These contributions were actually an investment and were collected with surprising ease and in great amounts.

The first major drive for funds for peninsular defense began in October, 1808, under Garibay, and in one week collected 353,000 pesos, almost entirely from Mexico City. In April, 1809, Garibay opened a second drive, which by July had collected 1.5 million pesos. A third drive, begun in July, 1809, received donations from some individuals in amounts as high as 200,000 pesos, which was only slightly less than the yearly income of

Mexico City. In the first half of 1809 alone New Spain collected, above its usual revenues for Spain, an additional three million pesos from private sources, and an equivalent amount was raised in 1810.[20]

The money raised in New Spain in 1808–1810 had to be transported to the peninsula in ships purchased from the British navy and repaired in New Spain. Special drives were therefore launched to pay for these repairs. In 1810, a loan to recondition the *Beluarte* drew quick response and large amounts. Diego de Agreda and the conde de la Cortina gave 50,000 pesos each; Juan Antonio de Cobian and the marqués de Santa Cruz de Inguanzo gave 25,000 pesos each. In less than a month, a total of 555,000 pesos was collected.[21] The records of this loan, however, show that the government was already having difficulties making prompt repayments. A few months later, repair of another British ship, the *Implacable*, required another subscription to send still more money back to Spain.

Smaller drives for local defense purposes further divided the contributors' fortunes. In April, 1810, the archbishop-viceroy appealed for contributions to establish rewards for the discovery of Napoleonic agents in New Spain. Four donors gave a special reward of 5,500 pesos. Special drives to support the troops were constantly made. The drive to provide rewards for soldiers who distinguished themselves in the Battle of Las Cruces and to aid the families of the dead collected more than 15,000 pesos in a few days. In another drive to support individual soldiers in Spain the cabildo pledged to pay for fifty soldiers and the viceroy for twenty-five.[22]

Spain's desperation pushed her to take financial measures of an increasingly stringent nature. In January, 1810, the government in Seville ordered an across-the-board reduction in salaries of civil and military personnel; called a contribution, the reduction ranged from 2 percent on a salary of 5,000 reales to 33 percent on a salary above 120,000 reales. This was implemented in New Spain, and by 1814 Viceroy Calleja was himself complaining that out of his ample salary he was allowed to keep only 24,000 pesos. In January, 1812, the Cortes extended these salary deductions to clerics.[23]

In May, 1810, Spain demanded a loan of twenty million pesos from New Spain, to be collected from the Consulados at Mexico, Guadalajara, and Veracruz. This was the largest loan ever demanded from the colony, and its payment was virtually impossible. The amount was greater than the total value of all imports from Spain to Mexico in 1810 (just over seventeen million pesos) and greater than New Spain's exports (sixteen million pesos). In Mexico City a committee met to plan the drive, with Gabriel de Yermo and the conde de la Cortina representing the capital's Consulado. They proposed a 2 percent increase in all customs duties and new tobacco taxes, which would provide an additional 500,000 pesos yearly. In addition, private persons were encouraged to loan not only cash, but even jewelry. Despite its heavy expenses the city council offered to turn over to the drive 25,000 pesos from its revenue on city property.[24]

On top of this loan came another request for a special loan for Spain in November, 1810, for two million pesos. Again, Viceroy Venegas sent out his usual "invitations" to potential donors. By then, however, the word *loan* was becoming a euphemism. He requested the archbishop to urge all priests to preach on the loan at mass. Mexico City's peninsular elite again contributed staggering sums. The conde de Bassoco gave 200,000 pesos, and others gave 50,000 to 100,000. More than the required amount was collected, over half of it from Mexico City alone.[25]

By the end of 1811, the insurrection in New Spain was costing so much, and normal revenues were so reduced, that the viceregal government had to turn most of its attention to meeting its own emergencies. The attitude of the government began to change as collections ceased to be voluntary and the matter of repayment began to be overlooked. The first forced loan of the war was instituted in February, 1812, with an order requiring persons to turn over worked gold and silver. Its purpose was to acquire new specie, now in chronically short supply. Viceroy Venegas created a special committee—the Junta de Arbitrios—to propose methods of raising new income.

The first of several imaginative new taxes created by the Junta de Arbitrios under both Venegas and Calleja was a 10 percent tax on the revenues of private buildings in Mexico City. It was, in essence, a property tax, though it was levied against the actual income produced from rental property or the estimated sum that would be produced from houses occupied by their owners. Mexico City had never seen such a tax. In the late eighteenth century, Viceroy Revillagigedo II had instituted a tax on houses for paving and street repairs, but it had been abolished by Viceroy Iturrigaray. This new tax, however, was for general revenue rather than improvements. All owners of rental properties paid the government 5 percent of the value of the yearly rent from that property, and the tenant paid 5 percent. Persons occupying their own houses paid the full 10 percent of the estimated rental that the houses might produce. Inhabitants of public buildings—hospitals, the university, convents, colleges, rectories, town council buildings—paid the 5 percent owed by the renter. Each of the capital's thirty-two quarters was assigned six commissioners to collect the tax, which remained in existence for the duration of the war.[26] Viceroy Calleja altered the payments, requiring the tenant to pay 8 percent and the owner only 2 percent. The last viceroy, Apodaca, found that formula unfair and in 1817 restored the equal 5 percent for both renter and owner.[27]

In August, 1812, Viceroy Venegas again acted on the proposals of his Junta de Arbitrios and imposed a special war tax on corn, chiles, and beans. This partly made up for the revenue losses occasioned by the exemption of grains and meats from the customs and sales taxes. The cabildo complained bitterly that it had not been consulted and warned that this would cause severe privation for the poor who depended on those very staples. The list of taxable foods was expanded until, by the middle of 1813, nearly every comestible was covered. In effect the viceroy was preempting food taxes that usually went to the city government.[28]

As these special duties piled up, a new contribution for the "urgent necessities" of the peninsula was requested in October, 1812. Scarcely had that gotten underway when General Calleja became viceroy, and he outdid his predecessor in the invention of new contributions. Upon his accession to office, he found there was a debt of more than thirty million pesos, with a monthly deficit of 260,000 pesos. The best sources of income were already being fully employed, and the kingdom was nearing bankruptcy. Consequently, on his first day in power he ordered a forced loan of 1.5 million pesos. The conde de Bassoco again led private contributors with 50,000 pesos. Gabriel de Yermo and the condes de la Cortina, Heras, and Agredo gave from 25,000 to 15,000 pesos, and the cathedral chapter gave 60,000 pesos. Only 960,000 pesos of the amount demanded by Calleja was collected. Of that sum, over 780,000 pesos came from only 175 persons, and 513,000 of that came from only 55 persons. Obviously, only a handful of extremely wealthy men, most of them peninsulars, were now willing or able to meet the government's demands for direct subscriptions.[29]

As old sources of revenue were exhausted, need increased. Calleja reported on the last day of 1813 that the viceroyalty's debt was now nearly thirty-two million pesos and the debt on the overseas locations New Spain was required to support— Cuba, the Floridas, Santo Domingo, and others—was over seventeen million pesos. The kingdom thus had an aggregate debt of forty-nine million pesos, and the debt was growing every day. As a result, the government ordered the levy of a tax called "forced direct contributions." It was, in fact, a type of income tax, invented by the Junta de Arbitrios and modeled on a special war duty currently in effect in Spain. Persons with incomes of over 300 pesos a year were taxed at a rate of from 3 to 12.5 percent of income. Persons who received room and board as part of their employment—as many civil, clerical and military personnel did—had to evaluate that at 150 pesos and add it to their taxable income. The contribution was in effect from January 1, 1814, in all places under royal control, and in October special committees were created in each locality to assign contributions and collect them. A person who refused to declare his income faced the threat of a committee estimation based on public hearsay. Letters from the Guadalupes attest to the unpopularity of this tax. Even the judges of the audiencia complained to the king about it, nervously suggesting that it might cause popular discontent.[30]

Forced contributions, even if unpopular, were necessary by 1814, for voluntary contributions had ceased to meet the need for additional revenue. A special loan collected from merchants and clerics by the Consulado in the first half of 1814 fell far short of its goal, and the city council by July was 14,000 pesos in arrears on two of its pledges. Other new duties imposed by Calleja included a tax of eight pesos a month on private carriages, a tax of fifty pesos a year on public carriages, and a tax of twelve pesos a year on riding a horse within city limits. With a total duty of ninety-six pesos a year, maintenance of a private carriage was a luxury indeed.[31]

These extraordinary exertions helped lower the viceregal deficit by the end of 1815 to 131,000 pesos a month. That was still far too great; Calleja announced the government needed at least one million pesos more a year merely to survive. To meet part of this, in December, 1815, he established the most unusual and imaginative of his new taxes—a forced lottery. Two distinct lotteries were created, one specifically for the capital city for half a million pesos a year, and one for the rest of the country, including the Intendancy of Mexico, for one million pesos. Tickets were distributed to parishes, the city council, the Consulado, corporations, and commercial establishments. All whites and members of the royal army could buy tickets, and in an unusual measure, Indian communities were allowed to purchase tickets, though individual Indians could not. For the first six months of every year the corporations to which tickets were assigned sold them voluntarily, but in the final six months of each year the unsold tickets were distributed by force. Any person with an income over 300 pesos was required to buy tickets to the value of 2.5 percent of his income. Exactly half the total collection was set aside as prize money; the rest was clear profit for the royal treasury. To operate the municipal and national forced lotteries the viceroy created a committee of three persons chosen by the archbishop, the city council, and the Consulado. It is not clear if this forced lottery ever worked. One author, at least, says that it did not and that only government employees ever suffered salary discounts because of it (no source for this information is cited).[32]

The forced lottery was the last of Calleja's emergency revenue measures. It brought the total tax burden of the well-off citizen—whether elite or bourgeoisie—to an all-time high. In addition to the taxes already enumerated, the citizen was subject theoretically to the tithe and, if he were a civil or military officeholder, to the tax of his office, the *media annata*. Besides his taxes and forced contributions, his food costs had risen by about 300 percent, and no doubt the cost of clothing and luxuries rose proportionately. He might also have lost his provincial property to the rebels. Merchants and landowners bore their share of the burden in increased property taxes and forced loans.

The viceregal regime was indeed hard pressed, but it faced the revenue crisis with the same skill and ability it brought to bear on military and political problems. In 1819 and 1820 Viceroy Apodaca was able to end the discounts of civil and military salaries as well as the forced lottery, and the king complimented him on maintaining financial stability "without the necessity of resorting to the odious recourse of taxes or contributions established by your predecessors." The viceregal government's power to create new taxes, to operate in the red, and to borrow on its credit made survival possible. The total national deficit, which was forty-nine million pesos in 1813, had grown to eighty million by 1816.[33]

The municipal government had no such powers and no such credit. It had to pay interest whenever it borrowed, whereas the national government often appealed to the patriotism of contributors to forego interest, and the city had no access to the immense private fortunes of the oligarchy. The total revenue of Mexico City during the insurrection was reduced to as little as one-third to one-half of its prewar level. This had a disastrous effect on city services.

In spite of the scarcity and disorder of records concerning municipal financial affairs (a gap exists for 1807–1816), it is possible to acquire some idea of the city's income by comparing statistics for 1816–1821 with those from before the war. Two reports, one written in 1801 and the other in 1812, give figures of city income for the years 1790 to 1807. The 1790s was a prosperous decade, and city income reached a yearly high of 323,000 pesos in 1794. The decade closed with a 1799 income of 306,000 pesos. The first seven years of the new century were almost as prosperous. City income in 1807 was 242,000 pesos.[34]

A third report, drawn up after independence, gives totals of city income from March, 1816, to the end of October, 1821. These totals indicate the extent of decline, for in 1816 (less the two months not included in the report), city revenue was only 141,000 pesos, over 100,000 pesos less than the last prewar figure available. Since by 1816 the worst of the war was over, it is probable that, as statistics for sales taxes and customs duties suggest, income for the five previous years was even lower. Incomes in 1811, 1812, and 1813 may have been less than 100,000 pesos a year. In 1817 income rose to 189,000 pesos; in 1818 it was up to 200,000; in 1819, to 216,000. However, income was still lower than before the insurrection. The published financial statements of the city council during the second period of constitutional government show the income for the year of June, 1820, through June, 1821, to be 230,000 pesos.[35]

The improvement noted in the last five years of the war was largely owing to increases from the capital's major source of income—taxes on goods introduced for sale in the city. Only 78,000 pesos were collected in 1817 from this source, but in 1818 the total rose to 108,000 pesos. In 1819 and 1820 it was 116,000 and 118,000 pesos. Income from public marketplaces—the second major source—reflected the same drastic decline for the early war years, with an attendant improvement after Morelos's defeat. In 1811 the income was only 25,000 pesos, and in 1812 it fell to its lowest level at 22,000. A steady improvement occurred after 1812; yearly market incomes from 1813 through 1816 were 30,000, 35,000, 40,000 and 56,000 pesos. In 1820 Viceroy Apodaca boasted to the Spanish government about the increase from this source.[36]

Nevertheless, the city suffered constant revenue deficits. It defaulted on a debt of 100,000 pesos owed to the Consulado and on one of 50,000 pesos owed to the Marquesate of the Valley of Oaxaca. In the case of the latter, the viceroy imposed a lien on the city markets, in reaction to which the cabildo threatened spending cuts in police, drainage, and pavement-repair programs. Since the same financial problems plagued all corporations in New Spain, various large debts owed to the city also went unpaid.[37]

While the general economic dislocation of the war was responsible for most of the municipal financial troubles, the cabildo's incompetent management exacerbated the problem. The cabildo was so fiercely jealous of its own treasury that it resisted any viceregal intervention. In 1788, as part of a controversy over auditing municipal records, the auditor of the Royal Tribunal of Accounts accused the city of "a great deal of arbitrariness, little or no formal structure in the keeping of accounts, and not a few abuses in the management of public rents."[38] Unfortunately, Viceroy Apodaca could still repeat that assessment as late as 1817. For thirty years the city struggled to keep its financial records from being audited by the Contaduría General. The audit was first ordered by José de Gálvez in his Ordinance of Intendants of 1786. Viceroy Branciforte in 1796, Viceroy Calleja in 1815, and Viceroy Apodaca in 1816 ordered the city council to submit its accounts for review, and each time it refused. Apodaca finally ordered the viceregal auditor to take over the duties of the municipal auditor and informed Spain that he had grounds to suspect that there was "something sinister" in the city's management. He charged it was padding its income figures, that one of its officials was guilty of graft, and that its treasurer had amassed a personal fortune beyond reasonable expectations. Three more orders, each an ultimatum, were required before the cabildo submitted its accounts in July, 1817. The accounts themselves were incomplete and of little value.[39]

There were considerable grounds for concern about the city fathers' conduct of financial affairs. In 1813 the administrator of markets and plazas, Rafael Villela, was removed from office on suspicion of theft. In 1814, regidor Manuel de Gamboa was arrested on charges of misusing the money of a widows' and orphans' gratuity fund. The cabildo even refused to testify as a character witness for him. When Gamboa returned to the council in 1817, the viceroy ordered that he not be permitted to handle public money. Viceroy Apodaca, for his part, was personally suspicious of the city treasurer of nineteen years, Bruno Larrañaga. At the time of his death in 1816, he left a fortune of 23,000 pesos, which the viceroy considered excessive for a man of his income. Larrañaga's son, Benito, was denied succession to his father's proprietary office, even though he had served as his assistant for twelve years. In turn, Benito accused the new treasurer, José Ignacio Náxera, former cabildo secretary, of playing politics to get himself the promotion.[40]

The cabildo cannot be excused on the grounds that it was unaware of the sad state of its financial management. In 1812 the syndic advised publication of statements of municipal expenses and income in order to allay public suspicions, but the information was not made public until 1820. In 1812 the cabildo asked the city attorney to draw up monthly financial reports for the councilors' own information and requested the intendant-corregidor to draw up a list of the major sources of revenue and to assign two councilors to supervise these and to keep a watch on each other. These proposals were motivated by a speech of regidor José Urrutia in February, 1812, asking the members to observe more careful practices in supervising public funds.[41]

During the time of the Constitution, the elected aldermen bore a particular onus to prove themselves competent. In 1814 the regidor Francisco Manuel Sánchez de Tagle proposed that the councilors in charge of financial matters should meet frequently "in order to clarify doubts about the accounts" and to protect themselves from accusations of mismanagement. But the record of the constitutional cabildo was no better than that of the proprietary, for it dissipated all of the surplus cash that was on hand when it took office. In 1813 and 1815 both the city treasurer and Sánchez de Tagle frankly criticized the cabildo for mismanagement of rents from city property.[42]

This combination of declining revenues and mismanagement resulted in a city debt in 1820 of between 640,000 and 680,000 pesos. In the absence of a budget and with no powers to create new income, the city was financially no better prepared at the beginning of the new era of independence than it had ever been. A letter from Viceroy Apodaca in 1819 referred to its continuing "income deficit," and in April, 1821, a regidor proposed the appointment of a special committee to discuss ways of salvaging the city "in respect to the deplorable state of the public funds." In the last trimester before independence only 46 pesos were applied toward the debt, while the extravagant sum of 27,432 pesos was spent for the triumphal entry on September 27, 1821, of the liberator Agustín de Iturbide.[43]

The viceregal regime survived these financial crises because the elite had no alternative but to keep up their contributions. Until the advent of Iturbide, all alternatives were rejected and royal authority held. Yet, everyone suffered. There were out-breaks of disease in 1813, 1814, and 1821, drainage ditches and sewers backed up into homes, packs of wild dogs roamed city streets unchecked, parks and highways deteriorated, crime increased, markets declined, medical and educational services virtually ceased, thousands faced the specter of hunger, and the general quality of life under the royal regime declined.

Chapter 6

The Fourth Threat Continued:
The Terrible Year 1813, and After

THE ROYAL regime's resiliency and its success in resisting the first phase of the insurrections were demonstrated in the terrible year of 1813, when one of the greatest civilian crises in Mexico City's history occurred. The capital was no stranger to natural disaster: serious floods occurred there with great frequency,[1] and it was swept by devastating epidemics in 1736–1739, 1761–1762, 1772, 1779, and 1797–1798.[2] Natural catastrophe had never before broken the city's resolve, and disaster alone would not do so now.

The troubles of 1813 were different. They were accompanied by armed insurrection in the countryside—Morelos's movement was at its very height—and by the threats of imperial disunion, confusion in authority, and governmental chaos that were provoked by the king's capture and by the Constitution of Cádiz. All of this limited the viceregal government's ability to respond to crisis. Furthermore, the city council—the royal authority that possessed first jurisdiction over civilian affairs in the capital—was on the verge of bankruptcy; at the same time, the first elective cabildo fought to prove its right to exist in the face of the hostility of both viceroy and audiencia. Underground sedition was rampant, loyal Mexicans were spilling their blood on the battlefield, food prices leaped by 300 percent, normal trade and commerce were paralyzed, and every political tenet that had previously sustained Mexicans in time of need was in danger of repudiation. Mexico City had survived all its previous catastrophes because, while individual viceroys might have been renounced, royal authority was never repudiated. In 1813 the imperial ethos itself was under attack.

In May, 1813, a contributor to the *Diario de México* summarized the general feeling of the population when, after reviewing the catastrophes that surrounded them, he said: "Our circumstances are the most calamitous America has seen since the Conquest."[3] However, the dubious honor of being the most calamitous year in Mexico City's history might as easily belong to 1629, when the city was so seriously flooded that Spain actually approved moving the capital to another site, or to 1692, when it was nearly destroyed in riots, or to 1736–1739, when it lost half its population in an epidemic. These and other catastrophes—from which not a single generation of Mexicans was spared—point to the population's remarkable endurance and capacity for suffering.

Under even the best of circumstances, Mexico City was an unhealthy place to live. The principal problem was the fact that the city was situated on the site of a former lake bed. The canals were slow moving, usually fetid, and always used for garbage disposal. The high water content of the earth made it immensely difficult to maintain pavements and drainage ditches in working order. At the very outset of the War of Independence the city was troubled, as usual, by extreme pollution. A viceregal committee in 1810 reported that the lakes themselves, mainly Lake Texcoco, were filled to overflowing with garbage from the city's canals.[4] Scarcity of funds during the war made it even more difficult than usual to maintain public facilities.

There was certainly no lack of legislation to deal with sanitation problems. Nearly every viceroy, as one of his first acts after assuming office, published series of regulations concerning public cleanliness, but he usually failed to enforce them. Viceroy Venegas, for example, ordered that all houses must have their sewers connected directly with the drainage canals, rather than with the streets, but many houses, even of the wealthy, had no connections at all. While the government distributed free smallpox vaccinations at all times—a practice initiated in 1803 by

Viceroy Iturrigaray when the precious vaccine was first imported into New Spain—no attempt was made to prohibit
various unsanitary usages that caused or spread disease, such as
the widespread practice of renting funeral effects, including
coffins and shrouds, to the poor.[5] And so it went; at all times the
chief complaint of persons concerned with public health and
cleanliness was that no enforcement of the many pertinent laws
was attempted at any level of government.

As in the Apocalypse, where there was war, famine, and
death, there also was pestilence. For Mexico City, it started, as it
had so many times before, with the news of an outbreak of
fevers at some other place, and the municipality hastened vainly
to put up its defenses against the spread of the peril. On
January 15, 1813, the cabildo informed the viceroy that there
was an epidemic of "fevers" in Puebla. It asked him to call
together the royal tribunal of the Protomedicato, the official
medical authority of the kingdom, in order to discuss what
measures should be taken. At the same time it proceeded to
establish the Junta of Health prescribed by the Constitution as a
municipal function, to manage the city's defenses against disease. The Protomedicato was charged with supervision of the
physicians, while the Junta of Health was charged with planning and paying for general relief work. Within a matter of days
the Junta of Health was functioning, and it mobilized the city's
trained medical practitioners and representatives of government
organizations to discuss methods of preventing the spread of
the contagion from Puebla. A quarantine at the city's gates was
immediately established. Every traveler or merchant arriving
from Puebla was detained for one or two days for fumigation of
his clothes, baggage, horse, and coach. Sick persons were
indefinitely quarantined. All mail and commercial products
coming from Puebla, particularly wool and cotton, were detained.[6]

But the plague had already struck the outskirts of the capital
and was beginning to infect the poor people in low-lying
districts. The city's leading physician, Dr. Luis José Montaña,
reported the disease was mainly attributable to the miserable
living conditions and inadequate diet of the poor, occasioned by
"the scarcity, high cost, and poor condition of meat in the city."
As Dr. Montaña indicated, the supply problems troubling the

capital encouraged and spread the epidemic, and the misery of the poor was linked to the disruptions of the war. Donald B. Cooper has determined that the fever, whose precise nature is not known, was principally typhus, and that several other diseases complicated the diagnosis.[7]

By mid-April the fever was established in the suburbs and was reaching epidemic proportions. The cabildo began to solicit donations from wealthy citizens and corporations, for its miserable financial condition made voluntary contributions essential. It hired four physicians to care for the sick and a few weeks later found it necessary to hire four more. The Junta of Health, composed of five members of the cabildo, had the responsibility of distributing food, clothing, and medicine, much of it provided at the city's expense on credit from apothecaries and merchants. To encourage contributions from the rich, the cabildo on April 26 asked four wealthy residents of each district of the capital to organize and support a relief society in their neighborhood, the implication being that these commissioners would pay for the necessary supplies. The city-hired physicians were authorized to distribute tickets for free food to needy victims. All normal agencies for feeding the poor had broken down. When the public granaries reported they were bankrupt and could not buy maize, the cabildo established public kitchens in each of the major quarters of the capital, at the expense of private charity.

Dr. Montaña urged the cabildo to remember to pay particular attention to the needs of prisoners in the municipal jail, a prime target for the contagion. He also called for every doctor in the city to be mobilized under the direct orders of the Protomedicato. A General Treasury of Charity was created by the cabildo to collect and distribute contributions. The cabildo itself simply did not have the cash on hand to meet the emergency. It desperately asked Viceroy Calleja for permission to confiscate the balance of 6,000 pesos in the treasuries of the two Indian communities of San Juan Tenochtitlán and Santiago Tlaltelolco, arguing that the Constitution no longer permitted the Indian communities to remain separate from the general municipality. The viceroy agreed. A special study commission of two physicians and two aldermen reported that the fever was not yet "malignant" but that it would soon become so because of the lack of food, clothing, housing, and medical care for the first victims. Some months later Viceroy Calleja admitted in a report to Spain that "for the purpose of containing the epidemic the steps taken at its beginning were insufficient."[8]

As with any natural catastrophe, the epidemic soon brought out both the best and the worst in the inhabitants. Unusual acts of individual heroism and sacrifice occurred side by side with unusual hoarding and speculation. The cabildo cited the work of Nicolás Antonio del Puerto y Gómez, a government employee, as an example of the high level of sacrifice some of the residents sustained to aid the poor and sick. Puerto y Gómez valiantly went among the sick to distribute food donated by one of the city's most noted philanthropists, Doña Ana María Iraeta de Mier. When the city council asked the hospitals of San Juan de Dios, Belén, and Jesús Nazareno to set aside wards for fever victims, only the first hospital agreed. Some people took advantage of the crisis to accuse the newly elected city council of failing to take adequate measures. The council replied that its members were exposing themselves to great danger by traveling abroad in the city ministering to the sick and that some inefficiency was to be expected. On May 28, the regidor the marqués de Valleameno died, apparently from the fever contracted in his charity work. This outbreak of fever, at the very moment the new constitutional cabildo was engaged in organizing itself, seriously damaged the cabildo's chance to reform city government. All the cabildo's resources for nearly six months were absorbed by the battle against the epidemic.[9]

The plague could not be contained. During May it spread further over the city. Devotionals and special novenas were offered by every parish. On May 11, Archbishop-elect Bergosa posted in all the parishes a decree asking for donations to the Treasury of Charity, but by the end of May the city council reported that so little money was available that it feared all relief operations would soon have to stop. In May the city council joined private initiative and established in seventeen of the city's quarters provisional hospitals, called lazaretos, which were associated with the soup kitchens. Here the sick could come for whatever aid was possible. The existing hospitals were of little help in a crisis of such vast proportions, for most of them were specialized in function or constituency—that is, hospitals existed for the Indians, for members of the clergy, for the poor, for the demented, and so forth—and none were equipped to deal with typhus. Besides, the city's medical practitioners were no longer functioning out of their hospitals but were moving throughout the town, usually seeing victims in the lazaretos. Many victims sought no help of any kind. The immensity of the crisis lies as much in the number of persons who were stricken as in the death toll. Viceroy Calleja later reported that 65,512 persons were known to have contracted the disease. This figure, however, represents only those who sought help of some kind and were therefore counted. Over half the city's inhabitants fell sick in the summer of 1813.[10]

The city council's valiant efforts soon ground to a halt as it ran out of money, and relief efforts collapsed just as the epidemic worsened. The council had scraped together the pitifully small sum of 27,000 pesos to fight the emergency, and that was all gone in a month and a half. On June 10 it began buying drugs from pharmacists on credit. It was reported that in the first ten days of June "the epidemic is three times greater than it was in May." Already 54,000 persons had been diagnosed by the public lazaretos and hospitals as having contracted the disease. On June 14 the city council desperately wrote the viceroy, "We have exhausted all our resources. . . . today we find ourselves compelled to suspend assistance, and one after another of the district kitchens has had to close."[11]

The city's total dependence on private charity in this crisis was its greatest weakness. In desperation to find funds, it asked the viceroy for several unusual favors. First was a request for a grant of 30,000 pesos from the property of the Inquisition, which, having been abolished by the Cortes, had turned its assets over to the royal government. The viceroy denied this request. The city next asked him to confiscate the 8,000 peso balance on hand in the royal granaries. This extraordinary proposal—which meant the bankruptcy of the granaries, themselves no less vital to public relief—was granted, and the granary system ceased to function. Then, after the Charity Fund reported that every peso of its relief money was spent, the council asked Calleja's permission to confiscate 8,000 pesos remaining from prize money in the National Lottery. The most extraordinary proposal, however, was made by the cabildo syndic José Rafael Marques, who asked that the Church be called upon to contribute some of its silver. The cabildo submitted this request, but no action of any kind was taken on the matter. This was the only instance during the War of Independence of a functionary of the royal government in Mexico City making such a suggestion. In addition to pleas to the viceroy, the council continued its direct appeals to wealthy citizens. On June 11 it commissioned three councilors to speak personally to the University and to the marquesa viuda de Vivanco.[12]

None of these financial measures helped much, and the epidemic was left to run its course. A pall of death descended over the New World's premier city. In the parish of San José, the inhabitants began burying victims in the streets and haphazardly in vacant lots. A special appeal went out for funds to provide a burial place for that parish and for the parish of San Pedro y San Pablo. Consequently, mass graves were opened, and the city council set aside two special carts to haul bodies from the lazaretos. Ultimately, the council prohibited the tolling of church bells for the dead because it spread panic and alerted the population to the extent of the deaths.[13]

As laborers died or fled their jobs, the city faced a sanitation crisis. The cabildo offered triple wages to garbage collectors, but to no avail. Viceroy Calleja finally consented to permit convicts to carry out essential jobs in drainage and garbage removal. Municipal sanitation at that time was in the hands of a private contractor, Rafael Morales, who was accused repeatedly by the city council of nonfulfillment of his contract. The regidor Ignacio Adalid conducted an investigation of the contractor and found that the basic problems were a shortage of laborers and the inhabitants' failure to cooperate. Nevertheless, on June 30 the cabildo rescinded Morales's contract and took over the job of street cleaning and garbage removal.[14] An inventory of the contractor's carts and mules showed half his equipment to be unusable, whereupon the city, though it had no money to pay for it, ordered thirty new carts to be constructed.

In the realm of sanitation, too, the city depended on private charity. Lacking money to pay sanitation inspectors, it requested the viceroy to permit it to appoint commissioners from among prominent citizens to supervise sanitation in their home districts. Since the plague was raging, it asked him to order that any man so selected could not be excused from performing the job on any grounds. The viceroy concurred, ordering the commissioners to be appointed on July 19.[15]

None of these measures helped. The regidor Adalid reported on August 14 that none of the thirty new carts he ordered had been delivered, because the city could not pay for them, and no workers could be found willing to risk their lives in cleaning the plague infested streets. He testified to the "intolerable filth of the streets," declaring most of the main thoroughfares to be impassable and admitting it was impossible to clean them.[16] The intendant and one regidor offered a loan of 2,500 pesos from their personal funds to help the city pay for the new carts. The sanitation commissioners were not doing their jobs, so, as an incentive, the cabildo decided to allow the inspectors to pocket any fines they might levy against persons disobeying regulations.

In this same horrible summer of 1813 Mexico City was endangered by its old enemy—flooding. In August it rained heavily, and the lakes and canals filled to overflowing. At the end of the summer, some of the rivers and canals were allowed to run off into fields and lowlands. The little Indian village of San Mateo Churubusco outside the capital was flooded until June, 1815, while its Indian governors continuously begged for some relief for their people. The administrator of the canals, Ramón de Llano, informed the viceroy that there was no other method of preventing the capital itself from flooding because the Constitution now forbade forced Indian labor drafts—the traditional means of making up for labor deficiencies. By February, 1814, the cabildo was forced to suspend cleaning the drainage canals for lack of funds. Another regidor in this instance came to the city's aid by offering to loan it 2,000 pesos to be repaid by a lien on one-third the income of the Parián market. Nevertheless, only the most important canals could be cleaned.[17]

Everything that was elegant and beautiful about colonial Mexico City fades in this scene of the great metropolis ravaged by disease and festering in its own garbage. As the plague began to subside, the capital was nearly overcome by packs of wild dogs. They roamed the streets at night raiding homes and gardens, attacking domestic animals and sometimes even people. A nightmarish scene, worthy of recounting by some colonial Dante, confronted the inhabitants as the dog packs invaded the shallow mass graves of the plague victims. The city council reacted with revulsion, ordering the night watchmen to pursue and kill the dogs. For several weeks groups of men, armed with guns, knives, and poison, slaughtered packs of dogs in the still of the night, as residents huddled in their homes listening to the sounds of the slaughter. In the mornings the streets ran with blood, and the dogs' bodies were hurled into the canals and drainage ditches or left in the sun to rot.[18]

The grisly epidemic began to ease with the coming of cooler weather, but its toll had been immense. In Mexico City, according to computations based on reports from the parishes and lazaretos, the epidemic killed 20,385 people. Of that number, 11,294 died in hospitals or lazaretos, the rest in their homes or in the street. This constituted a death toll of one out of every eight of the city's residents. No epidemic since that time has caused as great a loss of life in Mexico City. That the royal regime survived 1813 is surely its most remarkable victory.[19]

The city council's finances were paralyzed by the epidemic. "The city's debts are so many," it said, "and the creditors insistently urge payment, but there is nothing with which to satisfy them." It received so little financial help from the viceregal government that when in September, 1813, Viceroy Calleja proposed the creation of a Junta of Charity under his, rather than municipal, auspices, the city council bitterly opposed the idea, saying that such a viceregal committee would end up getting all the credit for the sacrifices the cabildo had thus far made. Proud and self-assured, desperately trying to prove the validity of its constitutional mandate, the cabildo turned its attention to the question of how it would pay the employees of the lazaretos, including the physicians, who had worked without salary since the epidemic began. It decided that all income from municipal properties outside city limits would be diverted directly to this task. It also had to pay the pharmacists who had provided medicine on credit, and the private individuals, convents, and hospitals who had taken in the sick, distributed food, or dispensed drugs. It owed one pharmacist

3,476 pesos; another, 4,182; another, 5,159; and yet another, 5,509. Its debt to the Hospital of San Andrés was not paid until 1819.[20]

It would be reassuring if one could report that this was the end of Mexico City's suffering, but it was not. Scarcely a year later it was struck with an outbreak of smallpox. The first cases were reported in April, 1814. With the memory of the 1813 epidemic still very much in mind, the cabildo in 1814 prepared itself with far greater care. Determined to end its dependence on private charity, it proposed a method by which 128,000 pesos might be raised from a series of temporary taxes to pay for emergency relief. The viceroy, however, vetoed the proposal because the population was already overburdened by taxation. The city council lowered its estimate of the amount of money required to deal with the smallpox to only 30,000 pesos, following a report in May from the Junta of Health that the smallpox was propagating itself only very slowly. The major threat became pneumonia, which affected many persons.[21]

Smallpox, unlike typhus, could be controlled with existing medical knowledge, for vaccine had been in general use in the capital since 1803. In the second week of July, 1814, the city council, rather than waiting for persons to come to medical authorities, began vaccinations in each district of the city. The vaccine made it possible to control the disease to such an extent that the city did not find it necessary to make an enumeration of deaths in this 1814 outbreak. That the rudimentary vaccine was dangerous and unpleasant is suggested by the general awe in which it was held by the inhabitants and the extraordinary pains the cabildo took to supervise its distribution. One regidor was assigned supervision over the vaccine, and the cabildo hired two special runners to carry the precious fluid out to the commissioners in the city. Evidently because of the risk involved, the runners received the astounding pay of six pesos a day. Children were vaccinated with the live fluid and apparently suffered severe reactions. The Junta of Health, in a major propaganda campaign to overcome popular fears of the vaccine, published a twenty-five page booklet—at the expense of the regidors themselves—describing the value of the vaccine, the course of the reaction to it, and the treatment of reactions in children. Despite its disadvantages, the vaccine saved lives and prevented a repetition of the catastrophic smallpox outbreaks of previous centuries. By August the disease was adequately controlled, and the cabildo reported that its victims were being cared for by volunteer relief agencies.[22]

In the summer of 1814 the city was again threatened by flooding, even as the smallpox outbreaks occurred. The grand canal of Huehuetoca, the principal drainage canal for the entire valley of Mexico, became hopelessly obstructed. In the previous winter various bridges and roads had already become impassable, and, following a thunder storm on August 14, massive flooding occurred. Worst of all, it appeared Lake Texcoco was about to overflow. This would truly have been a catastrophe, since the lake served as the city's principal garbage dump. The canals, therefore, were once again opened to allow flooding of fields and villages. Rebel bands preyed upon the flooded regions. One band robbed the house and office of the official in charge of the Huehuetoca canal, giving rise to fears of rebel sabotage.[23]

Every summer throughout the remaining years of the War of Independence, flooding of varying degrees occurred in and around Mexico City. In 1814 and 1815 the municipality experimented with a method to prevent blockage of the canals. Night soil was usually dumped into the San Lázaro canal, which was the city's main sewerage, and allowed to flow into Lake Texcoco. In these two years the city tried dumping the waste on dry land so that the sun and air would absorb and neutralize its "putrid miasmas." The experiment was a failure, for the stench of it filled the air and turned the viceroy's stomach. Therefore, on May 8, 1815, Calleja ordered it once again dumped into the water. As a result, in September, 1815, several blocks of the city were flooded by the choked ditches.[24]

The cabildo, which had continued to manage garbage collection for two years after the 1813 epidemic, decided to return collection once again to private concessionaires. Pedro Prieto won the contract by virtue of agreeing to all the city's conditions. He held it for the next four years, all the while complaining about a lack of cooperation from both the inhabitants and the cabildo. In January, 1819, the contract was taken over by

Francisco Bustamante, who announced that some sections of the capital were so filthy they could not be cleaned under any circumstances in less than two months. Bustamante's contract with the city shows that the municipal garbage system consisted of fifty-four carts and an equal number of mules—some owned by the city, some by the concessionaire, and all stored in a municipal corral. During the day, eight carts were detailed for general daytime cleaning of public squares and twenty-three worked in pickup of garbage. Twenty-three others worked at night, collecting nightsoil. There were three garbage collection points on each block, to which residents brought their containers when the workers arrived and rang a bell. The concession was let by public bidding. Like Prieto, Bustamante begged the cabildo to order that inhabitants stop throwing trash on the streets, and he asked the night watchmen to cooperate with the garbage collectors. All to no avail, however, for he found the city intransigent. As late as April, 1823, he was threatening to sue the city for failing to comply with the contract.[25]

The worst flooding of this period occurred in 1819. By July and August several highways were impassable. In September, Viceroy Apodaca informed Spain that a dangerous situation existed. Torrents of water streamed down the mountains, flooding the east and north of the city. The viceroy himself rode forth to view the flooded region, and found standing water, to a depth of six to nine feet, from the village of Tanepantla to Lake Texcoco, an area shaped like a crescent nineteen leagues long and five leagues wide. He immediately dispatched forty canoes from the capital, which rescued more than six hundred people from the waters and distributed over three thousand tortillas. As late as February, 1820, the level of Lake Texcoco remained dangerously high.[26]

As a direct result of the flooding, Mexico City experienced a third outbreak of disease. In July, 1820, a regidor reported that the barrio of Santa Cruz Acatlán, primarily an Indian district, was stricken with "a pestilence of fevers so ferocious that many have died." On July 21, three members of the Junta of Health reported that there was indeed a fever rampant in that section, "and although it does not deserve the name of pestilence, the circumstances of the sick, their nakedness, the lack of any succor or of medicines or food, . . . and the spoiled water they drink, make the disease progress to a putrid and contagious form." The cabildo immediately instructed the Hospital of San Andrés to receive all the sick at the expense of the city treasury.[27]

The fevers reached their peak in October and November, 1820. The Junta of Health published at private expense one thousand copies of a treatise on their cure and prevention. Dr. Ignacio García Jove later reported that the fevers were not contagious, although he recommended vaccination as a precaution in case his diagnosis was incorrect. The fevers did not subside until about March, 1821.[28]

The 1819 floods produced a second outbreak of wild dog packs in the capital. In August the cabildo ordered the night watchmen to kill a minimum of one hundred dogs a night. The watchmen responded in fine form, this time even keeping count: they slaughtered 1,326 dogs in one week. The sound and fury of this slaughter, and the revulsion felt by the populace on awakening in the morning to find the streets filled with carcasses, so roused the people that the syndic, Manuel de Noriega, was required to justify it in a speech to the cabildo. He recounted a number of popular misconceptions about dogs: "It is said that their excrement is an excellent material for tanning hides; that they clean the streets . . . of dead animals and bones; that they protect property from thieves; that they are loyal and grateful; and lastly, that they constitute part of the harmony of the universe." He replied to these charges: the poor people who collected and sold dog excrement should collect the bones and dead animals instead; wild dogs did not defend against robbery; and lacking natural predators they did not share in the harmony of the universe, but merely upset it.[29]

This woeful story of misery was played out in the context of declining city services in other fields besides health and sanitation. Two other municipal functions—crime control and education—suffered noticeable deterioration and attest to the declining quality of life in the capital.

The social and economic disruption of the insurrections caused a tremendous increase of crime in the capital city that the cabildo, despite large expenditures, was powerless to control. In

1820, for example, the audiencia in Mexico City brought down 386 convictions for homicide. The municipality increased its weekly budget for the night watchmen and for street lighting from seven hundred to nine hundred pesos in 1814, making it the only area of municipal activity to enjoy an increased appropriation. The city collected an average of 43,000 pesos a year for lighting and watchmen from a tax of three reales on each load of wheat. Approximately 38,000 pesos a year was spent on street lighting alone. From 1809 to 1815 the cabildo undertook a major project to replace the city's candle street lamps with oil lamps, and 1,216 oil lamps were installed.[30]

Despite these exertions, and despite the existence of the viceregal police force from 1811 to 1813, the offenses of vagrancy and robbery continued. In the summer of 1814, the residents of District No. 8 complained that the area was "so infested with thieves" that "no one can go out without risk at any hour of the night." In August of that year Viceroy Calleja wrote the cabildo concerning the "extraordinary and continuous scandalous robberies that are perpetrated in the streets and houses of this capital." He expressed his suspicion that "if the lamp-lighters are not the authors [of the robberies], at least they are not free of complicity." He ordered the cabildo to redouble its efforts to stop the robberies and a few months later sent the same order to the corregidor. In 1820 the royal government, in an attempt to clear the city of the thousands of vagrants, ordered all vagabonds to be imprisoned for periods not exceeding two years in the public work houses. This was no solution at all, for the treasury could hardly afford to support these men, and it is not clear if the order was ever implemented.[31]

The decline in services is also to be seen in the capital's educational system during the War of Independence. The virtual collapse of the university has already been noted. A similar process occurred in the city's primary and secondary schools. In Mexico City there were two types of schools—those operated by the clergy, the city, or lay corporations, and those operated privately by licensed teachers (called maestros if they taught boys or maestras de amiga if they taught girls). All primary schools were under the jurisdiction of the cabildo in matters of curriculum and teacher accreditation. Church schools were supported and controlled by ecclesiastical authorities, but they had to conform to the general regulations set down by the city council as well. In 1811, when a newly arrived teacher from Spain proposed a new ordinance for primary education, the city's maestro mayor, or chief teacher of elementry education, Rafael Ximeno, scornfully rejected the proposal on the grounds that only the municipality could form new ordinances.[32]

In 1813 the current maestro mayor, Juan Espinosa de los Monteros, submitted a report saying that, although an 1803 plan had shown that more than 20,000 children in Mexico City should be attending school, in 1813 all the city's schools together—including the private ones, those of the parishes and convents, and those supported by the city or other charitable funds—had less than 5,000 students.[33]

In a second report, submitted in 1816, Espinosa declared that primary education was completely disorganized, and he accused three of the city's leading teachers of being rebel sympathizers. The regidor charged with supervision of primary education, León Ignacio Pico, investigated these charges. He found the three teachers innocent of rebel sympathies but agreed that "the state of public instruction is indeed sad, and it tortures every careful father, for he does not know what to do nor where to send his sons when they come of age to be educated." Pico found the girls' teachers to be "almost all very old, very ignorant or fanatical, or visionary, without education and without principles, pursuing this career only because they cannot get along in any other." He thought the Church-supported and charitable schools for poor children and foundlings were especially badly organized and funded, and he called their teachers "charlatans who, afflicted by hunger, take up this career for lack of any other." In conclusion, he pointed out that Mexico City's statutes relating to the examination and certification of school teachers were 216 years old: "Think back to those days, I do not have to say more." In response, the city council appointed a Junta of Primary Education to consider revisions of the statutes, but nothing seems to have come of it.[34]

An 1818 report from the archbishop corroborated Pico's pessimistic views, finding that the Church maintained only five free schools for poor boys and only three for poor girls, although at least three more of each was deemed absolutely essential.

Before the war, however, nearly every parish and convent had operated some sort of school for the poor.[35]

Mexico City's oldest and most famous primary school, the Colegio de San Juan de Letrán, announced its bankruptcy in 1817. Founded in 1528 by Mexico's first archbishop and first viceroy, it normally accommodated several hundred boys. In May, 1817, its rector, Juan Batista de Arechederreta, told the cabildo that his school's income was so small that he would have to close it unless the city came to its aid. Nearly a year later, Arechederreta informed the king that nearly 5,000 pesos in teachers' salaries had been left unpaid. He begged to be granted some type of tax revenues. Well over a year after that, Viceroy Apodaca reported to the royal government that the school, which at the time had 103 boarding students, 140 day students, and 13 teachers, was still unable to pay teachers' salaries or buy ink and paper for the students. The cabildo finally came to the school's aid by uniting it with the much smaller San Ramón school run by the city for poor mestizo boys. Although the viceroy approved the concordat between the city council and San Juan de Letrán in 1818, minor difficulties delayed it from going into effect until 1820.[36]

Final evidence of the breakdown of the city's educational system comes from a census taken in 1820 in accordance with a Cortes decree. The city council sent out circulars to all the schools and teachers in the city requesting reports on enrollment and curriculum. The total enrollment reported in all schools amounted to only 2,773 children—a further radical decrease from 1813, when Espinosa estimated it at 5,000. For boys there were seven colegios sponsored by the city or civilian corporations (Abogados, Minería, Escribanos); ten primary and secondary schools combined, sponsored by regular orders; and twenty-four private maestros. For the girls there were only three public colegios and thirty-five maestras de amiga, most of whom did not reply to the questionnaire. In addition, there were eight parish schools, half of which had fewer than twenty students. Many parishes and convents reported that they had been forced by lack of funds to close their schools: the parish of Santa Catarina Martír replied it lacked the money for a school; the parish of Santa María Redonda said that it formerly had rather a large school but enrollment fell so drastically that it closed; and the parish of San Miguel closed its school in 1810 for lack of funds. Other parishes that had once had large schools reported only a handful of children. San Antonio de las Huertas, for example, had only eighteen children. Of a total school-age population of perhaps 30,000 children in the city, only 2,800 were receiving any kind of education as Mexico neared the moment of its independence.[37]

The queen city of the Americas began to show the strain caused by the war's privation. Pasqual Azpeitia, a private citizen, summarized the deterioration in a letter to the alcalde in 1820 complaining about the general quality of life in Mexico City. He said that "the maintenance of this capital, its districts and suburbs, is in the most decadent state." He said the city was filthy, its pavement and embankments decaying, its market system disordered, its bridges, aqueducts, roads, and highways decomposing, its ditches and canals in ruins. He complained about the shortage of food and the high prices, the failure of the city to keep the Indians well provided for and well disciplined, the increase in vagrancy and crime, and the inability of the city's work houses and penal system to cope with the general collapse of law and order. His letter was petulant and filled with complaints about things over which the city council had no control and problems caused more by the war than by anybody's neglect of duty, but it illustrates the fact that, even though Mexico City was never the scene of a battle, it was still deeply affected by the rebellions.[38]

The picture that emerges at this point is of a royal regime that had martialed its human and financial resources in a variety of ways and had been able as a result to beat back and resist wave after wave of rebellion, subversion, confusion, and danger. Yet, the costs were beginning to show. The costs came in the form of human misery occasioned by disease, starvation, insupportable food prices, and fear. The political price came in the form of militarization, disproportionate dependence on force, refusal to implement limited reforms, and confusion in the channels of authority. The economic price was a government on the brink of bankruptcy, a capital city unable to respond to the normal, much less unusual, needs of its inhabitants, and a population submitted to ever newer and heavier taxes.

Chapter 7

Victory

FEW HISTORIANS, except perhaps Alamán, have given sufficient emphasis to the fact that the royal regime actually defeated the rebels. Spain won the War of Independence. Five years elapsed between the defeat of the rebellion in 1816 and the Plan of Iguala in 1821. These were years in which the royal regime reestablished itself, spread its effective control gradually over all the nation, abolished some of the special war-time taxes, extended amnesties to 17,000 rebels, and turned its thoughts to reconstruction. The last year of Viceroy Calleja's administration and the first years of Viceroy Apodaca's were a time for tying up loose ends, for freeing the nation of the last vestiges of armed insurrection, and for restoring peace. All in all, the restoration of royal power over New Spain was a remarkable achievement, one of the Spanish empire's greatest victories. It was not, however, an enduring victory, for while Spain restored its power over New Spain, it did not restore its authority.

Spain restored its power in New Spain because the formula for independence proposed by all the leaders and movements in the first phase of the war was unacceptable to the policy-making portion of the Mexican population. Hidalgo, Morelos, Rayón, and the other early leaders failed because radical lower-class rebellion could not win independence.

Hidalgo's movement wavered after Las Cruces, crumbled after Calderón, and collapsed at Baján, as Hamill says. Before Hidalgo died he repudiated the rebellion he had led and is alleged to have signed a formal retraction in which he echoed the cry of the Prophet Jeremiah, "Oh that my head were waters, and my eyes a fountain of tears, that I might weep day and night for the slain of the daughter of my people" (9:1). But Hidalgo phrased it even more pitifully, asking, "Who will give water for my head and fountains of tears for my eyes?" as he agonized over "the multitude of souls who, for having followed me, are in the abyss." The mandate to Jeremiah—"I have set you this day over nations and over kingdoms, to pluck up and to break down, to destroy and to overthrow, to build and to plan" (1:10)—was denied Hidalgo and his followers. It remained the burden of Spanish sovereignty.[1]

Nor had Morelos inherited the mandate. Like Hidalgo, he failed to receive creole support. After his brilliant victories in the south, his military campaign ground to a halt in the long siege of Acapulco, allowing Calleja to regroup his forces and launch a massive campaign against the rebels. In late 1813 Morelos's forces suffered a grievous defeat at Valladolid. Thereafter, the Congress he organized wandered the countryside, keeping one step ahead of the royal armies. Throughout 1815 Morelos lost power and the rebellion lost its way. Morelos was captured and condemned, and he was shot in December, 1815, outside the capital.

By 1816 the rebellion was effectively over. In the following two years, most remaining rebel leaders sought the amnesty offered freely by Viceroy Apodaca's government. The expedition of Xavier Mina in 1817 failed miserably in its efforts to provide new leadership and a rallying point to the rebellion. Eventually only two rebel leaders continued in the field, and their power was negligible. One was Vicente Guerrero, a mestizo, who with about 2,000 ragged and hungry men roamed the Sierra Madre del Sur, managing an occasional skirmish with royal forces and resisting the viceroy's frequent offers of amnesty. Guadalupe Victoria continued undaunted to inhabit the forests between Puebla and Veracruz, but he had lost his army and constituted no threat to the authorities. The rebels were little more than bandits—an inconvenience from which New Spain had always suffered.

On September 16, 1816, Viceroy Calleja turned his command over to the newly arrived viceroy, Juan Ruiz de Apodaca. Apodaca's arrival in Mexico City was unexpected because the news of his landing at Veracruz was intercepted by rebels. On the road overland, he was attacked by a rebel band, leading him to proclaim that he was the first viceroy of New Spain "ever to be greeted by a hail of bullets."[2] Calleja and his family left Mexico City in October. Their convoy also carried the former archbishop-elect of Mexico, Antonio Bergosa y Jordán, who was traveling to Spain to assume the bishopric of Tarragona. Bergosa's appointment by the constitutional government had not been recognized by Ferdinand VII on his restoration to the throne. The king appointed as archbishop Pedro de Fonte, a strong advocate of the peninsular viewpoint.

Alamán summarized the state of the kingdom upon Calleja's departure:

Calleja left his successor a revolution discredited, defeated and beaten, and although there still remained fortified points to take and groups to be disbanded, he left him a numerous and flourishing army, composed of troops accustomed to the incessant fatigues of campaign, and even more accustomed to winning; he left him an organized treasury with revenues increased by new taxes; mercantile traffic was reestablished in frequent convoys that circulated from one end of the kingdom to the other, and the mails were in regular circulation.[3]

Alamán concluded that "if Spain had not lost its dominion over these countries by later events, Calleja would have been recognized as the reconqueror of New Spain and the second Hernán Cortés." Most important, Calleja had convinced the rebels "that it was impossible to obtain [independence] by the means they had employed, for these led only to the ruin and annihilation of the country." As he prepared to leave New Spain after twenty-seven years of residence as royal officer and viceroy, Calleja wrote the government at home to say he was leaving in Apodaca's hands a country that was well on its way to recovery, "and I have no doubt that his talents will further perfect [the recovery], if the methods that have served me so well are continued."[4]

Apodaca, however, was a man of rather different disposition from his predecessor. He was far more cosmopolitan, far more attuned to the recent changes and fresh ideas that had swept the peninsula. While certainly not a liberal, he was not an absolutist either. He did not fear change or reform, for he had been an intimate witness of the changes that had occurred in Spain's long struggle to free itself from the foreign conqueror. During the Napoleonic wars, he had served as a naval commander and had held the highly sensitive position of Spanish ambassador to London. He came to New Spain directly from his post as governor and captain general of Cuba. Whereas Calleja, who had lived in New Spain since 1789, was a product of the Spain of Charles III,[5] Apodaca was a product of the Spain of the Napoleonic struggle. Whereas Venegas and Calleja had boldly disobeyed the Constitution in an era when Spain was supposedly devoted to reform, Apodaca was not averse to change in an era when Spain was devoted to a restored absolutism.

While not naïve, Apodaca definitely lacked Calleja's political sagacity. Though a naval commander of considerable merit, he lacked Calleja's total personal dedication and involvement with the army, and he later proved himself considerably less skilled as a military tactician. Apodaca's forte was administration. In six years as viceroy he churned out so much correspondence that the index alone of his letters in office, preserved in the Spanish Royal Academy of History, numbers over sixty volumes. For most of his administration he sent to Spain regular and detailed monthly reports on the state of the kingdom. In 1818 he was granted the title conde del Venadito in reward for his role in capturing the expedition of Xavier Mina.

Where Venegas had been the buffer and Calleja the reconquerer, Apodaca set for himself the task of being the reconciler. His government was consciously conciliatory. His job was to restore New Spain to the prewar status-quo. He set himself to heal, through the limited means available to him, the wounds of civil war, to cut back on New Spain's massive war-time expenditures, to restore loyalty, and to reaffirm Spain's authority on the foundation of Calleja's military victories. His was the greatest opportunity of all the viceroys, for he had the chance— denied to his two predecessors—of strengthening Spanish authority, of renewing the ties that bound New Spain to the mother country, of reaffirming the international ethos of Hispanism. Indeed, if he had been left to his own devices, he might well have achieved these high goals. But he was governing in the name of a Spain that had restored the absolutism of the eighteenth century and in behalf of a king who repudiated reform, turned on the liberals who had saved his throne from the French, and was unworthy of the loyalties of a colonial people. Up to the restoration of the Constitution in 1820, it was Spain's intransigence, its refusal to consider change in an overseas kingdom where change was obviously long overdue, that prevented Apodaca from the total restoration of royal authority.

Apodaca's actions appear particularly mild in comparison with his predecessor's "fire and sword" regime. Though royal troops remained active in Veracruz province and wherever bands of rebels were sighted, Apodaca rejected Calleja's policy of terror. Manuel Palacio Fajardo, summarizing the state of the Spanish American insurrections in 1817, wrote, "Apodaca . . . has entirely changed the policy of the preceding viceroys by endeavoring to gain the affection of the Mexicans instead of inspiring them with terror. The plan has been crowned with success." Most gratifying to the new viceroy, no doubt, was the rapid response to his offer of amnesty to former rebels. In his monthly report for February, 1817, he announced that many rebels were coming forward to accept the amnesty and that he had ordered their names published in principal gazettes at the beginning of every month "with the idea that their numbers . . . will attract others little by little." In February, 1,345 persons accepted the amnesty, and in July, 1,016. Similar numbers were recorded throughout most of 1817. H. G. Ward says that Apodaca granted over 17,000 amnesties during his rule.[6]

Apodaca's letters were filled with other good news. In his first report to Spain, dated October 31, 1816, he announced that all the territory between Querétaro and the capital was tranquil, free of rebel activities, and engaged in normal commerce. In November he reported that the district of Chalco and the road from the capital to Puebla was free and that weekly mails with Puebla were reestablished. In his report for December he announced that the silver convoys from Pachuca and Zimpapán were moving freely and Cuernavaca and Riofrio were back to normal. He also reported that his reorganization of the patrols in the capital and the taking of a secret census of vagrants and suspected criminals for conscription into the army had brought about a notable reduction in murders and robberies in the city. In February, 1817, he announced the dispatch of two hundred infantry troops and a corps of cavalry to reopen the mines of Temascaltepec and Sultepec. He was able to report that for the first time in years the army was fully supplied with rifles, owing to his reorganization of the arms factory in the capital. The viceroy did not cover up the bad news. He was particularly concerned by the fact that his government owed thirty million pesos to corporations and private persons within New Spain and fifty million pesos to other royal treasuries and offices. And by late 1817 the danger of a breakdown in Spanish negotiations with the United States over the cession of Florida turned the viceroy's thoughts to the possibility of border troubles. The main object of the regime, however, had been accomplished—the rebellion was over.[7]

Spain had achieved a stunning victory. Yet in 1821, when Iturbide raised his new insurrection, Mexicans flocked to his banner and the royal regime breathed its last. The collapse of the regime is all the more startling because of its apparent strength in the period from 1816 to the Plan of Iguala. How can this extraordinary fact be explained?

The scenario that had unfolded thus far within the royal regime was truly remarkable and filled with paradox. During the terms of Venegas and Calleja, New Spain was converted into an armed camp, fighting to maintain loyalty to "the desired one"—the unknown entity who was Ferdinand VII. The only thing Mexicans knew about him was that he had overthrown the corrupt regime of Manuel Godoy. He had been taken from them before they could discover any of his true qualities, and he existed only as the symbol of royal authority. Yet, in the years in which two viceroys struggled to preserve the king's patrimony intact, the empire was governed by radical self-mandated government in the Cortes and Constitution of Cádiz, a government that the viceroys refused to give their full allegiance. In the king's name, Venegas and Calleja made reformism the equivalent of treason. In the name of legitimacy, they refused to obey the legitimate law. Just as the rebellion was being overcome in New Spain, the symbol of legitimacy—the sovereign—returned to the throne. He failed, in the flesh, to fulfill the promises that his actions before capture by the French had implied, and he restored divine absolute monarchy.

After 1816, New Spain was governed by a viceroy who, although a loyal servant of his king, desired to reconcile the contradictions that now jarred and weakened royal authority in the colony. What Apodaca needed was time for the wounds to heal and no new source of contention to divide the empire and confuse popular perceptions of who possessed authority and in whose name. He was denied the luxury of time, for in 1820 the Constitution was restored. It gave the final lie to the symbolism of king and viceroy and established in Spain the most radical government in contemporary Europe. And yet, that same radical government did nothing to provide the type of effective reforms—autonomy and free trade—that Americans wanted. Spain had stood for so many things, so many contradictory things, in so short a time, that it was impossible for anyone to know what royalism represented. The imperial ethos, delicate and fragile as any idea, could not survive these contradictions and inconsistencies.

New Spain, meanwhile, had been presented with a wide array of alternatives and had rejected each. Hidalgo had proposed terrifying and bloody Indian insurrection. Morelos had offered violent reform leading to racial equality and profound social revolution. These were found wanting by the elite and bourgeoisie, indeed by all creoles, as well as by royalists. The Constitution had next offered limited reform and parliamentary sovereignty, but this was unacceptable to extreme royalists, to the two viceroys who possessed the military and political power to enforce their views, and even to some radicals and rebels, for parliamentary imperialism was still imperialism. The Cortes had no intention of voluntarily divesting Spain of the empire. Once constitutionalism failed, New Spain was offered the alternative of Calleja's government of force, ultraroyalism, and decision by fiat bordering on tyranny—in short, viceregal despotism. That was unacceptable to creoles, rebels, and even some moderate royalists, but it did save the state. At that point Ferdinand VII returned to power. He offered the old ways, divine absolutism, and niggardly ingratitude toward his rescuers. He turned with a vengeance upon reform and upon constitutionalism, and his policies were unacceptable to all but the most hard-line royalists. After having tasted constitutionalism, Mexicans had no desire to return to absolutism, but Calleja's military victories had the effect of preempting open opposition from a war-weary people. Viceroy Apodaca then took office, offering reconciliation and a quietly competent government such as New Spain had possessed before its time of troubles. His emphasis on administration, normalcy, and calm might have achieved success, but a reactionary Spain ignored the possibility of reform, and a last precious opportunity to recreate the badly corroded authority of the mother country was lost. Inheriting a regime dependent on force, Apodaca chose not to use force; believing that the "deceitful calm," as Ward called it, constituted normalcy, he rejected viceregal despotism. When the next crisis occurred, the regime found itself unprepared. New Spain's elite and bourgeoisie still sought an acceptable alternative, one that they had initiated, that they could live with, and that lay somewhere between radical reform and niggardly absolutism. They sought a formula that would be neither revolutionary nor counterrevolutionary. Spanish imperial absolutism belonged to the eighteenth century and was defunct even in Spain itself, but Morelos's social revolution would not be manifest in Mexico until the twentieth century.

The period from 1816 to 1821 was a time of intensity and great drama, for it would show whether a policy of reason could solidify the gains won by relentless force, whether authority could be re-created after terror had taken its place, whether Spain still had a right to govern. The onus was on the imperial power to prove to Mexicans that they should obey it and that it had something to offer. It was Spain's job to restore the legitimacy of its own authority. Not only was independence not inevitable, it was farther from realization than it had been in many years. The fact that independence swept the country in only a few months in 1821 is evidence that Spain failed in its task. It failed because Spain and its agents did not recognize that the reconquest of Mexico was not the same thing as the reaffirmation of royal authority.

For Mexicans the authority of the Crown had been disintegrating for some time. It was seriously damaged by the depravity (as Americans viewed it) of the Godoy era, by the forced abdication of Charles IV at the hands of his heir, by the overthrow of Iturrigaray in 1808, by the usurpation of the throne by Joseph Bonaparte, by the creation of self-mandated government at Cádiz, and by the mindless reaction of the restored Ferdinand VII. Was this not sufficient evidence of the system's profound disorder? More important, the legitimacy of the king's government in Mexico was discredited by the viceroys' refusal to obey the Constitution or to permit more than token reform, and by the fierceness with which they polarized the loyalists to a do-or-die struggle between absolutism and any alternative to it. This converted the delicate strands of loyalty, faith in the monarch, and sense of brotherhood of all Spaniards into tyrannical government by foreigners and eliminated the possibility of compromise. A last straw was needed, however, for New Spain's elite still recognized an essential unity of interest with the royal system in the face of the other alternatives thus far presented to it. The last straw was provided when the peninsula restored the Constitution in 1820 and provoked, not a counterrevolution, but a final realization of the irrelevance of king, Crown, hispanism, imperialism, and motherland. Mexicans in 1820, as they had in 1812, liked what the Constitution did; they did not like what it said about the mother country.

The movement for independence did not destroy Spanish authority in Mexico. Until the Plan of Iguala presented a politically acceptable program, the insurrection was not sufficiently attractive to many Mexicans, because it threatened their lives, security, and welfare. The threat to Spanish imperial control posed by the insurrection was great, but Venegas and Calleja defeated the insurrection. Spain won the war, but it lost the country, because it lost its right to govern. In politics, economics and social affairs, Spain contradicted its own expressed ethos, disabusing the subject peoples as rapidly as it could of any residual belief in the right of the imperial regime to govern them. The restoration of the Constitution in 1820 was the ultimate contradiction that proved to Mexicans the irrelevance of Spanish sovereignty.

Part II
LOSING THE COUNTRY

Chapter 8

The Ultimate Contradiction
and Its Resolution

In the history of the Mexican War of Independence, the most confused issue is the question of whether Mexico's elite and bourgeoisie rejected the restored Constitution in 1820–1821. The fact that the reestablishment of the Constitution was a precipitating factor in bringing about the final break with Spain is undisputed. The question, however, is whether independence resulted from rejection of the Constitution—which would constitute counterrevolution—or whether there were other, less obvious factors at work in the move toward independence.

The final achievement of independence in 1821 constituted the culmination and final victory of the autonomist urge that was first articulated by the city council in 1808, restated by successive delegates to the Cortes, and reaffirmed in the reaction of Mexican creoles in the first constitutional era. As such, it obviously represents a conservative rejection of the radical reforms advocated by the violent lower-class insurrections of 1810–1816. However, the lower-class formula for independence had been fully rejected by 1816 and was not of major significance in the events of 1821. Reinstitution of the Constitution in 1820 gave a new opportunity to the advocates of commonwealth status, or autonomy, for Mexico. They had a fresh chance to be heard. Those elements in Mexican society that represented moderate reform, autonomy, and constitutional monarchy in place of absolutism were now victorious. Independence therefore cannot be said to represent counterrevolution. It represents limited reform, compromise, corporatism, liberalism, and the achievement of the long-displaced political goals of the Mexican creole elite and bourgeoisie. By definition, these goals were conservative, not reactionary.

Mexico's rejection of Spanish sovereignty is the central fact in the widespread misinterpretation of the causes of independence. Because Mexico rejected a Spain that in the brief period from 1820 to 1823 possessed Europe's most radical government, the assumption has been easily made that it was also rejecting the Constitution. That is not true. Mexico made two fundamental political decisions when it became independent: it threw out Spain and her imperialist agents, and it adopted Spain's Constitution and even attempted to extend it. The Spain it was rejecting was the imperialist, absolutist mother country, the Spain of Ferdinand VII, which had overturned reform in the past and would do so again in 1823.

Why did Mexicans, who for so many years had clung to Spanish legitimacy in order to defend their interests against internal insurrection, make the decision to abandon the Crown? Quite simply, because in 1821 the internal insurrection did not threaten the interests of the elite and bourgeoisie but was perfectly consistent with their frequently stated goal, while the Spanish Crown, by reinstating the Constitution in 1820, gave the final lie to its own ethos. In yet another example of the unending succession of contradictions and confusions that had battered the imperial ethos for the past twenty years, Spain again revealed its weakness. The wonder is that a political system that so often made itself vulnerable to attack should have survived so long.

Why did the first implementation of the Constitution in 1812–1814 not effect the total destruction of Spanish power? Because the only alternative to Spain in 1812–1814 was unacceptable radical insurrection. In 1820 and 1821, however, lower-class rebellion was not a factor, so the elite and bourgeoisie had the option—which they previously had lacked—of proposing what form of government should fill the void created by the fall of Spanish imperialism. In addition, in 1812–1814 the viceroys in charge of the defense of Spanish legitimacy, Venegas and Calleja, were ruling through viceregal despotism and force. In 1820–1821, the viceroy, Apodaca, failed to see the danger and failed to take the necessary steps in time to prevent collapse of the royal regime.

Why did the Mexican elites, who favored the general principle of the Constitution, not give the Constitution more chance to prove itself? Because the government of the Cortes, radical though it might have been in comparison with previous governments, still took no action to meet the chief demands of Americans. Overseas territories were still not allowed equal proportionate representation; peninsular deputies still outnumbered American ones; and the Cortes, though it professed conciliatory intentions, still did not recognize American home rule or free trade with foreign powers. The Cortes might have been radical, but it remained a peninsular government dedicated to peninsular well-being. It might have proposed all kinds of reforms, but to Americans it remained an imperial regime; it did not fulfill American demands.

The Constitution was restored in Spain in early 1820 as a result of a series of spontaneous uprisings among the disaffected peninsular troops. The uprising first broke out among the soldiers being gathered at Cádiz, under command of Félix Calleja, to make up the expeditionary force for the reconquest of America. Calleja himself was arrested by his own troops at Arcos de la Frontera. The uprisings spread, and in March, 1820, the king was forced to restore the Constitution.[1]

For Spain itself, the "revolution" of 1820 was the beginning of a time of nearly incalculable disaster. Restoration of the Constitution was not so much the cause of the new time of troubles as it was a symptom of the profound internal political crisis—the struggle between conservatives and liberals—that would dominate peninsular affairs for the remainder of the century. This struggle eventually led to the Carlist civil wars, economic and commercial collapse, and a more or less permanent legitimacy crisis. The immediate consequences were just as significant. The king and his advisers had spent years preparing the huge

Expeditionary Army that was to be hurled against Buenos Aires and that they hoped would spark the reconquest of all of South America. The revolution, by eliminating any chances of sending the Expeditionary Army, guaranteed the loss of South America. In his anger and fury, the king looked for support to the only Spaniards he trusted, the extreme conservatives and militarists, and with their help he began to appeal to the Holy Allies for money and an army to overthrow the Constitution. Ferdinand became convinced that the peninsular revolution and the American independence movements were intimately related. As early as June, 1821, he confided to the Russian emperor Alexander I his conviction that France and, especially, England were "the secret promoters of the disturbances in Spain." England's motive was clear: "England has for many years worked secretly for Spanish American independence . . . in order to . . . undertake direct trade . . . and to dismember Spain of such rich and powerful possessions." France's motives were the same "because with the emancipation of America . . . Spain would be reduced to the ten million souls who live on the peninsula."[2] In a handwritten letter to the Russian emperor in 1822, Ferdinand combined all his accusations in one sentence: "The revolution in Spain was the work of the machinations of those who desired the separation of the Americas from the Metropolis." He added, "That has happened. They are now lost."[3] If ever a king betrayed his own people, Ferdinand did. He spent three years in secret negotiations with the Holy Allies, begging them to send an army to restore his absolute power. The French king, Louis XVIII, responded, and in April, 1823, an army of 100,000 crossed into Spain and overthrew the constitutional regime. Ferdinand launched a massive campaign of terror against the liberals, imprisoning and executing those who fell into his hands.

If the restoration of the Constitution revealed, as Richard Herr said, "the disappearance of a commonly accepted authority" in Spain itself, the effect on Mexico could hardly be less.[4] The minister of war wrote Viceroy Apodaca that His Majesty had "freely and spontaneously" accepted the Constitution and therefore New Spain was to do so as well.[5] The viceroy, audiencia, city council and other leading officials of the kingdom took the oath of allegiance on June 1, 1820. As in 1812, all possible ceremony was employed in the publication and oath-taking. The Constitution was read in its entirety during the mass on June 10, and each parish swore allegiance to it. There followed three days of public festivities, at a total cost to the city of 15,985 pesos.[6]

Viceroy Apodaca, unlike his predecessors, proposed no objections or impediments to the reestablishment of elected corporations. On June 14 he ordered the election of the new city council. The electors were chosen in the parishes on June 18, and on June 21 the cabildo was selected. The new ayuntamiento was composed of alcaldes Ignacio Aguirrevengoa and the conde de Alcaraz; regidors Juan Ignacio Guerra González Vertis, Manuel Noriega Cortina, Francisco Manuel Sánchez de Tagle, Ignacio Mendoza, the conde de Bassoco, Alejandro Valdés, José Manuel Cadena, Gabriel Patricio de Yermo, José María Cervantes, Ramón Nava, José María Casasola, Andrés del Río, Ignacio Adalid, Juan Pérez Juárez, Manuel Carrasco, and Miguel Calderón; and syndics Benito Guerra and Agustín de la Peña y Santiago. On June 22 Apodaca ordered that, "because we want not only to fulfill the letter of the Constitution but its spirit as well," the new members should immediately be installed. The cabildo's first duty was to ask city treasurer José Ignacio Náxera, who had been secretary during the first constitutional era, to assume that position again. Since he declined, the cabildo chose José Miguel Guridi y Alcocer, one of the city's leading liberals and a former deputy to the Cortes. Elections for Cortes deputies and members of the Provincial Deputation followed on August 11 and 18. In both sets of elections, the creole autonomists swept the field.[7]

The cabildo published a proclamation to the people making it clear that constitutional government would work this second time around. It said it intended to search out and eliminate all the old abuses, petty tyrannies, and failures of the hereditary cabildo. It promised change, but urged patience, pointing out that hundreds of years of abuse could not be corrected overnight. This was a remarkable statement, and of a kind with those that were being made all over the empire as the new constitutional bodies admitted publicly the sins of their predecessors and promised to correct abuses. The city council again divided its responsibilities up into a series of commissions and promised to hold a special meeting once a week to formulate the new municipal bylaws required for a complete reform of government. Every hope of thorough reform and complete implementation of the Constitution was held out to the people.[8]

More than any promises, however, the members of the new council were sufficient indication of the resurgent impulse toward autonomy. Some of Mexico's leading liberals—the new secretary Guridi y Alcocer and the regidors Francisco Manuel Sánchez de Tagle, Ignacio Adalid, and Andrés del Río—sat on the cabildo. They were joined by young representatives of the old nobility—the new conde de Bassoco and Gabriel Patricio de Yermo, both Spaniards, both nephews of the Bassoco and Yermo who were active in 1808. The presence of these representatives of the bourgeoisie and elite in common support of the Constitution is the first indication of the establishment of that all-important alliance of interests among the white population of New Spain that Villoro sees as having brought about the ideological climate that allowed for independence. Two other elements of this alliance, the high clergy and officers, were still missing, but they were to join the alliance in a few months.[9]

Once again the question of who should be president of the city council was brought up, since the regidors refused to accept the presidency of Intendant Mazo. According to a decision handed down by the Cortes at the end of 1813, but never put into effect in Mexico City, the viceroy was supposed to preside in his role as superior political chief of the whole province but could appoint a representative to take his place. Apodaca did not want to preside because, as he told Spain, "it would compromise my authority," but he adamantly agreed with the cabildo that Mazo should not be president. After repeated protests from Mazo, the viceroy decided he had no choice but to serve himself, though he attended very few meetings. The hapless intendant was forced to vacate the free chambers he occupied in the city building.[10]

Yet another indication of the city council's new sense of independence came in disputes over how to pay for the transportation of Mexico's Cortes deputies to Spain. Viceroy Apodaca ordered the capital cities of each province to make a loan to the Provincial Deputation of 3,000 pesos for each deputy from that province. For Mexico City this required raising a sum of 30,000 pesos for ten deputies. A commission of the city reported that "neither do we have the money, nor do we expect ever to have it." As to whether a method of finding it could be devised, the commission bluntly informed the viceroy that according to the Constitution such a question was no longer under his jurisdiction and it was not constitutional for him to make any proposals concerning it. Never had the ayuntamiento so treated a viceroy.[11]

This reassertion of autonomism was encouraged by statements from the Crown itself. A remarkable manifesto of the king, published in Mexico City on July 24, 1820, indicated clearly the extent to which royal authority had been curtailed by the peninsular uprisings and liberal restoration to power. Entitled "Proclamation of the King to Overseas Inhabitants," it was a plea to dissenters and rebels all over America to return to the Spanish cause, for the new order of constitutional guarantees would give them all the things they had been fighting for. The king publicly apologized for his abrogation of the Constitution in 1814 and admitted he had been mistaken. He prayed his subjects to remember "that errors in judgment are not crimes," and he urged them "quickly to forget all past evils."[12] This regal *mea culpa* made it very difficult in the future to believe in the divinity of royal authority.

Many other decrees and orders throughout August and September, 1820, implied fundamental reforms and a widening of the sources of power. The removal from office of all government personnel who refused to take the oath to the Constitution was decreed, and a few offices and positions were abolished.[13] Spain ordered that proof of nobility was no longer necessary for admittance into military colleges or academies or into any unit in the army and navy.[14] The penalty of scourging was abolished. The Inquisition was again suppressed, the free press instituted, and Indian tribute cancelled. The clergy was ordered to preach the principles of constitutionalism in the parishes.[15] And the king ordered the city councils to remove from their buildings all carvings, insignias, or plaques showing vassallage to the sovereign, as a sign, he said, "that the Spanish nation does not and will not recognize any other lord than the nation itself."[16] These reforms, and others, touched nearly every level in society. Although many of them had been decreed originally in 1812, they frequently were being implemented for the first time in 1820 under the cooperative regime of Viceroy Apodaca.

What did Apodaca think he was doing? Did he not recognize, as Calleja had, that even token concessions to regional autonomy weakened the viceregal regime? Apparently, he did not. Having lived in New Spain only since 1816, he possibly was not aware of the depth of support for autonomy among the upper classes. Or, if he was, he did not fear it. It is important to remember that he was a product of the Napoleonic struggle and that he had been appointed to most of his earlier positions by self-mandated peninsular regencies and juntas. He did not fear the Cortes or the Constitution; he did not react with the stark terror exemplified in the letters of Calleja and the audiencia, or even the scornful haughtiness of Venegas. Since the rebellions were over, Apodaca felt there was no need for viceregal despotism. This was not naïveté, for it corresponded to the reality of the Mexican situation as he viewed it.

Viceroy Apodaca's own evidence sets to rest the thesis of independence as a counterrevolution. For example, he reported early in the year that the restoration of the Constitution in 1820 caused no unrest of any kind in Mexico. He continued throughout 1820, and even well into 1821, to offer no objection to full implementation of the Constitution, including the free press and other highly volatile articles. At the end of the first year (December, 1820), he presided over the election of a second constitutional city council. (The members of the last ayuntamiento were: alcaldes José Ignacio de Ormaechea and Juan José de Acha; regidors returned from the 1820 cabildo Juan Ignacio González Guerra Vertis, Manuel Noriega Cortina, Francisco Manuel Sánchez de Tagle, Ignacio Mendoza, the conde de Bassoco, Alejandro Valdés, José Manuel Velázquez de la Cadena, and Gabriel Patricio de Yermo; and newly elected regidors Eusebio García, Juan Arce y Acevedo, Manuel Balvontín, Manuel Ochoa, Francisco Xavier Heras, Miguel Dacomba, Ramón Gómez Pérez, and Mariano Dosamantes. The syndics were Benito José Guerra, from the year before, and Juan Francisco Azcárate, newly elected.) In January, 1821, Apodaca surveyed the state of the kingdom and concluded that the revolution was over. As late as March, 1821, after the publication of Iturbide's Plan of Iguala, Apodaca took the successful completion of elections for deputies to the 1822–1823 Cortes as an encouraging sign pointing to the continued soundness of constitutional government even in the face of the new insurrection.[17]

How should the viceroy's lack of concern about the Constitution's effects be interpreted? Either he was a hopeless fool who did not recognize the erosion of the very foundation of royal power, or he was correct in his assessment that the Constitution provoked no serious opposition.

There are two reports upon which historians have based the thesis that implementation of the Constitution caused a counterrevolutionary reaction among Mexico's elite, leading to the establishment of independence in order to prevent execution of a series of radical Cortes decrees that were received in Mexico in January, 1821. These reports are the one submitted to the minister of justice in October, 1820, by the fiscal of the audiencia, José Hipólito Odoardo, and the one submitted to the city council in January, 1821, by liberal alderman Francisco Manuel Sánchez de Tagle. The Cortes decrees that, according to the traditional historiography, set in motion a chain of counterrevolutionary reactions to the Constitution, were five in number: (1) the suppresson of all monasteries of the monastic (as distinguished from the mendicant) orders (including the Benedictines, Hieronymites, Carthusians, Augustinians, and the hospitalers), combined with restrictions on the growth of the powerful mendicant orders; (2) suppression of the Jesuits; (3) prohibitions on all property entail and prohibition on the acquisition by civil and ecclesiastical institutions of further real estate; (4) abolition of ecclesiastical immunity from civil prosecution; and (5) abolition of military immunity from civil prosecution for militiamen serving in America. All these decrees were passed in September, 1820, and received in Mexico in January, 1821. Odoardo, therefore, could not have heard of them, and Sánchez de Tagle wrote at about the same time as their receipt.[18]

In October, 1820, Odoardo reported that New Spain's commerce and trade had returned to a near normal level, but "New Spain is not what it was in January or February of this year. The public spirit has changed entirely." He explained what he meant by specifying various elements of society: "The military and the clergy, who were and are the power of the Government, are resentful, and if we can believe appearances, they do not all concur with that same efficacy as in former times in sustaining the Government and defending it from the attacks that are being newly prepared." The clergy's complaints were simple: "The regular and secular clergy, in view of public papers and the reforms that are projected in certain religious things, fear changes in their way of life, and in their incomes and personal immunities." Odoardo said both the clergy and the military were resentful of the lack of recognition and reward from the king for their efforts during the rebellions, and all of them were afraid of losing their privileges. Continuing with his listing of the vocal classes in society, he said, "The Europeans, who in the past united in order to sustain the Government with their persons and their fortunes, are not today animated by the same sentiments. . . . The country landowners have more or less the same feelings; they also consider the success of any new revolution to be inevitable." The constant anxiety in which everyone lived contributed to these dangers, "giving life to the same fantasies and fears." The city councils were far exceeding their powers and were spreading disunity and the desire for independence throughout their jurisdictions, he said, and "the same thing that Mexico City is doing is being repeated in the capitals of the provinces."

Odoardo concluded that there would be another insurrection: "I would not dare to suggest the time of the catastrophe which many expect to be realized any moment; but if things continue following their natural course, we shall not come out of this year without some more or less general commotion." He was prepared to suggest, however, that the greatest danger of renewed revolt lay in those rebel chieftains who accepted the amnesty, or in the disaffected clergy, or perhaps it might be imported from the United States. From whatever quarter it might come—and it finally came from among the disaffected military—he felt that another rebellion was inevitable and that the vocal elements of the city's inhabitants agreed it would succeed.[19]

Sánchez de Tagle's report, submitted on January 9, 1821, was centered around his pessimistic feeling that "the constitutional system loses more and more ground every day, and its enemies make very rapid conquests." This was chiefly because "the feminine sex, and all the people generally in the lower and middle classes," had turned against the Constitution for fear that it was antireligious. Many ecclesiastics, he reported, were preaching against the Constitution, telling the people that the Cortes was set upon the overthrow of religion. The clerics were powerful, he said, because this was "a people who give blind credit to anything they hear any ecclesiastic say."

When his report was submitted to the viceregal government, it carried the approval of the cabildo syndics, who added that the elements the councilor saw endangering the Constitution were real and that "the evil is positive and fearful." The syndics said, "It is well known that when the secular and regular ecclesiastics . . . speak of the constitutional institutions and of the reform, especially with respect to the ecclesiastical fuero, they manifest their distaste."[20] Sánchez de Tagle's report was next read by the audiencia attorney, and then by the Provincial Deputation, which approved it for higher action and sent it to the viceroy. Apodaca, however, took no action. Iturbide's revolt was already underway, and, by the time the viceroy read this report, Iturbide was drawing near the village of Iguala, where he would draft in unison with the rebel chieftain Vicente Guerrero his Plan of Iguala.

These two reports, then, are the foundation of the theory that the upper classes reacted against the liberal reforms of the Constitution and opted for independence under Iturbide as the best means of defending their interests and privileges. According to this thesis, independence was a counterrevolution and a betrayal of all the blood and tears shed in the war years.

Both reports have been misinterpreted. The fact that viceregal authorities took no action on them suggests that other eyewitnesses viewed the reports, as Sánchez de Tagle himself feared would be the case, as "hypochondriacal." As of October, 1820, the radical Cortes reforms concerning entail, religious communities, and the military fuero were not yet known in New

Spain, though it was known that they were under consideration. Odoardo, therefore, was primarily summarizing the long-
term anxieties of the elite rather than stating any new grievances,
and he was quite clear in admitting that the generally excited
state of politics led to widespread rumors and ungrounded
fears. At any rate, he was not writing about specific reactions to
the Constitution, but about long-standing public complaints
now being openly voiced for the first time because the Constitution allowed them to be. Odoardo and Sánchez de Tagle both
agreed that the clergy were afraid for the loss of their fuero, and
that the clergy accused the Cortes of being irreligious. Of this
there can be little doubt, though Sánchez de Tagle admitted that
some priests were "seducers" while the rest were merely "seduced."[21] Neither report specifically ascribed anti-Constitutional attitudes to any group other than the clergy. Sánchez de
Tagle's report referred only to the clergy and to their influence
over only the lower and middle classes. At no point did he refer
to anti-Constitutional reactions among the elite or creoles—from
whom independence came. Furthermore, the one priest he cited
specifically as having held novenas to pray for the overthrow of
the constitutional system wrote the city council denying the
charge.

The widespread dissatisfaction expressed in these reports
originated long before the Constitution and was not directed
against the Constitution but against the long-term inequalities
and anxieties of the royal system. Sánchez de Tagle, as a liberal,
genuinely feared that the Constitution was losing support, but
any liberal, especially before the Plan of Iguala, would have
expressed that fear, for the Constitution was the source of the
liberals' restoration to power. He was not talking about independence or counterrevolution, but about a weakening of the
power of the Constitution, which—before the Plan of Iguala
came along to propose a better way—would have been a
profound disaster to anyone of autonomist persuasion. Sánchez
de Tagle himself would become a fervent supporter of Iturbide.

Careful consideration of the Odoardo and Sánchez de Tagle
reports suggests that Viceroy Apodaca is the better witness
when it comes to assessing the Mexicans' reaction to the
Constitution in 1820 or early 1821. Indeed, the viceroy's total

surprise at the Iturbide uprising suggests that he foresaw no cause for alarm as late as the end of 1820. Except for certain groups predisposed to paranoia in questions of status and rank, such as the capital's hysterically status-conscious clergy, Apodaca saw no adverse reaction against the Constitution. If Apodaca was guilty of naïveté, it was for not recognizing the depth of disaffection with the imperial regime as a whole, for evidence of that surrounded him.

Doris Ladd argues that the government established after the achievement of independence did not indicate any excessive fear or worry about the Cortes decrees it was supposed to have been created to defeat. Mexico, she says, avoided very little threatening legislation by proclaiming autonomy under Iturbide. The decree limiting the growth of mendicant orders was abrogated in November, 1821, by the Junta Soberana, and the decree requiring disentailment of all Church property was simply ignored by viceregal and independent regimes alike. On the other hand, a surprising amount of radical anti-Church legislation remained in effect after independence, all of it endorsed by the Mexican delegates to the Cortes. The disbandment of the Inquisition, the Jesuits, and the Hospitaler orders was affirmed after independence by the Sovereign Junta and the Congress. The property of these orders, plus that of the Philippine missions and the Jerusalem Crusade, as well as all pious funds that paid dividends to exiles, were seized by the independent government.[22]

Many other radical reforms originally initiated by the Cortes were maintained or furthered after independence, while others were newly adopted. All tend to suggest that the assumption that independence was achieved in order to forestall implementation of reforms in status or privilege cannot be correct. Ladd cites the following examples. Some of Iturbide's officers voluntarily offered to give up their military fuero. Several leading elite gentlemen proposed the abolition of slavery. Mayorazgos unanimously agreed to give up the institution of entail. Iguala gave full citizenship to people of all racial backgrounds—including Indians, Africans, Orientals and Europeans—whereas the Spanish Cortes had denied citizenship to blacks and castes. Iturbide officially abolished racial definitions for citizenship in

1822. Iguala opened offices in the bureaucracy to all citizens, not only to proved hidalgos as the Spanish regime had. Ladd concludes, "The desire to preserve a social status quo was not as rigid as heretofore supposed. . . . It is not clear that Spanish liberalism ever threatened the position or function of any elite sector of the Mexican society except the Church, or, if some decrees appeared to do so, the interested sectors responded favorably to the change."[23] Where, then, is the counterrevolution?

There was no counterrevolution. Independence was achieved because Mexicans wanted it, viewing it as a positive step forward, not as a reaction against anything. They desired it because the Constitution itself showed Mexicans how easy would be the acquisition of total autonomy. The Constitution, however, did not set at rest the desire for autonomy among the creoles because the Cortes, no matter how liberal, still maintained New Spain in colonial dependence. That was the source of the dissatisfaction, that was the objection, not reform. Mexicans could foresee two critical aspects of the constitutional regime: first, the Cortes had no intention of granting genuine autonomy to America; second, political divisions between moderates and radicals within the regime in Spain suggested that constitutionalism itself would be shortlived.[24] Sánchez de Tagle's report of January, 1821, shows that even Mexicans who were well disposed toward the Constitution feared it would soon be overthrown and absolutism restored.

More important, the Constitution served to point out to Mexicans the emptiness of the imperial ethos. The Spanish sovereign was not divinely endowed to possess absolute authority. If he were, he would not be reduced to a figurehead by the Cortes. The great fear was not of the Constitution, but that viceregal despotism might at any moment reassert itself, as it had under Venegas and Calleja, to deny Mexicans their constitutional guarantees. The general thrust of Iturbide's rebellion, as expressed in its propaganda, was to overthrow viceregal government, not the Constitution. Manuel de la Bárcena, Iturbide's leading propagandist, declared, "We swore fealty to the King, not to Viceroys, and obedience to the law, not to despotism. . . . The Constitution is useless, because the viceroy can defy it with impunity."[25] Following publication of the Plan of Iguala in

February, 1821, Viceroy Apodaca was forced—chiefly by pressure from his peninsular military officers—to disobey the Constitution by abolishing the free press and other provisions concerning public political activities. When the final rejection of Spain came, Mexicans were reacting to abuses of power; they were supporting the Constitution, not rejecting it.

Iturbide himself supported the Constitution. The Plan of Iguala proclaimed it the law of the land, and it remained in force until December, 1822. Even after the creation of Iturbide's imperial government, Mexico decreed that all Spanish laws promulgated between the restoration of the Cortes and the proclamation of the Plan of Iguala were valid and in effect.[26] After Iturbide, in his turn, was overthrown, the republican Constitution of 1824 was modeled, at least in its creation of a federalist state, on the Spanish Constitution of Cádiz. For the rest of the century Mexican courts looked to the Spanish Constitution to provide basic precedents in political, economic, and legal disputes.

The final achievement of independence was the product of elite and bourgeois efforts to clarify and guarantee the long-sought autonomy of the country. It was not a counterrevolution against the Constitution. The Plan of Iguala, proclaimed on February 24, 1821, consisted of the following major points: New Spain was to be separate from Spain; the religion of the country was to be the Catholic religion; its government would be a limited monarchy under the supervision of the Constitution of Cádiz until such time as a separate Mexican Constitution could be written. Ferdinand VII would be invited to become emperor, and if he refused, the Infantes Carlos and Francisco de Paula would be asked, then the Archduke Carlos. A Mexican Cortes would eventually meet, but in the meantime a provisional Sovereign Junta would be formed, and a Regency would be chosen to await the arrival of the monarch. The new government would be sustained by the Army of the Three Guarantees. The three guarantees were Religion, Independence, Union. Iturbide further guaranteed that all persons and property would be respected and protected, the secular and regular clergy would be preserved in its fueros, and all government, clerical, and military personnel would be guaranteed their positions unless they manifestly refused to accept the Plan. The army,

Iturbide promised, would be orderly; officers would remain at the rank they held in the royal army, and all volunteers would be welcomed. Iguala praised Spain as "the most pious, Catholic, heroic and magnanimous nation on earth."

As evidence of the extent to which Iturbide hoped to unite various political groups in support of his Plan, he proposed the fourteen men who would compose the Sovereign Junta. Twelve of them were residents of Mexico City. He suggested the viceroy be chairman of the Junta, though Apodaca naturally refused. Vice president would be Miguel Bataller, regent of the audiencia and old foe of Hidalgo and Morelos. Full members would be José Miguel Guridi y Alcocer, priest of the Sagrario parish, former Cortes delegate, and, at this date, secretary of the cabildo; the conde de la Cortina, prior of the Consulado; Matías Monteagudo, former rector of the university and canon of the cathedral; Isidro Yáñez, oidor; José María Fagoaga, who was serving on the Provincial Deputation at the time; Juan Espinosa de los Monteros, teacher and now fiscal of the audiencia; Juan Francisco Azcárate, currently the cabildo syndic; and Rafael Suárez de Pereda, judge of the Censorship Board. Among the three alternate members were two from the capital, regidor Francisco Manuel Sánchez de Tagle and oidor Ramón Osés. The only two members who were not full-time residents of the capital were Juan Bautista Lobo, who served on the Provincial Deputation of Veracruz, and alternate Juan José Pastor Morales, who served on the Provincial Deputation of Valladolid. These were the junta members listed in the published Plan of Iguala on March 1.[27] Some changes were made in the final membership. The proposed membership was almost equally composed of liberals and conservatives.

In effect, the Plan of Iguala called for the establishment of an autonomous Mexico under a limited constitutional monarchy, governed by the Constitution of Cádiz and headed by a member of the Spanish royal dynasty; it guaranteed the creation of a Mexican resident Cortes and the extension of official equality to all classes and colors, all to be blessed by the official Church and defended by the Army of the Three Guarantees composed of former royalists serving in the same ranks as they held in the royal army. It is difficult to understand how this formula could be described as counterrevolution.

It was, in fact, a remarkably astute compromise that achieved instantaneous success because it offered something to everyone, whether privileged elite or caste, whether white or nonwhite, whether old revolutionary or new dissident. The clergy supported it because it guaranteed religion, the creoles and lower classes because it brought independence, and the elite and even some Spaniards because it guaranteed them protection. It thus forged a new alliance of political forces that brought the Spanish imperial regime crashing down.[28]

On the one hand, the elite, who for ten years had been the source of survival for the viceregal regime, defected. Whether creole or European, they recognized that Iguala was advantageous. The moderate majority, who in 1808 and again in 1812–1814 had desired autonomy but were unwilling to break their deeply rooted attachments to the throne, had been forced by Spanish obstinance to realize that as long as the attachment to the peninsula remained, New Spain would be nothing but a colony. Suddenly to be a royalist meant simply to be in favor of government by Spaniards. The Crown had proven itself irrelevant. Spanish intransigence, combined with Iturbide's tempting formula, brought New Spain's creoles together at last. The Plan of Iguala was the alternative the elite and bourgeoisie had been waiting for.

On the other hand, dedicated rebels, whether creole or mestizo, could now find common cause with their oppressors. Life-long rebels like Guerrero, who had resisted amnesty, as well as the majority of the rebels who had accepted amnesty, joined Iturbide because there was a possibility of success, and because the Plan, even though it abandoned their long objective of a republic, was nonetheless reformist. In the years ahead, of course, these groups would provide the factions that kept the independent nation in turmoil, but for the moment they all entered an alliance to achieve autonomy. Iturbide was speaking the truth when he observed to the viceroy: "Any country is free that wants to be free."[29] Mexico finally had a consensus; it knew what it wanted. For the first time, independence became a reasonable alternative to Spanish imperialism.

Few countries can boast of such a logical and entirely consistent achievement of self-determination. All the elements had been present since 1808; they now coalesced in a program that brought victory. Iturbide's Plan of Iguala was not unique, and it was not a miscarriage. It was moderate, it was achievable, it did not require rivers of blood or Hidalgo's "fountains of tears." Even the most dedicated modern nationalists—those who today honor Hidalgo—need feel no embarrassment that it was Iturbide who prevailed. To require independence to have been achieved in 1821 by more radical means is to impose twentieth-century values upon what was an essentially colonial, politically undeveloped, conservative society.

Once the Plan of Iguala is recognized to be neither counterrevolutionary nor revolutionary, the question of whether Iturbide's uprising itself was the product of a reactionary conspiracy to overthrow the Constitution becomes irrelevant. The idea that Iturbide was sent out on his mission of achieving independence by a coterie of reactionary clerics, nobles and merchants who met in the ex-Jesuit chapter house, La Profesa, is based only on hearsay evidence.[30] This unsubstantiated idea is not significant. What is important is that Iturbide represented a genuinely broad cross-section of political opinion in Mexico City—Masons, merchants, Guadalupes, churchmen, Cortes deputies, nobles, and, most important of all, creole army officers. The clergy, the nobles, the mercantile plutocrats, the scholars, the miners, all collaborated in his uprising. Iturbide himself later insisted that the Plan of Iguala was his work alone; "I alone conceived it, extended it, published it, and executed it."[31] No magical or conspiratorial explanation for either its origin or its success is required.

The most important thing about the Plan of Iguala is its consistency with past Mexican aspirations. It was the fulfillment of the political objectives of the cabildo in 1808 and of the American Cortes deputies after 1811. A plan very similar to the Plan of Iguala was presented to the Cortes on June 24, 1821, by the Mexican delegates, including the marqués de Apartado, Francisco Fagoaga, Lucas Alamán, and José Mariano Michelena. It advocated autonomous governments in each capital of Spanish America, each with its own parliament, executive, and ministries. As usual, the Cortes ignored this proposal. The most significant contribution of the Mexican Cortes delegates to eventual independence was their successful effort to have Lieutenant

General Juan O'Donojú (a liberal and Mason and former minister of war during the first constitutional period) appointed as next captain general of New Spain and superior political chief of Mexico. Although the appointment was made in December, 1820, O'Donojú did not reach New Spain until eight months later, by which time the country's future was largely decided.[32]

The only regard in which the Plan of Iguala seriously deviated from creole autonomist proposals issued in 1808 or 1811 is that it was being advocated by the military and the officers would guarantee it. Having been given short-shrift over the past thirteen years by a succession of royal governments, the idea of autonomy needed armed support to prevail.

Spain's restoration of the Constitution in 1820 helped precipitate the achievement of independence by proving to Mexicans the irrelevance of the imperial ethos, thus motivating them to aspire to total autonomy in place of half measures while simultaneously providing them the constitutional forms upon which to build a separate state. Peninsular administrators in New Spain, from the viceroy down, failed to understand this contradiction and were thus unprepared for the solution about to be enacted by the Mexican people.

Chapter 9

Dénouement

THE VICEREGAL regime collapsed only seven months after publication of the Plan of Iguala. It collapsed; it was not defeated.
The core element in this collapse was surprise. On March 7,
1821, Viceroy Apodaca informed the Spanish government of
Iturbide's uprising and Plan of Iguala and admitted that "this
unexpected event has filled both me and everyone else in the
capital with surprise and consternation." He had simply not
foreseen the threat, nor had he understood the extent to which
royal authority was weakened. Months later he wrote from his
refuge in Cuba, "I had a feeling of presentiment about this
misfortune in the middle of last year, 1820, but not about the
terms in which it would come about nor the means by which it
would be effected, because they are so extraordinary that it was
not possible to imagine them."[1]

Spanish expeditionary troops also showed their shock and
surprise. Throughout March, various corps in the capital dispatched oaths of loyalty and support to Apodaca, indicating
their reactions to Iturbide's stunning coup. The National Corps
of Engineers swore not to succumb to Iturbide's infamous machinations; the Dragoons of the King proclaimed their desire to
die in the defense of the capital; the naval squadrons gathered in
the capital promised the same; the Battalion of Barcelona decried

the shame Iturbide's treason brought to royal arms and promised to make up for it by their loyalty. Francisco Novella, subinspector general of the Artillery Corps and member of the Council of War, published a proclamation implying censure of Apodaca's easy-going policies of the past, which Novella, together with many other militarist officers, considered to be the fundamental cause of Iturbide's uprising.[2]

Viceregal leadership was effectively paralyzed by the combination of Apodaca's surprise and his growing discredit among the troops. In the ensuing months the viceroy took no firm military action against the rebels; instead, he pursued a policy of concentrating various veteran army corps in the capital, in preparation for an expected assault against the city. As a result, other regions of the country were left virtually undefended and rapidly went over to the rebels. In the city itself, Apodaca's orders were not willingly obeyed by civilian authorities. The royal government was adrift. On July 5, 1821, a mutiny of peninsular troops deposed Apodaca and replaced him with Francisco Novella in a last-ditch stand against independence.

Iturbide's first statement to the befuddled Apodaca was an assertion of superiority and the certainty of victory. With a copy of the Plan of Iguala, Iturbide sent a covering letter informing Apodaca that independence was inevitable and asking him to accept the presidency of the Sovereign Junta. "Public opinion is decided," he said. "I do not have to repeat that to Your Excellency. Neither Your Excellency nor I, nor any other person, can alter it. Nor does Your Excellency have the power to oppose it." Iturbide reminded the viceroy of the support for Iguala among the militia and even some of the European troops, and of the rapid spread of conspiracy in favor of independence. He wrote: "How many plans, sir, are being formed this very moment in Oaxaca, in Puebla, in Valladolid, in Guadalajara, in Querétaro, in Guanajuato, in San Luis, in the capital itself, around your person, perhaps within your own household? Is there anyone who can undo the opinion of an entire kingdom?"[3]

After consultation with his War Council, the viceroy replied by sending Iturbide a plea to desist and to return to royal service. In a public proclamation he told the people that Iturbide was a traitor whose only motive was personal ambition for power. Rather lamely, he pointed out that he and the Council of War agreed the insurrection would ruin the constitutional government and the process of peace and recovery. In letters to Spain, Apodaca several times agonized over the sheer gall of Iturbide. Apodaca was certain the rebel leader was simply wrong, that he was deluded by personal ambition and by false ideas of what independence would mean, that he had "lost his mental judgment." Angry, embarrassed, even a little ashamed, the viceroy clearly did not understand what Iturbide was about or where his tremendous popularity came from.[4]

Iturbide replied to Apodaca's refusal to accept the Plan of Iguala on March 2 in a short statement that was icily cold and daring: "Your Excellency has not had the kindness to answer the letter I sent you on the twenty-fourth. I shall approach the capital to await your answer." On March 3 he added a note asking the viceroy to send him two trusted persons to begin negotiations for the capitulation of the royal government. Thus the capital became, as it was in 1810, the declared objective of the rebels.[5]

An immediate difference in purpose between the viceroy and the city council appeared. On March 5 the viceroy informed the municipality that an attack was near. He ordered the council to provide twenty carts and forty mules, one hundred pack mules with their handlers, and twenty-five horses with saddles to help the army prepare for attack. He further requested it to take particular care to guard the public peace and quiet. The cabildo replied that it would increase the night watch but said nothing about providing the carts and mules. Shortly thereafter the viceroy asked to take over the city jail to house two army battalions and warned the cabildo of his desire to put the National Local Militia, required by the Constitution, into the field in battle readiness. However, what concerned the cabildo was not defense of the capital but the danger that Iturbide's revolt might force the viceregal regime to overturn some of the Constitution's personal guarantees. In a proclamation to the inhabitants on March 3, it urged them not to follow Iturbide in order not to endanger the Constitution. This was the chief concern of civil authorities during the next months.[6]

In fact, Iturbide was not yet prepared to make good his promise of marching on the capital. He wanted first to gain control of as many regional centers as possible in order to isolate the royal power in Mexico City. Apodaca continued massing what forces he could in the city and, on March 6, ordered all members of urban troops who had been released from service to present themselves immediately to take up arms. This included the artillery brigade and the city battalions of infantry and cavalry.[7]

The city council hastened to clarify the question whether aldermen would be required to serve in their patriotic regiments. The question came to a head when councilman Gabriel Patricio de Yermo received an order to come to arms and to pay a monthly contribution to his regiment. Yermo refused to do either and was promptly arrested. A commission of the city asked the viceroy to release him, and the viceroy, showing definite signs of strain, replied that it was all a mistake, that another person of the same name was supposed to have been arrested, that Yermo should not have been seized, and that he would be released immediately. The viceroy affirmed that elected officials would not be required to join their regiments, since their higher duty was to the Constitution.[8]

Owing to this insistence on scrupulous observation of the Constitution, on March 10 the regularly scheduled elections for deputies to the 1822–1823 session of the Cortes took place peacefully and quietly. On March 11, as Viceroy Apodaca proudly announced to the public, a vanguard of the royal army under command of Field Marshal Pascual Liñán drew up near Iguala and forced Iturbide to flee to the village of Tlacotepec. The viceroy declared Iturbide an outlaw, making all communication with him a crime. A circular from Archbishop Fonte, a staunch Spanish supporter, endorsed the viceroy's boast that the Iturbide movement would soon be destroyed.[9]

The Iturbide movement, however, did not collapse. Throughout April, May, and June, 1821 it grew stronger. Apodaca could not send out a large expeditionary force, because the rebels were not concentrated in any one or two locations and the loyalty of the royal troops could not be counted upon. By the end of May, Iturbide could not be stopped. Amnestied rebels came out to join his forces, royalist troops began to desert to him, creoles responded to his call and flocked to him, and garrison after garrison capitulated without firing a shot. Throughout June his forces moved through the rich Bajío section of the kingdom—the heartland of Hidalgo's revolt—and the survivors of that first movement joined him in what by now had become a crusade. Even the troops in the capital went over in considerable numbers, provoked by the widespread publication of the Plan of Iguala there under cover of constitutional freedom of the press. On the night of June 5, three of the city's gates were abandoned by their guards, numbering more than two hundred men and ten officers.[10]

Viceroy Apodaca was disconsolate. On May 29 he wrote Spain saying that "the majority of troops in the kingdom with many of their officers . . . have been seduced and passing to the rebels have left me in the greatest agony, and the kingdom is on the verge of being lost." More serious still, an internal division within his administration endangered his personal leadership. His chief military advisers, notably members of the Council of War, became convinced he was not taking sufficiently strong action against the rebellion and turned against him. Since the decrees of the rebels were still being freely published in the capital under the protection of the Constitution, the officers demanded abolition of the free press. On May 31, therefore, admitting he was under heavy pressure from the officers, Apodaca wrote the city council announcing that he was about to suspend the free-press article as well as all other constitutional provisions concerning public political activities. These suspensions, he promised, would be in effect only one month, and he asked the council's approval of his proposed measure.[11]

It was over this question that the constitutional civilian corporations began publicly to withdraw their support. The city council chose a commission to draw up an answer to the viceroy's request, and on June 1 it presented for discussion a statement declaring, "The commission is of the opinion . . . that Your Excellency does not have the power to suspend any article of the Constitution, nor does the ayuntamiento have the power to consult with you about it." The letter that was finally drafted and sent to Apodaca phrased this rather more discreetly, asking rhetorically, "Does Your Excellency, in the current circumstances, have the right to suspend even temporarily any article of the Constitution?"[12]

Iturbide's advance, however, left Apodaca no choice but to act, thus provoking an outright break with the city council. On June 1 the viceroy ordered, without consultation with the audiencia, that Articles 8 and 9 of the Constitution be activated, calling for all citizens to take up arms and contribute to the defense of the state. Every man aged sixteen to forty was requested to come to arms. In response, on June 2 four members of the city council—Sánchez de Tagle, Arce, Guerra, and Azcárate—presented a draft resolution that indicated the thinking of the members. The draft resolution, which was not immediately acted upon because of its drastic statements, declared that the council, as the corporation responsible for defense of human rights and protection of the Constitution, could not ignore the viceroy's arbitrary actions. Accusing the government of trying to create panic and of ignoring the indication on all sides of the public desire for independence, it insisted that the general enlistment of troops infringed on the city's rights, for constitutionally the council was permitted to be consulted in such questions. Proclaiming that a state of general anarchy existed in the government, the councilors said that the viceroy could not count upon any further cooperation in his illegal actions and proposed four questions for the consideration of the full council: Could it ignore such an open and public infraction as that which the viceroy proposed to commit by annulling parts of the Constitution? Could it submit to the decree? Could it remain apathetic in the face of a danger of such magnitude, or should it protest to the Cortes? Should the city make its decisions unilaterally, or should it not perhaps await further indication of the general will of the nation on the question of independence?[13]

The viceroy in turn responded by suspending the free press on June 5, and on June 7 he ordered general mobilization for all men from sixteen to fifty years of age, with no exclusions; a special junta was appointed to administer the mobilization. In order to prevent a general exodus of the peninsulars he simultaneously annulled all licenses for travel to Spain.[14]

This was exactly the program adopted in 1813 by Viceroy Calleja. In fact, Apodaca merely repeated the decrees that Calleja had promulgated on October 26, 1813. Apparently against his will, Apodaca was following precisely the course Mexicans most feared—viceregal annullment of portions of the Constitution, viceregal despotism. The reaction of the Mexican elite, who favored the Constitution, was entirely predictable. They were faced, at last, with the two clearly articulated choices that the traditional historiography assumes had always faced them—viceregal despotism versus an acceptable type of self-determinism. Iturbide could not have sought a more advantageous turn of events if he had planned it himself.

Some members of the city council could no longer restrain themselves. The protestations of alderman Gabriel Patricio de Yermo were so loud that on June 9 he was again arrested and declared an outlaw. On June 14 the city council presented Apodaca with a ringing statement of denunciation and a final declaration of its withdrawal of support. "There is no doubt," it said, "that the health of the people constitutes the supreme law; but the true health of the people is comprised of the exact observation of the fundamental laws of the state." In its opinion, the viceroy had outraged the fundamental law and was no longer deserving of the support of the citizenry. Apodaca's reply to this was to appoint Field Marshal Francisco Novella, the spokesman of the military clique, as interim military governor of Mexico City. The battle lines were drawn, the city council had taken its stand. When the viceroy demanded the collection of all private arms and horses in the city on June 16, the city council again denounced him. [15]

While these events transpired in Mexico City, the remainder of the country was going over to Iturbide. By the end of June the rebel forces had overtaken the garrisons of most of the major cities of New Spain. Most of the others capitulated in the following two months, and finally only Veracruz and Mexico City were left in royalist hands. In June and July Iturbide completed the isolation of Mexico City so that it became the last bastion of Spain.

Viceroy Apodaca was remarkably slow to respond to the Iturbide uprising. The Plan of Iguala itself circulated freely in the capital for three months before freedom of the press was abolished, no army went forth to meet the rebels, and by June the viceroy had lost the confidence of civilian corporations. No royal government could regain this confidence, but the peninsular expeditionary troops, convinced that Apodaca's conciliatory policies enhanced Iturbide's success, determined to depose him.[16]

Writing from Guanabacoa in Cuba, where he recuperated from the voyage from New Spain after his overthrow, Apodaca described what happened. On June 25 the last count of royal troop strength in the capital showed there were 5,300 trained expeditionary soldiers and an additional 6,000 men belonging to various militia. All the troops and their officers were still being paid, and the royal treasury contained 135,790 pesos. According to Apodaca, Mexico City was well enough supplied and garrisoned to resist Iturbide. In addition, the principal avenues entering the city were fortified, and the surrounding towns of Tanepantla, Chalco, San Angel, San Agustín de las Cuevas, and Cuernavaca were still loyal. Apodaca reported that on the night of July 5, 1821, he was meeting with his Council of War to discuss "the forthcoming formation of an army corps that could go out on campaign against the enemy."[17] This plan, or hope, was frustrated when a significant portion of the expeditionary forces mutinied on the very night of the meeting.

The mutiny was led by Francisco Buceli, an officer of the Regiment of the Infante Don Carlos, who came out between the hours of nine and ten at night with approximately 800 to 1,000 troops from the regiments of Don Carlos, Castilla, and the military orders. They arrested their commanding officers in their quarters. Together with troops of the Urban Infantry Corps, the Dragoons of the King, and naval forces, they entered and occupied the palace. At that very moment the permanent Council of War—consisting of the viceroy; the subinspector-general of infantry, Field Marshal Pascual Liñán; the subinspector-general of artillery, Field Marshal Francisco Novella; the subinspector of engineers, Juan Sociat; and four brigadiers—was meeting on the main floor of the palace. The council members came out to receive the demands of the troops, who, professing their lack of confidence in the viceroy, asked for his resignation in favor of one of the subinspectors. General Liñán informed the troops that effective war plans were even then being made. Apodaca himself told them that, although he would like nothing better than to surrender the burdens of office, he nevertheless feared that his resignation might bring complete chaos. Unmoved, the troops replied they could not guarantee Apodaca's safety unless he resigned. Bustamante said that their first choice to take the viceroy's place was General Liñán, although Apodaca's own account of the coup did not mention that fact.[18] The viceroy apparently felt the mutiny from the very beginning was directed toward placing Novella in charge. Convinced of his own failure and long since ready to retire from office, Apodaca capitulated to their demands.

The mutineers asked the viceroy to sign a decree, which they had prepared beforehand, giving bad health as the reason for his resignation, but he refused to accept it and actually tore it up. Calling for pen and paper, he sat at a desk and wrote by hand his own decree turning power over to General Novella on the request of the expeditionary forces. The leading officers then signed a guarantee of the viceroy's personal safety and permission for him to travel to Veracruz as soon as possible. The Apodaca family was moved to the Villa of Guadalupe, but the chaotic conditions in the provinces did not allow for their transfer to Veracruz. The family was returned to the capital, and the former viceroy was lodged in a Franciscan school, where he remained until September 25 without communication or visitors. He was thus within the city during its final capitulation but took no part in that event.[19]

Field Marshal Novella now claimed for himself the offices of viceroy, captain general, and superior political chief, but none of the civilian authorities were prepared to recognize him. The city council told Novella that it recognized him as "Chief General and Political Captain of New Spain"—a strange combination of titles meant to imply its lack of recognition. The Provincial Deputation was more explicit. On July 6 it informed Apodaca that it did not recognize his resignation, "first because . . . notoriously it was the result of violence, and second because Your Excellency does not have the power to turn over command to any persons except those who are designated by law." The city council applauded the Deputation on this stand and referred to

Novella merely as "the Field Marshal." According to O'Donojú, not even the audiencia accepted Novella.[20]

Undeterred, Novella moved forcefully to shore up royal defenses. He took the oath as viceroy of New Spain on July 8. He created a military committee to help maintain the fast-vanishing discipline of the army. Each battalion was represented on the committee by an officer elected by the troops. He issued a proclamation urging the troops not to listen to the insidious propaganda of the enemy and not to desert. He prohibited all public meetings and political discussions and the carrying of arms on the street. He ordered the third and final general mobilization of all men in the capital, this time from the ages of sixteen to sixty. All of this had little effect, although the capital did remain quiet. Many people went out to the rebels, as Novella himself admitted in a public decree, while others hid in their homes to escape the exactions of the government.[21]

On August 3, the city of Puebla capitulated to the rebels, removing the last major defense outside the capital. Novella warned the city council that a siege was imminent and ordered the collection of all livestock and grain in the vicinity. A solemn novena to the Virgin of Los Remedios began in the cathedral to implore divine aid for royal arms.[22]

During the first week of August, Iturbide's forces took Oaxaca, and, under Antonio López de Santa Anna, they took the province, but not the city, of Veracruz, thus closing communications between the capital and the coast. The anticipated rebel siege of Mexico City might have been the next order of business except that at this crucial point General Juan O'Donojú, newly appointed captain general of New Spain, arrived at Veracruz. The royal army of which he was to be commander had deserted everywhere except in Mexico City and Veracruz, and, with the territory between the two cities in rebel control, he was presented with a fait accompli. He announced that he was a man of liberal opinions and asked for a conference with Iturbide.[23] Iturbide accepted, designating the village of Córdoba near Veracruz as their meeting place. As Iturbide passed near Mexico City on his way there, he paused to establish a headquarters and gave orders for surrounding the capital. The flood of royal desertions became intense, and Novella's forces were reduced by nearly half. At Córdoba on August 24, Iturbide and O'Donojú signed the so-called Treaty of Córdoba, by which New Spain became independent.

The treaty, which Spain later refused to accept, was based on the Plan of Iguala and made very few changes in Iturbide's original program. It declared the creation and independence of the sovereign Mexican Empire. Article 17, considering the problem of Mexico City, declared that the capital's occupation by Spanish troops was an obstacle to fulfillment of the treaty; Iturbide, however, had no desire to drive them out by force, since they had neither the means to defend themselves nor the support of the capital's inhabitants. He thus promised that O'Donojú, using his authority as captain general, would attempt to induce them to an "honorable capitulation."[24]

On August 31, O'Donojú wrote the Spanish government his reasons for signing this treaty without authorization. He said resistance to independence was useless, for Iturbide had an army of 30,000 well-armed and disciplined troops, while nearly every major garrison and town had capitulated. Only Veracruz, Acapulco, and Perote remained in royal hands outside of Mexico City, and none of the three was disposed to resist much longer. He wrote: "There remains only Mexico City, but what a state it is in. The viceroy is deposed by his own troops, their numbers do not exceed 2,500 veterans and another 2,000 patriots; the city is governed by a usurping authority that is not recognized by the most important corporations like the Provincial Deputation and the audiencia; and the rest of the population wants to unite itself with the rebels."[25] To hold out much longer in the capital was "a vain hope."

In the first two weeks of August, the frantic pace of preparation for defense of the capital continued unabated, but, while promulgations flooded the city, while officers galloped about, and while priests intoned their prayers, the civilian population either joined the rebels or waited to see what would happen. When Novella published a decree for the confiscation of privately owned horses, the populace failed to obey it. On August 4 he repeated the decree, declaring that "since July 25 . . . not one single individual has voluntarily presented any of the many horses that are to be seen in this city." He restricted his own troops in their use of the few horses that remained.[26]

Novella's last effort to keep the royal regime from collapse was his project to raise the sum of 100,000 pesos a month from the tremendously reduced area under his active control. He created a special commission to propose means of raising the money. The city council, which on August 9 suspended all payments for lack of funds, responded to Novella's request that it appoint two members of this special commission by replying, "This ayuntamiento, being charged with the security of the neighborhood and of the persons and property of the citizens, considers that you cannot realize as you wish the collection of 100,000 pesos a month." Novella answered the city on August 15, saying he had merely asked the council to name two members of the junta, not to offer any other advice. After a long debate, the cabildo members voted to withhold the city's cooperation in the matter and duly notified Novella that it would not choose two men to sit on the commission. On August 31 Novella informed the city council that it would be charged with collection of half of the proposed total donation, to which the cabildo replied on September 4 with outright refusal. It said its determination not to cooperate in the collection had not changed but had been strengthened by the continued deterioration in the city's position. Thus the cabildo made clear its refusal to cooperate further in the royal regime.[27]

On August 30 Novella, who had received a copy of the Treaty of Córdoba from General O'Donojú's adjutant, called a meeting of the various corporations of the city.[28] What happened at the meeting is not known, but Novella apparently asked the opinion of the civil authorities and did not like what he heard, for the cabildo noted in its records that the meeting "broke up tempestuously." On September 3 the city council sent Novella its final statement on the crisis, urging capitulation. It complained that the government had not listened to its opinions in the August 30 meeting, but it felt "that the public health now requires that we speak the language of truth, and that ignoring any public danger . . . we say what is necessary to save this populous capital." The party of independence, said the city council, now had three factors on its side that were conclusive: the general will of the nation, financial power, and the acquiescence of the legitimate royal authority, General O'Donojú. Most of the capital accepted the inevitability of independence. Further resistance was therefore illegal, "because the will of the nation cannot be more decisive, and no legitimate opposition to it can be made." In the absence of any hope of victory, the ayuntamiento urged Novella to accept the Treaty of Córdoba, which was mutually beneficial to both Mexico and Spain and which would preserve the honor of the dynasty and the good name of the troops.[29] Faced with such unequivocal support for independence, the royal resistance died.

On the morning of September 7, Novella's representatives conferred with officers representing Iturbide and O'Donojú and announced a six-day armistice. During those six days, Novella took stock of the city's defensive position and found it wanting. Public opinion in support of independence was clear, as many rebel propagandists proclaimed. José Joaquín Fernández de Lizardi, a late recruit to the Iturbidista forces, wrote a long polemic on the peaceful nature of Iturbide's intentions, his desire to establish a branch of the Bourbon dynasty in Mexico City, and the suicidal results of resistance. The program Mexico City was asked to accept was the program of limited constitutional monarchy under a member of the dynasty—autonomy. This is the program that Lizardi accepted and the one that O'Donojú accepted.[30]

At the end of the six-day truce, on September 13, Novella capitulated. In the company of the members of the city council and representatives of other corporations, he met with O'Donojú and Iturbide near the Basilica of Guadalupe. He perused O'Donojú's credentials, recognized him as the legitimate captain general, and placed the royal garrison under his command. There was no formal surrender or capitulation, no ceremonial degradation of the royal standard. In keeping with the treaty, the royal officers were not humiliated.[31]

Iturbide determined to await his thirty-eighth birthday to make his formal entry into the capital. Meanwhile, General O'Donojú ordered the royal troops to prepare for evacuation, and Intendant Ramon Gutiérrez del Mazo was appointed interim political chief of the capital. Mazo abolished the use of passports and the licenses to ride horses in the city. On September 17 O'Donojú announced that the government stipulated by the Treaty of Córdoba was now installed and formed the legitimate authority. On

September 24 he led one of Iturbide's divisions into the city to take formal possession. One division was all that was required to enact this second conquest of Mexico City, exactly three hundred years to the month after the original Spanish Conquest.[32]

On September 24 Iturbide announced the members of the Sovereign Junta, a majority of whom were residents of Mexico City. Among them were incumbent city council members Azcárate, Sánchez de Tagle, and Veláquez de la Cadena; cabildo secretary Guridi y Alcocer; former aldermen Cervantes y Padilla, García Illueca, and the conde de Regla; the conde de San Miguel de Aguayo; several members of the audiencia; Bishop Pérez of Puebla; and several high churchmen from the capital.[33]

As the city council prepared for the triumphal entry of the 16,000-man Trigarante Army, the royal garrison evacuated the capital on September 23 and 24. After a brief stay in Toluca, the evacuees moved toward Veracruz to take ship for Spain or to join the governor of Veracruz, who had refused to accept independence and had established a stronghold in the fort of San Juan de Ullua in the harbor. So many royal troops took Iturbide up on his offer of membership and equal rank in the Imperial Army that only 2,000 of them evacuated the capital. Field Marshal Novella left on September 24 and at Veracruz embarked on the *Diamante* for Havana. Former viceroy Apodaca and his family left the capital on September 25 with three aides and a bodyguard of twenty naval troops and thirty dragoons. He left Veracruz a month later on the *Asia*.[34]

Iturbide made his triumphal entry on September 27. Under an arch erected by the city council, he received the keys of the city from José Ormaechea, first alcalde. The city council gave a banquet for two hundred guests in the palace, where councilor Sánchez de Tagle read a sycophantic ode to the liberator.[35] That night Iturbide attended a special program in his honor in the theater, while outside the city was brightly illuminated. The city paid for it all, at a cost of 27,432 pesos.

After Iturbide's entry, mobs roamed the streets and pulled the royal coat of arms, the lion and the castle, down from the façades of buildings. In a week and a half General O'Donojú, who sacrificed his career for a people he did not know in order to preserve legality and stability, died from pleurisy, and before long Iturbide strutted across the stage in the ridiculous garb of Emperor Agustín I.

It took twelve long years, but eventually the autonomist program advocated in 1808 by a handful of creole liberals in Mexico City was achieved in the Plan of Iguala and independence. Because Iturbide proposed a formula consistent with the limited reformist goals of the creoles, he was endowed by the nation with the mandate that Spain had lost. The fact that his mandate was short lived does not alter the universal enthusiasm with which the nation greeted him in September, 1821, though it does signify the beginning of the problem of legitimacy that was to trouble the independent nation for a century to come.

Spain hesitated for years to face up to the reality of its loss of sovereignty in America. Former viceroys Venegas and Apodaca were members of the Spanish Council of State that as late as 1828 was still debating methods by which to "pacify" the "rebellious American provinces."[36] This failure to recognize that the Americans had rejected Spain's right to sovereignty characterized much of peninsular thinking for years to come and helps explain Spain's hesitance to recognize American independence during the lifetime of Ferdinand VII. Until the mid-1830s there was an air of suspended animation in peninsular policy toward the new republics, as if the Spaniards expected to be called back.

The autonomist urge, which survived through so many years and so many vicissitudes, did not reach a successful conclusion. Autonomy did not work and was never actually implemented because it had one great weakness—it depended upon Spanish approval. As ever, the Spain of Ferdinand VII was intransigent. King and Cortes alike refused to recognize the Treaty of Córdoba, that remarkably skillful face-saving device signed without authorization on Spain's behalf by O'Donojú. Furthermore, the enthusiasm and optimism with which Mexico greeted the moment of independence quickly waned. Ocampo has shown that in the first two months of independence the nation's joy was replaced by profound pessimism and, regarding every question except independence itself, deep and dangerous division of opinion. Although the proposal of the Plan of Iguala and Treaty of Córdoba to create a moderate constitutional monarchy had widespread support, there was no agreement as to what course to take in meeting the immense problems facing the new nation: what form the new government should take, whether there should be a free press, what status the Indians and castes should have, who should be allowed to vote, whether the Cortes should be bicameral or unicameral, what the status of the church temporal should be, and what economic and social reforms should be adopted. The utopian ideals of reform that characterized all political thinkers at the moment of independence ran up against the harsh reality of the real Mexico, while the Sovereign Junta, which governed the nation from September 28, 1821 to February 25, 1822, failed to come to grips with or act upon the critical questions of the day. Political activists immediately divided between traditionalists and liberals, and enthusiasm turned to pessimism, union to factionalism, concord to fear.[37] Unable to find a member of the Spanish dynasty to establish the autonomous throne, Iturbide himself took the throne in 1822, thoroughly substantiating Viceroy Apodaca's charge that he was power hungry. For a few brief months a separate monarchy, still using the Constitution of Cádiz, functioned in Mexico, but in 1823 it was overthrown in favor of a clean break with the past political norms and the establishment of a republic. If a miscarriage occurred, it was the assumption of the throne by Iturbide, not the Plan of Iguala itself.[38]

Authority slipped out of Spain's grasp because of the countless contradictions between the imperial ethos and the actual fact of Spanish administration. One moment advocating constitutional reform, the next moment advocating absolutism, then returning to constitutional reform; teasing Mexican political aspirations with the hollow promise of reform but not the reality; forced by the European war to squeeze every penny out of New Spain, but refusing ever to reward its generosity—Spain toyed with Mexican loyalty until the habits of centuries were broken and aspirations that in 1808 were hardly spoken aloud became the public consensus of 1821. The rebellion for independence did not defeat Spain. Until 1820, Spain had defeated the rebellion. But in the process of doing so, it converted legitimacy to force and disproved its own ethos. After years of brilliant defense, the viceregal regime eliminated the radical alternatives, clearing the way for Mexicans to agree on the more limited option presented by Iturbide. Then under Apodaca, Spain was unable to sustain the level of force of earlier years, and the Iturbidist formula filled the vast chasm that now existed between imperialist objectives and domestic aspirations.

The way in which Mexico achieved its independence played an essential role in the three-quarters of a century of political chaos that ensued. It was not that independence was counter-revolutionary or that it miscarried, but that independence, when it came, came too easily and in disguise. Iturbide did not have to defeat anybody, for his enemy collapsed. Having defeated a whole series of lower-class insurrections, the royal government itself made Iturbide's victory possible and quick. There was no time to think out the consequences of victory, no body of political thought forged out of years of struggle against the common enemy. Spanish imperialism was rejected, but there was no agreement on what should take its place. The Spanish political ethos was gone, but there was as yet no fresh body of theories, ideals, myths, illusions to take its place. There was only a negative rejection of the old, not a positive acceptance of the new. The very thing that made the Plan of Iguala achievable—its being all things to all men—was its weakness. Many wars would have to be fought before the meaning of independence would be revealed.

Notes

PREFACE

1. Lucas Alamán, *Historia de Méjico desde los primeros movimientos que prepararon su independencia en el año de 1808 hasta la época presente*, 4:308.

2. A revealing example of the insights to be gained from integrating peninsular and colonial studies is Margaret E. Crahan, "Spanish and American Counterpoint: Problems and Possibilities in Spanish Colonial Administrative History," in Richard Graham and Peter H. Smith, eds., *New Approaches to Latin American History*, pp. 36–70.

3. As I have argued in "The Last Viceroys of New Spain and Peru: An Appraisal," *American Historical Review* 81, no. 1 (February, 1976): 38–65.

4. John Lynch, *The Spanish American Revolutions, 1808–1826*, pp. 317–18; Luis Villoro, *El proceso ideológico de la revolución de independencia*; Romeo Flores Caballero, *La contrarevolución en la independencia*, pp. 66–82. For other advocates of the counterrevolution thesis, see Luis Chávez Orozco, *Historia de México, 1808–1836* (Mexico: Editorial Patria, 1947), p. 134; Howard F. Cline, *The United States and Mexico* (Cambridge, Mass.: Harvard University Press, 1953), p. 138; Lesley Byrd Simpson, *Many Mexicos*, pp. 225–27; Arthur P. Whitaker, *The United States and the Independence of Latin America* (Baltimore: Johns Hopkins University Press, 1941), p. 371; Felipe Tena Rodríguez, in Congreso Hispanoamericano de Historia, *Causas y carácteres de la independencia hispanoamericana* (Madrid, 1953), p. 291; Luis Martin, "Lucas Alamán, Pioneer of Mexican Historiography: An Interpretative Essay," *The Americas* 32, no. 2 (October, 1975): 239–56; and several of the essays in Nettie Lee Benson, ed., *Mexico and the Spanish Cortes, 1810–1822: Eight Essays*.

5. Enrique Florescano, *Precios del maíz y crisis agrícolas en México (1708–1810)*; D. A. Brading, *Miners and Merchants in Bourbon Mexico, 1763–1810*; D. A. Brading, "Government and Elite in Late Colonial

Mexico," *Hispanic American Historical Review* (hereafter cited as *HAHR*) 53, no. 3 (August, 1973): 389–414.

6. Villoro, *El proceso ideológico*, p. 191.

7. Doris M. Ladd, "The Mexican Nobility at Independence, 1780–1826," (Ph.D. diss., Stanford University, 1971). This work has been published by the Institute of Latin American Studies, University of Texas.

8. Ibid., p. 242.

9. Peter H. Smith, "Political Legitimacy in Spanish America," in Graham and Smith, eds., *New Approaches*, 225–55.

10. Hugh M. Hamill, Jr., "Royalist Counterinsurgency in the Mexican War of Independence: The Lessons of 1811," *HAHR* 53, no. 3 (August, 1973): 470–89.

11. Viceroy Juan Ruiz de Apodaca to Minister of Ultramar, Mexico, March 7, 1821, Archivo General de Indias, Seville (hereafter cited as AGI), Mexico 1680.

12. Carl J. Friedrich, *Tradition and Authority*.

13. Ibid., pp. 97–98. Exactly such a situation prevailed in the Mexican War of Independence.

14. Ibid., pp. 55–56, 115–17. Friedrich calls this the "power for reasoned elaboration."

15. Frank Jay Moreno, "The Spanish Colonial System: A Functional Approach," *Western Political Quarterly* 20 (June, 1967): 308–20. For further discussion of the patrimonial qualities of traditional authority in the Spanish empire see Magali Sarfatti, *Spanish Bureaucratic-Patrimonialism in America*, Institute of International Studies (Berkeley: University of California Press, 1966); and John Leddy Phelan, *The Kingdom of Quito in the Seventeenth Century: Bureaucratic Politics in the Spanish Empire* (Madison: University of Wisconsin Press, 1967), pp. 320–37.

16. Richard M. Morse, "The Heritage of Latin America," in *Politics and Social Change in Latin America: The Distinct Tradition*, ed. Howard J. Wiarda, pp. 25–69.

17. Smith, "Political Legitimacy in Spanish America," p. 235.

18. Moreno, "Spanish Colonial System," pp. 312–16.

19. Glen Dealy, "Prolegomena on the Spanish American Political Tradition," *HAHR* 48, no. 1 (February, 1968): 37–58.

20. Charles A. Hale, "The Reconstruction of Nineteenth-Century Politics in Spanish America: A Case for the History of Ideas," *Latin American Research Review* 8, no. 2 (Summer, 1972): 53–73.

21. Jaime E. Rodríguez O., *The Emergence of Spanish America*, pp. 6–46.

22. David A. Brading, *Los orígenes del nacionalismo mexicano*, p. 125.

CHAPTER 1

1. Alamán, *Historia de Méjico*, 1:61.

2. Charles Gibson, *The Aztecs under Spanish Rule*, pp. 107, 337; Jacques Soustelle, *Daily Life of the Aztecs on the Eve of the Spanish Conquest*, p. 32; Jorge Hardoy, *Pre-Columbian Cities*, p. 160; Juan de Viera, *Compendiosa narración de la ciudad de México*, p. 91; G. A. Thompson, *The Geographical and Historical Dictionary of America and the West Indies . . . of D. Antonio de Alcedo*, 4:91; Alexander von Humboldt, *Ensayo político sobre Nueva España*, p. 129. The anglicized spelling of *gachupín* will be used throughout.

3. "Resumen de las operaciones de la nueva policía desde el día 26 de agosto último en que fué instalada," January 6, 1812, Archivo General de la Nación, Mexico (hereafter cited as AGN), Historia, vol. 454. A general summary of these figures, and figures for other Mexican cities, is Keith A. Davies, "Tendencias demográficas urbanas durante el siglo XIX en México," in *Ensayos sobre el desarrollo urbano de México*, Sep Setentas 143 (Mexico: Secretaría de Educación Pública, 1974), pp. 131–174. However, see note 5 below.

4. Originally the Indian inhabitants of the capital were required to live in these parcialidades, but the requirement was rarely carefully enforced (Gibson, *Aztecs Under Spanish Rule*, p. 371).

5. "Memoria sobre la población del reino de Nueva España, escrita por D. Fernando Navarro y Noriega," (Mexico: Juan Bautista de Arizpe, 1820), in AGN, Impresos oficiales, vol. 60, no. 48. Davies, "Tendencias demográficas," p. 152, errs in saying that Navarro said the 1811 census excluded residents of parcialidades. The original copy of Navarro cited here declared that the figure included those Indians.

6. Navarro y Noriega, "Memoria"; Joel R. Poinsett, *Notes on Mexico, Made in the Autumn of 1822 by a citizen of the United States*, p. 49; "Resumen de las operaciones de la nueva policía," AGN, Historia, vol. 454.

7. Humboldt, *Ensayo político*, p. 132; *U.S. Census, 1810* (Washington, D.C., 1811); John Preston Moore, *The Cabildo in Peru under the Bourbons* (Durham; Duke University Press, 1966), p. 47.

8. Navarro y Noriega, "Memoria"; *U.S. Census, 1810*; *U.S. Census, 1820* (Washington, D.C., 1821).

9. Ladd, "The Mexican Nobility," p. 113.

10. Thompson, *Geographical and Historical Dictionary*, 3:106; Viera, *Narración de la ciudad*, p. 107.

11. See Fanny Calderón de la Barca, *Life in Mexico*.

12. From *El Periquillo Sarniento*, quoted in Jefferson Rea Spell, *The Life and Works of José Joaquín Fernández de Lizardi*, p. 84; *El Pensador Mexicano*,

no. 3 (1812), in ibid., p. 95; *El Pensador Mexicano*, no. 9 (1812), in ibid., p. 97.

13. Ladd, "The Mexican Nobility," pp. 46, 48, 317–19; Brading, *Miners and Merchants*, pp. 95–128, 208–19; see also Brading, "Government and Elite in Late Colonial Mexico," pp. 389–414.

14. Ibid., p. 39.

15. Alamán said simply that "the division between Europeans and creoles was the cause of the revolutions" (*Historia de Méjico*, 1:22).

16. Brading, *Miners and Merchants*, p. 304.

17. Ladd, "The Mexican Nobility," p. 52.

18. Information on Villoro's view of the social classes is from his *El proceso ideológico*, pp. 16–31.

19. Quoted in Lynch, *Spanish American Revolutions*, p. 298.

20. María Dolores Morales, "Estructura urbana y distribución de la propiedad en la ciudad de México en 1813," *Historia Mexicana* 25 (January–March, 1976): 363–402.

21. Viceroy Félix María Calleja to Luis Salazar, Mexico, October 31, 1814, AGI, Mexico 1484.

22. Ladd says that three nobles rented their mansions to other nobles or to Spanish officials at rents of 1,000 to 2,000 pesos a year ("The Mexican Nobility," p. 116).

23. See Leon G. Campbell, "A Colonial Establishment: Creole Domination of the Audiencia of Lima during the Late Eighteenth Century," *HAHR* 52, no. 1 (February, 1972): 1–25; Mark A. Burkholder, "From Creole to *Peninsular*: The Transformation of the Audiencia of Lima," *HAHR* 52, no. 3 (August, 1972): 395–415; and M. A. Burkholder and D. S. Chandler, "Creole Appointments and the Sale of Audiencia Positions in the Spanish Empire under the Early Bourbons, 1701–1750," *Journal of Latin American Studies* 4, no. 2 (November, 1972): 187–206.

24. Romeo Flores Caballero has the most complete discussion of this figure and of Humboldt's very different estimate that there were 75,000 peninsulars (*La contrarevolución*, pp. 15–24). Humboldt's figure is generally rejected on the grounds that he was projecting the proportion of Europeans in the capital to the rest of the country. Alamán, following Humboldt, said there were 70,000, but he also said he thought this to be an exaggerated figure (*Historia de Méjico*, 1:15). A further 8,448 Spanish expeditionary troops came to New Spain during the war.

25. Flores Caballero, *La contrarevolución*, p. 22.

26. Ibid., pp. 23–24. The Consulado of Mexico City controlled import-export commerce and was the preserve of peninsulars, who in turn divided politically between Montañeses and Vizcaínos (Alamán, *Historia de Méjico*, 1:45). Brading has shown that the same two groups

of peninsular immigrants struggled for control of the Mining Deputation of Guanajuato in the last decade of the eighteenth century (*Miners and Merchants*, pp. 329 ff.), though Alamán says the Mining Tribunal in Mexico City was predominately creole (*Historia de Méjico*, 1:49).

27. As can be seen from the fact that Viceroy Calleja's forced contribution based on incomes in 1813 chose 300 pesos as the floor income for taxation purposes (Regulations of the direct contribution, Mexico, December 19, 1813, AGN, Impresos oficiales, vol. 36).

28. Ladd, "The Mexican Nobility," pp. 113–16.

29. Morales, "Estructura urbana," pp. 363–402.

30. Ladd, "The Mexican Nobility," pp. 117, 177. Aguayo owed 450,000 pesos.

31. Brading, *Miners and Merchants*, pp. 169–207.

32. Ladd, "The Mexican Nobility," pp. 152–85; Michael Costeloe, *Church Wealth in Mexico, 1800–1856*.

33. Flores Caballero, *La contrarevolución*, pp. 28–65. See also Asunción Lavrin, "The Execution of the Law of *Consolidación* in New Spain: Economic Aims and Results," *HAHR* 53, no. 1 (February, 1973): 27–49; and Brian Hamnett, "The Appropriation of Mexican Church Wealth by the Spanish Bourbon Government: 'The Consolidación de Vales Reales,' 1805–1809," *Journal of Latin American Studies* 1, no. 2 (November, 1969): 85–113.

34. According to the testimony of Bishop-elect Manuel Abad y Queipo, quoted in Ladd, "The Mexican Nobility," p. 175.

35. Ibid., p. 167. The importance of the elite's role in accounting for the initiation of social mobilization in the Mexican and other Latin American movements for independence has recently been restated in Jorge S. Domínguez, "Political Participation and the Social Mobilization Hypothesis: Chile, Mexico, Venezuela, and Cuba, 1800–1825," *Journal of Interdisciplinary History* 5, no. 2 (Autumn, 1974): 237–66.

36. Brading, *Los orígenes*, pp. 59–148.

37. Poinsett, *Notes on Mexico*, p. 48.

38. Quoted in Donald B. Cooper, *Epidemic Diseases in Mexico City, 1761–1813*, pp. 163–64. For an attempt to categorize the lower classes in Querétaro see Torcuato S. Di Tella, "The Dangerous Classes in Early Nineteenth-Century Mexico," *Journal of Latin American Studies* 5, no. 1 (May, 1973): 79–105.

39. Poinsett, *Notes on Mexico*, p. 48.

40. Florescano, *Precios del maíz*, p. 153.

41. Ibid., pp. 143–44. The incomes of 8 or 10 reales a day would be for very specialized work by highly skilled craftsmen, who might well overlap with the bourgeoisie, since this would amount to an annual income of about 400 pesos.

42. Ibid., pp. 160–63.

43. Ibid., pp. 197, 224, 235. A fanega was about 1.5 bushels.

44. Humboldt, *Ensayo político*, p. 132.

45. Clark W. Reynolds, *The Mexican Economy: Twentieth-Century Structure and Growth* (New Haven: Yale University Press, 1970), pp. 311–14; Henry G. Aubrey, "The National Income of Mexico," *Estadística* (Journal of the Inter-American Statistical Institute), June, 1950, pp. 185–98; Fernando Rosenzweig Hernández, "La economía Novo-Hispaña al comenzar el siglo XIX," *Ciencias Políticas y Sociales* (UNAM), 9 (July–September, 1963), 455–94. Their per capita income figures are based on Aubrey's adjustments of Humboldt's statistics and Rosenzweig's adjustments of the figures of José María Quiros, whose *Memoria de Estatuto* (1817) is published in Enrique Florescano and Isabel Gil, comps. *Descripciones económicas generales de Nueva España, 1784–1817*, Fuentes para la historia económica de México, 1 (Mexico: Instituto Nacional de Antropología e Historia, 1973), pp. 231–64. It should be added, however, that after converting these income figures into value equivalents for 1950, Reynolds found that per capita income actually declined after independence and throughout the entire nineteenth century. Gross per capita figures are not very helpful, since they do not distinguish between work force, children, and the elderly. For detailed income figures for employed persons in Querétaro in a later period see Di Tella, "The Dangerous Classes," pp. 100–1.

46. Its birth rate of 1:22.5 and death rate of 1:26.5 compared unfavorably to the nation's overall birth rate of 1:17 and death rate of 1:30 (Humboldt, *Ensayo político*, p. 131).

47. Royal cedula, Madrid, November 14, 1819, AGN, Reales cédulas originales, vol. 221, no. 259.

48. Alamán, *Historia de Méjico*, 1:45.

49. "Expediente sobre la división de esta ciudad en quarteles," Mexico, November 21, 1782, AGN, Ayuntamientos, vol. 221, no. 5.

50. Brading, *Miners and Merchants*, p. 348.

51. Calleja to Juan José Fagoaga, Mexico, January 16, 1815, AGN, Historia, vol. 459; duplicate in Archivo del Ex-Ayuntamiento, Mexico (hereafter cited as A. Ex-A.), Actas de Cabildo, vol. 135, January 17, 1815; "Sobre que el Sr. Intendente . . . desocupe la habitación que como corregidor disfrutaba en las casas capitulares," Mexico, June, 1815, AGN, Ayuntamientos, vol. 225, no. 9.

52. Royal Cedula, Madrid, September 5, 1817, AGN, Ayuntamientos, vol. 227.

53. "Informe que hizo el Dr. D. José Beye de Cisneros a Las Cortes como diputado de este Exmo. Ayuntamiento de México," A. Ex-A., Elecciones de diputados a Cortes, vol. 870, no. 9.

54. See Fredrick B. Pike, "The Municipality and the System of Checks and Balances in Spanish Colonial Administration," *The Americas* 15, no. 2 (October, 1958): 139–58.

55. See Timothy E. Anna, "The Finances of Mexico City during the War of Independence," *Journal of Latin American Studies* 4, no. 1 (May, 1972): 55–75.

56. "Colección de los Generales que cada trimestre se dan al público del ingreso y egreso de caudales de esta N.C.," A. Ex-A., Hacienda, Aduana, vol. 2000, no. 9.

57. For monthly income lists see A. Ex-A., Hacienda, Aduana, vol. 2000, no. 10.

58. "Sobre que el Tesorero mayordomo de la N.C. forme un estado de las fincas," 1802, A. Ex-A., Fincas de ciudad en general, vol. 1085, no. 7; "Sobre que se valuen las fincas urbanas y rusticas y sitios eriazos de la municipalidad," 1830, ibid., no. 11.

CHAPTER 2

1. Ladd, "The Mexican Nobility," p. 182.

2. Ibid., p. 185.

3. "Abdicación del rey Carlos IV," A. Ex-A., Reales cédulas y órdenes, vol. 2979, no. 306. The most thorough study in English of the long Napoleonic struggle is Gabriel H. Lovett, *Napoleon and the Birth of Modern Spain*, 2 vols. (New York: New York University Press, 1965); the best Spanish treatments are Miguel Artola Gallego, *La España de Fernando VII* (1968), vol. 26 in Ramón Menéndez Pidal, ed., *Historia de España* (Madrid: Espasa-Calpe, 1947–), and Miguel Artola Gallego, *La burgesía revolucionaria (1808–1869)*, Historia de España Alfaguara, vol. 3 (Madrid: Alianza Editorial, 1973).

4. "La N. Ciudad ofrece a S.M. que en caso de trasladarse a otra parte lo haga a esta ciudad," A. Ex-A., Historia, en general, vol. 2254, no. 32.

5. *Gazeta de México*, July 16, July 29, and August 1, 1808. Some of the documents cited from the original throughout this chapter can be found in vol. 2 of Genaro García, ed., *Documentos históricos mexicanos.*

6. The most thorough study of Iturrigaray is Enrique Lafuente Ferrari, *El Virrey Iturrigaray y los orígenes de la Independencia de México.*

7. Tomás Antonio Campomanes to Ferdinand, Prince of Asturias, and to the Duke of Medinaceli, Xiquipilco, January 2, 1808, Archivo Histórico Nacional, Madrid (hereafter cited as AHN), Estado 57.

8. See Francisco Santiago Cruz, *El Virrey Iturrigaray, Historia de una Conspiración*, p. 94.

9. "Relación sucinta y rasonada de muchos hechos antecedentes, y circunstancias que se tubieron presentes la noche del 15 y madrugada del 16 de septiembre para acceder el Real Acuerdo a la separación del Exmo. Sr. D. José de Iturrigaray," November 8, 1808, AHN, Consejos 21081. This is the audiencia's statement in Iturrigaray's *residencia*.

10. Faustino de Capetillo to his brother, Jalapa, July 19, 1808, AHN, Estado 57, E.

11. A. Ex-A., Actas de Cabildo, vol. 127, July 14, 1808.

12. "Oficio que la N.C. dirigio al Exmo. Sr. Virrey sobre que durante la ausencia del Señor D. Fernando VII govierne estos dominios Su Excellencia," July 19, 1808, A. Ex-A., Historia, en general, vol. 2254, no. 34; identical phrasing in "Testimonio de las representaciones que esta N. Ciudad presentó al Exmo. Sr. D. José de Iturrigaray, promoviendo . . . la conservación y defensa del Reyno," AHN, Consejos 21081.

13. Ladd, "The Mexican Nobility," p. 193.

14. Ibid., p. 196; Hugh M. Hamill, Jr., *The Hidalgo Revolt: Prelude to Mexican Independence*, pp. 94–97.

15. Juan Martín de Juanmartineña to Tomás Calderón, Mexico, October 31, 1808, AHN, Consejos 21081.

16. After discussing the radical ideas of Talamantes, Alamán makes just this assumption: "The Congress would have declared itself sovereign, just as happened later under identical circumstances in Buenos Aires, Santa Fé and Caracas" (*Historia de Méjico*, 1:176–77). Surely this remains a moot question.

17. Villoro, *El proceso ideológico*, p. 47.

18. The problem in interpreting Talamantes is that in his *Congreso Nacional* he spoke of New Spain establishing its independence from France (Hamill, *The Hidalgo Revolt*, p. 94).

19. Both in Villoro, *El proceso ideológico*, pp. 37–38.

20. Brading, *Los orígenes*, p. 102. The point of view was very similar to that which brought the peninsular regional juntas into existence. It should be remembered that the peninsula was entering a period of regional drives for autonomy too. See also Margaret E. Crahan, "Spanish and American Counterpoint", pp. 36–70.

21. Villoro, *El proceso ideológico*, p. 39.

22. Manuel Veláquez de Leon to Tomás Calderón, Mexico, October 26, 1808, AHN, Consejos 21081. It should be noted that Veláquez de Leon had no clear personal motive for supporting Iturrigaray. He had no fear of imprisonment, and his office was a royal appointment, not the personal appointment of the viceroy. He remained in office, and in 1811 Venegas raised him to the status of *intendente de provincia* (Alamán, *Historia de Méjico*, 1:175, 2:307).

23. "Protesta de la ciudad con motivo de la abdicación del Sr. D. Carlos IV al Emperador Napoleon," July 23, 1808, A. Ex-A., Historia, en general, vol. 2254, no. 36.

24. Testimony of José Juan Fagoaga to Guillermo de Aguirre, Mexico, October 20, 1808, AHN, Consejos 21081.

25. Ladd, "The Mexican Nobility," pp. 190–91; Royal Accord, August 8, 1808, AHN, Estado 57, E.

26. Ladd, "The Mexican Nobility," p. 191.

27. Royal Accord, September 6, 1808, AHN, Estado 58, E.

28. "Testimonio de la relación de los pasages mas notables ocurridos en las Juntas generales que el Exmo. Sr. D. José de Iturrigaray convocó en los días 9 y 31 de agosto, 1 y 9 de septiembre de este año," November 9, 1808, AHN, Consejos 21081; "Junta general celebrada en México el 9 de agosto de 1808," A. Ex-A., Historia, en general, vol. 2254, no. 34; Alamán, *Historia de Méjico*, 1:134.

29. *Gazeta de México*, August 10, 1808; Alamán, *Historia de Méjico*, 1:141. Jáuregui's testimony bears out their orders (Report of Jáuregui, Cádiz, August 20, 1809, in Genaro García, *Documentos históricos mexicanos*, 2:292–96).

30. Fabián de Miranda to Supreme Junta of Seville, Seville, November 22, 1808, AHN, Estado 58, E.

31. Alamán, *Historia de Méjico*, 1:142.

32. Ibid., 1:139–40; Faustino de Capetillo to his brother, Jalapa, August 18, 1808, AHN, Estado 57, E; John Rydjord, *Foreign Interest in the Independence of New Spain*, p. 278.

33. "Relación sucinta . . . del 15 y 16 de septiembre," AHN, Consejos 21081; Alamán, *Historia de Méjico*, 1:139, 140. Alamán says there is no firm proof that rock throwing occurred.

34. Ladd, "The Mexican Nobility," p. 192.

35. Ibid., p. 194. Many of the individual opinions of participants are published in Genaro García, *Documentos históricos mexicanos*, 2:77–135.

36. Ladd, "The Mexican Nobility," p. 194.

37. Royal Accord, September 6, 1808, AHN, Estado 58, E.

38. Alamán, *Historia de Méjico*, 1:147.

39. "Testimonio de las Juntas generales," AHN, Consejos 21081.

40. Ladd, "The Mexican Nobility," p. 197; Gabriel de Yermo to the Supreme Junta of Seville, Mexico, November 12, 1808, AHN, Estado 57, E.

41. "Observaciones que presenta a S.M. la Junta Central el Capt. de Navio D. Juan Jabat," Seville, December 27, 1808, AHN, Estado 58, E.

42. Faustino de Capetillo to his brother, Jalapa, August 18, 1808, AHN, Estado 57, E.

43. Gabriel de Yermo to the Supreme Junta of Seville, Mexico,

November 9, 1808, AHN, Estado 57, E. Brian R. Hamnett, *Politics and Trade in Southern Mexico, 1750–1821,* pp. 121–47.

44. This account of the events of September 15–16, 1808, comes from "Relación de lo ocurrido en México el 15 de septiembre de 1808 con motivo de la prisión del Sr. Iturrigaray," in Juan E. Hernández y Dávalos, *Colección de documentos para la historia de la Guerra de Independencia de México,* 1:660; and from Francisco de Paula de Arrangoiz y Berzábal, *Méjico desde 1808 hasta 1867,* 1:57; and from the letters of Yermo and the audiencia to the Supreme Junta of Seville, AHN, Estado 57, E, and Consejos 21081. Jáuregui's role in all this was ambivalent. Though a last minute substitute commissioner for Seville, he apparently did not consult with Jabat, knew nothing of the conspiracy, and was shocked and tearful on that night. He was lodged with the virreina in custody and left Mexico with her. See Report of Jáuregui, Cádiz, August 20, 1809, in Genaro García, *Documentos históricos mexicanos,* 2:292–96.

45. "Noticia Historica . . . ," by Vicente Iturrigaray, in Genaro García, *Documentos históricos mexicanos,* 2:361–90.

46. *Recopilación de Indias,* bk. 2, title 20, law 36.

47. Carlos María Bustamante, *Cuadro histórico de la revolución mexicana,* 1:7.

48. Azcárate's case was a long one. In September, 1811, he was released from prison following repeated requests from the city council and the College of Lawyers ("Informe de esta ciudad al Exmo. Sr. Virrey a solicitud del Lic. Juan Francisco Azcárate," A. Ex-A., Ayuntamientos, vol. 395, no. 126). Then the city council began a long legal battle to have his right to practice law and to resume his council seat restored (A. Ex-A., Actas de Cabildo, vol. 130, September 12, 23, 27, 1811; "El Lic. D. Juan Francisco Azcárate sobre que le restituya a su empleo de regidor honorario de esta ciudad," AGN, Ayuntamientos, vol. 183). He was seated on the city council at the end of 1814 for the 1815 term, but his right to practice law was not restored until the viceroy in 1816 granted his permission (A. Ex-A., Actas de Cabildo, vol. 135, May 17, 1816).

49. *Gazeta de México,* March 29, 1809; "Bando en que se inserta el real orden en que se dan las gracias a los sugetos que concurrieron a mantener el buen orden despues de la prisión del Sr. Virrey Iturrigaray," AGN, Impresos oficiales, vol. 29, no. 3; "Carta de la Infanta Doña María Carlota de Borbón al Sr. D. Pedro Garibay," in Hernández y Dávalos, *Colección de documentos,* 1:690.

50. "Apuntes de las gracias que D. Gabriel de Yermo propuso verbalmente en el Real Acuerdo de la Mañana de 16 de septiembre de 1808 . . . y a que accedió el Real Acuerdo," AHN, Estado 57, E; Yermo

to Supreme Junta, Mexico, November 9, 1808, AHN, Estado 57, E;
Order of Garibay to Treasury, Mexico, April 10, 1809, in Genaro
García, *Documentos históricos mexicanos*, 2:256–57.

51. Ladd, "The Mexican Nobility," p. 197.

52. Alamán, *Historia de Méjico*, 1:170–73; "Extracto de la sentencia
pronunciada por el Consejo de Indias contra el virey Iturrigaray,"
Appendix, Doc. 14, 1:365 (the records of the *residencia*, two volumes in
length, are in AHN, Consejos 21081 and 21082).

53. Ladd, "The Mexican Nobility," p. 199.

54. Friedrich, *Tradition and Authority*, pp. 97–98.

55. Brading, *Los orígenes*, pp. 107–9.

56. "La verdad sabida y buena fé guardada por Don Juan López
Cancelada," "Discurso que publica Don Facundo de Lisarza vindican-
do el Exmo. Sr. Don José de Iturrigaray," and "El ayuntamiento de
México pide se asegure a López Cancelada" in Hernández y Dávalos,
Colección de documentos, 1:725 and 3:765; and Juan López Cancelada,
*Conducta del Exmo. Sr. Don José Iturrigaray durante su govierno de Nueva
España*.

57. "Observaciones que presenta a S.M. . . . Juan Jabat," Seville,
December 27, 1808, AHN, Estado 58, E; "Voto consultivo del Real
Acuerdo sobre extinsión de los oficios de regidores del ayuntamiento
de México," AGN, Ayuntamientos, vol. 161.

58. Alamán, *Historia de Méjico*, 1:177.

59. Audiencia to Supreme Governing Junta Central of Seville,
Mexico, April 29, 1809, AGI, Mexico 1662. This long report includes
eight attached documents and, although opinionated, is the best single
source on the 1808 coup (with the exception of Iturrigaray's *residencia*
proceedings in the AHN).

60. Villoro, *El proceso ideológico*, pp. 55–59.

61. Alamán, *Historia de Méjico*, 1:193.

62. "Proclama del arzobispo virrey," January 23, 1810, in Hernández
y Dávalos, *Colección de documentos*, 2:11.

63. Isidoro Saínz de Alfaro to Archbishop-viceroy, Mexico, February
3, 1810, AGI, Mexico 1474; Archbishop-viceroy to Benito Hermida,
Mexico, February 12, 1810, AGI, Mexico 1474.

64. Alamán, *Historia de Méjico*, 1:195, 199–201, 202; Archbishop-
viceroy to Benito Hermida, Mexico, August 30, 1809, AGI, Mexico
1472; "Orden de la plaza de 3 de noviembre de 1809," in Hernández y
Dávalos, *Colección de documentos*, 1:715; Hamill, *The Hidalgo Revolt*, p.
27.

65. Alamán, *Historia de Méjico*, 1:209; A. Ex-A., Actas de Cabildo,
vol. 128, April 17, 1809.

66. "La Junta Superior de Cádiz al real audiencia de México,"

February 28, 1810, A. Ex-A., Reales cédulas y órdenes, vol. 2979, no. 261; see Benson, ed., *Mexico and the Spanish Cortes*, p. 12.

67. Lillian Estelle Fisher, *Champion of Reform, Manuel Abad y Queipo*, p. 117.

68. A. Ex-A., Actas de Cabildo, vol. 129, August 27, 1810; "Expediente instruído en virtud del oficio remitido al Sr. Alcalde ordinario," AGN, Ayuntamientos, vol. 136; "Cuenta del recibimiento del Exmo. Sr. Virrey D. Fr. Xavier Venegas," AGN, Ayuntamientos, vol. 129.

69. See Jesús Romero Flores, *México, historia de una gran ciudad*, p. 481.

70. Alamán says Yermo would have had to create a mayorazgo of 100,000 pesos for his primogeniture, which he did not choose to do (*Historia de Méjico*, 1:220). In addition, Regent Pedro Catani was retired and Guillermo de Aguirre served as Regent until his death which occurred shortly after his appointment. These were precisely the measures proposed by Juan Jabat in 1808.

CHAPTER 3

1. Hamill, "Royalist Counterinsurgency," pp. 470–89.

2. Fisher, *Abad y Queipo*, p. 155.

3. Alamán, *Historia de Méjico*, 1:254; A. Ex-A., Actas de Cabildo, vol. 129, September 24, 1810; Hamill, *The Hidalgo Revolt*, p. 170.

4. Fisher, *Abad y Queipo*, p. 152.

5. Christon I. Archer, "To Serve the King: Military Recruitment in Late Colonial Mexico," *HAHR* 55, no. 2 (May, 1975): 226–50.

6. "Expediente formado a virtud de la acta celebrada por los señores de la Junta de Alistamiento, sobre levantar Batallones de soldados voluntarios de Fernando VII," A. Ex-A., Milicias cívicas, vol. 3272, no. 66.

7. "Testimonios de otros tantos cuadernos y dos originales de la causa instruída contra D. Luis Rodríguez Alconedo y su hermano D. Ignacio por infidencia," "Testimonios duplicados de la causa instruído contra D. Luis Rodríguez Alconedo," and "Sobre D. José Ignacio y D. José Luis Alconedo," AGN, Historia, vol. 108, nos. 3, 4, and 9; Viceroy Garibay to Martín Garay, Mexico, June 30, 1809, AGI, Mexico 1472; "Pieza formada en el Consejo conveniente a la causa formada en México contra D. Antonio Calleja," AHN, Consejos 21212.

8. "Denuncias y anónimos remitidos en octubre, noviembre y diciembre de 1810 sobre la revolución de independencia," AGN, Historia, vol. 108, no. 29.

9. Hamill, *The Hidalgo Revolt*, p. 151.

10. The best summaries of the propaganda will be found in ibid., pp. 151–79; in Hamill, "Early Psychological Warfare in the Hidalgo Re-

239
Notes

volt," *HAHR* 41, no. 2 (May, 1961): 206–35; in Bustamante, *Cuadro histórico de la revolución mexicana*, 1:57–65; and in José María Miquel i Vergés, *La independencia mexicana y la prensa insurgente* (Mexico, 1941). The best treatment of public opinion in general is Javier Ocampo, *Las ideas de un día: el pueblo mexicano ante la consumación de su independencia*.

11. Hamill, *The Hidalgo Revolt*, p. 167.

12. Ibid., p. 176.

13. Perhaps the clearest proof of this is one notable example in which royal propaganda actually backfired. On May 24, 1815, Viceroy Calleja issued a detailed attack against the rebel Constitution of Apatzingán which, in effect, constituted the first widespread distribution of the constitution, for the rebels had not been able to publish it. Anna Macías cites this as an example of royalist overkill (*Génesis del govierno constitucional en México: 1808–1820*, pp. 154–59).

14. Niceto de Zamacois, *Historia de México, desde sus tiempos mas remotos hasta nuestras días*, 6:503.

15. Alamán, *Historia de Méjico*, 1:475, says 1,400; Servando Teresa de Mier, *Historia de la revolución de Nueva España*, p. 325, says 1,300; and José María Luis Mora, *Méjico y sus revoluciones*, 1:73, says 2,500.

16. Zamacois, *Historia de México*, 6:500; "Proclama del ayuntamiento de México," October 20, 1810, in Hernández y Dávalos, *Colección de documentos*, 3:911.

17. Hubert Howe Bancroft, *History of Mexico*, 4:185; José María de Liceaga, *Adiciones y rectificaciones a la historia de México que escribio D. Lucas Alamán*, p. 148; "Informe rendido por el Sr. García Conde al virey," December 8, 1810, in Hernández y Dávalos, *Colección de documentos*, 2:273. See also Alamán, *Historia de Méjico*, doc. 19, 1:375.

18. Hamill, *The Hidalgo Revolt*, 161; Luis Castillo Ledón, *Hidalgo, La vida del héroe*, 2:97.

19. So said the marqués de Rayas in a letter from Mexico to former viceroy Iturrigaray, November 12, 1810, in Hernández y Dávalos, *Colección de documentos*, 1:722.

20. Hamill suggests Hidalgo may have sent a final plea to Venegas for the surrender of the city only a few hours before his retreat (*The Hidalgo Revolt*, p. 178).

21. Ibid., p. 179.

22. Alberto María Carreño, "Hidalgo, Morelos, y el Capitán José María Landa," *Boletín de la Sociedad Mexicana de Geografía y Estadística* 76 July–December, 1953): 47–60. This article reprints the letter to Landa from Hidalgo, dated Celaya, November 13, 1810.

23. "Bando en que la Novilísima Ciudad de México comunica el aniversario . . . de la batalla memorable del Monte de las Cruces," October 6, 1811, AGN, Impresos oficiales, vol. 32, no. 160.

24. Henry George Ward, *Mexico in 1827*, 1:129; Hamill, *The Hidalgo Revolt*, p. 183.

25. Zamacois, *Historia de México*, 6:516; A. Ex-A., Actas de Cabildo, vol. 130, October 5, 1811.

26. Hamill, "Royalist Counterinsurgency," pp. 478–79; Calleja to Secretary of War, Madrid, February 20, 1818, AGI, Ultramar 834.

27. Ibid.

28. For a study of the process by which Oaxaca, for example, struggled to separate itself from the political and economic supremacy of Mexico City in the late colonial period see Hamnett, *Politics and Trade in Southern Mexico*.

29. Brading, *Los orígenes*, p. 114.

30. Hamill says, "The basic fact remains that the rebels were struggling under the onus of the Hidalgo revolt" (*The Hidalgo Revolt*, p. 218).

31. For Morelos and his program see: Wilbert H. Timmons, *Morelos: Priest, Soldier, Statesman of Mexico*; Alfonso Teja Zabre, *Vida de Morelos*; Ernesto Lemoine Villicaña, *Morelos, su vida revolucionaria a través de sus escritos y de otros testimonios de la época*; Luis González, comp., *El Congreso de Anáhuac de 1813*. Anna Macías clarifies the point that the Constitution of Apatzingán was not written by Morelos and his military leaders but was, rather, an attempt by several civilians, chiefly lawyers, to submit Morelos's power to civilian control (*Génesis del govierno constitucional*, pp. 108–17). It should thus be viewed as yet another alternative presented to the Mexican people. And Timmons, in a masterly bit of detective work, found that it would be an overstatement to call Morelos a true agrarian revolutionary ("José María Morelos: Agrarian Reformer?" *HAHR* 35, no. 2 [May, 1956]: 183–95).

32. Bancroft, *History of Mexico*, 4:331; Jesús Romero Flores, *México, historia de una gran ciudad*, p. 484.

33. "Oficio de D. Vicente Ruiz, al virey, sobre la causa de la conspiración de abril de 1811," December 7, 1813, in Hernández y Dávalos, *Colección de documentos*, 5:244.

34. Venegas to Minister of State, Mexico, November 26, 1811, AGI, Mexico 1476: "Causa remitida por el virey de México formada por la Junta de Seguridad de aquel reyno contra Fray Manuel Suarez y Fray Pedro Rivera," AHN, Consejos 21212.

35. A. Ex-A., Actas de Cabildo, vol. 130, August 3, 1811.

36. "El virey avisa al público de que se ha sofocado el movimiento revolucionario en la capital," August 3, 1811, in Hernández y Dávalos, *Colección de documentos*, 3:332.

37. Statements of the two points of view concerning whether a civil court could try the Augustinians are printed in ibid., 3:435, 441.

38. N. M. Farriss, *Crown and Clergy in Colonial Mexico, 1759–1821*, pp. 203–10.

39. Ibid., pp. 221–23.

40. Ibid., p. 211.

41. "Bando sobre pasaportes," February 13, 1811, in Hernández y Dávalos, *Colección de documentos*, 5:867.

42. "Expediente formada en virtud de Superior Oficio de S.E. en que exorta a esta N.C. para que contribuya a los gastos del nuevo establecimiento de Policía," A. Ex-A., Policía, en general, vol. 3629, no. 171.

43. "Expediente formada en virtud del mandato del Exmo. Cabildo de esta N.C. para constancia de los puntos de la nueva policía que dentro se contienen," A. Ex-A., Policía en general, vol. 3629, no. 173.

44. "Resumen de las operaciones de la nueva policía desde el día 26 de agosto último en que fué instalada," January 6, 1812, AGN, Historia, vol. 454.

45. "El ayuntamiento de México representa a V.E. lo que le parece conveniente sobre la nueva policía," October 25, 1811, AGN, Historia, vol. 454; "Expediente instruído sobre el nuevo Reglamento de Policía, y seguridad pública, de mandato del Superior Govierno, y representación que le hizo la N.C.," A. Ex-A., Policía, en general, vol. 3629, no. 176.

46. "Resumen de las operaciones de la nueva policía," AGN, Historia, vol. 454.

47. "Bando de Apodaca sobre pasaportes, repitiendo el bando de Venegas," November 11, 1818, AGN, vol. 43; A. Ex-A., Actas de Cabildo, vol. 669, July 13, 1820; Ayuntamiento to Viceroy Apodaca, Mexico, August 29, 1820, AGI, Mexico 1679; "Del Venadito, sobre usando los pasaportes y manteniendo el orden," March 23, 1821, AGN, Impresos oficiales, vol. 44; "Aviso al público para que ninguna persona de este reyno transite de un lugar a otro sin el correspondiente pasaporte," April 1, 1821, AGN, Impresos oficiales, vol. 44.

48. Pedro de la Puente to Minister of Grace and Justice, Mexico, February 1, 1813, AGI, Mexico 1664.

49. Fisher, *Abad y Queipo*, p. 135; Arrangoiz, *Méjico desde 1808*, 1:400; A. Ex-A., Actas de Cabildo, vol. 130, January 18, 25, and 28, February 4, 1811.

50. Ibid., April 9 and April 26, 1811; Archer, "To Serve the King," pp. 226–50.

51. Alberto María Carreño, *La real y pontificia universidad de México, 1536–1865*, pp. 428–31.

52. Quoted in Arrangoiz, *Méjico desde 1808*, 1:137.

53. "Comunicación del Sr. Calleja al virrey, acusando de falta de patriotismo a los europeos," January 28, 1811, in Hernández y Dávalos, *Colección de documentos*, 2:354; "Expediente sobre que dentro del término de ocho días se completen mil hombres para el regimiento de

Milicias," Mexico, July 31, 1811, A. Ex-A., Milicias cívicas, vol. 3273, no. 72.

54. "Oficios de Pedro de la Puente," AGN, Historia, vol. 456.

55. "Bando sobre colección de fusiles particulares en la ciudad," September 23, 1811, AGN, Historia, vol. 105, no. 20; "Bando en el que fijan penas a los particulares que no entreguen las armas que tengen en su poder," October 5, 1811, in Hernández y Dávalos, *Colección de documentos*, 3:393.

56. "Oficios de Pedro de la Puente," AGN, Historia, vol. 456.

57. Archer, "To Serve the King," pp. 226–50; idem, "Pardos, Indians and the Army of New Spain: Inter-relationships and Conflicts, 1780–1810," *Journal of Latin American Studies* 6, no. 2 (November, 1974): 231–55.

58. Alamán, *Historia de Méjico*, 2:304–5,308; A. Ex-A., Actas de Cabildo, vol. 131, February 14, 1812.

59. Alamán, *Historia de México*, 2:301–5, 340, 347.

60. Ladd, "The Mexican Nobility," p. 216.

61. The most complete biography of Calleja is Carol C. Ferguson, "The Spanish Tamerlaine?: Félix María Calleja, Viceroy of New Spain, 1813–1816," (Ph.D. diss., Texas Christian University, 1973). Ferguson rejects the term Tamerlaine, coined by Carlos María Bustamante in his *Campañas del General D. Félix María Calleja del Rey*, as inappropriate, on the grounds that Calleja, at least before the events of 1808 threw him into the center of events, had not sought the viceroyalty, but aspired to retire and settle on his estate near San Luis Potosí. See also José de Núñez y Dominguez's biography of Calleja's creole wife, *La virreina mexicana: Doña María Francisca de la Gándara de Calleja*. Brief biographies of Calleja and other viceroys appear in Lucas Alamán, *Semblanzas e ideario*, reedition (Mexico, 1939), and Artemio de Valle-Arizpe, *Virreyes y virreinas de Nueva España*. See also Timothy E. Anna, "The Last Viceroys of New Spain and Peru: An Appraisal," *American Historical Review*, 81, no. 1 (February, 1976), 38–65; and Anna, "An Essay on the Mexican Viceroys during the War of Independence: The Question of Legitimacy," Peter Gillis, ed., *Historical Papers, 1975*, pp. 59–78.

62. "El Sr. Virey nombra Governador militar de esta capital al Brigadier Olazabal," April 23, 1814, A. Ex-A., Historia, en general, vol. 2254, no. 74; Alamán, *Historia de Méjico*, 2:349; Mexico City ayuntamiento to Minister of Grace and Justice, Mexico, April 5, 1816, AGI, Mexico 2770; Royal decree, Madrid, June 17, 1818, AGI, Mexico 1322.

63. Juan Friede, *La otra verdad, la independencia americana vista por los españoles*, 2d ed. (Bogotá, 1972).

64. Calleja to Secretary of War, Madrid, February 20, 1818, AGI,

Ultramar 834; José de la Cruz to Secretary of Hacienda, Guadalajara, February 8, 1819, AGI, Ultramar 834; Miguel de Castro Araoz to Secretary of Hacienda, Mérida, March 16, 1819, AGI, Ultramar 834.

65. Calleja to Minister of Hacienda, Mexico, December 31, 1814, AGI, Mexico 1480.

66. "Bando en que se manda que todos los ciudadanos de esta capital desde la edad de 16 años se presenten al alistamiento de Patriotas," October 1, 1813, AGN, Impresos oficiales, vol. 36; A. Ex-A., Actas de Cabildo, vol. 132, May 28, 1813, and vol. 133, November 3, 1814; "Consulta al Exmo. Sr. Virrey sobre que se sirva declarar exentos del servicio militar a los individuos que reunan el cargo de Regidor y el de oficiales urbanos," March 2, 1821, A. Ex-A., Milicias cívicas, vol. 3273, no. 73.

67. "Providencia del Exmo. Sr. Virey sobre que se recojan los ociosos para el regimiento provincial de esta ciudad," January 20, 1815, and "Sobre que se complete la baja del regimiento provincial de esta capital," December 14, 1816, A. Ex-A., Milicias cívicas, vol. 3273, no. 76 and 77; Actas de Cabildo, vol. 136, July 28, 1817. Referring to the prewar era, Archer says; "Residents of Mexico City were by far the greatest experts on draft evasion" ("To Serve the King," pp. 226–50).

68. A. Ex-A., Actas de Cabildo, vol. 133, March 23, 1814.

69. Ibid., vol. 132, July 14, September 3, October 18 and 24, 1813, and vol. 133, June 3, 1814. There was a long history of enlisted men abusing Indians. Archer comments, "Soldiers had little regard for people whom they considered to be their social inferiors" ("Pardos, Indians and the Army of New Spain," pp. 231–55).

70. "Sobre no deberse dar alojamientos a la oficialidad y tropas en las casas particulares de esta capital," A. Ex-A., Milicias cívicas, vol. 3273, no. 74.

71. AGN, Hacienda, Mercedes y salarios, Legajo 546. These letters, in order, are numbers 43, 52, 55, 65, 73, 74, 80, 78, 87, 89, 91, 83, 103, 81, and 66. Most were written by public *escribanos* for their illiterate customers. Even more cases like these can be found in "Oficios de Pedro de la Puente," AGN, Historia, vol. 456.

72. "Oficios de Pedro de la Puente sobre la administración de la policía," AGN, Historia, vol. 454; Alamán, *Historia de Méjico*, 2:280; "Resumen de las operaciones de la nueva policía desde el día 26 de agosto último en que fué instalada," AGN, Historia, vol. 454; Farriss, *Crown and Clergy*, p. 208; "Real orden de las Cortes en quanto el modo de juzgar y castigar a los espios y demas reos de infidencia," February 6, 1812, AGN, Impresos oficiales, vol. 33, no. 8.

73. Mexico, La Junta Directiva del Desagüe, *Memoria histórica, técnica y administrativa de las obras del desagüe del valle de México, 1449–1900*, 1:

252, 258; *Diario de México*, February 9, 1806, December 14 and 28, 1810; Alamán, *Historia de Méjico*, 2: 236–37; Apodaca to Minister of Hacienda, Mexico, September 7, 1817, AGI, Mexico 1493. The most recent studies of hydrology in the Valley of Mexico are Richard E. Boyer, *La gran inundación: Vida y sociedad en la ciudad de México, 1629–1638* (Mexico: Secretaría de Educación Pública, 1975); and Louisa S. Hoberman, "City Planning in Spanish Colonial Government: The Response of Mexico City to the Problem of Floods, 1607–1637," (Ph.D. diss., Columbia University, 1972).

74. Hamill, "Royalist Counterinsurgency," pp. 470–89.

75. Friedrich, *Tradition and Authority*, pp. 45–56, 79–88, 113.

CHAPTER 4

1. For the effects of the Constitution and Cortes on Mexico see Benson, ed., *Mexico and the Spanish Cortes*; Benson, "The Contested Mexican Election of 1812," *HAHR* 26, no. 3 (August, 1946): 336–50; Benson, *La diputación provincial y el federalismo mexicano*; and James F. King, "The Colored Castes and the American Representation in the Cortes of Cádiz," *HAHR* 33, no. 1 (February, 1953): 33–64.

2. Rodríguez, *The Emergence of Spanish America*, pp. 7–10.

3. "Dos certificaciones sobre la elección del Sr. D. José Beye Cisneros para diputado en Cortes," A. Ex-A., Elecciones de diputados a Cortes, vol. 870, no. 3; "Decreto de las Cortes," León, September 24, 1810, A. Ex-A., Reales cédulas y órdenes, vol. 2979, no. 248; "Acta solemne de la instalación de las presentes Cortes," A. Ex-A., Reales cédulas y órdenes, vol. 2979, no. 244.

4. "Sr. Cisneros al Sr. Presidente Regidor y Regidores del Ayuntamiento de México," Cádiz, April 18, 1812, A. Ex-A., Elecciones de diputados a Cortes, vol. 870, no. 3.

5. "Representación de la diputación americana en las Cortes," August 1, 1811, AGN, Impresos oficiales, vol. 60, no. 44. For another discussion of this representation and of Cisneros's, see W. Woodrow Anderson, "Reform as a Means to Quell Revolution," in Benson, ed., *Mexico and the Spanish Cortes*, pp. 188–92.

6. "Informe que hizo el Dr. D. José Beye de Cisneros a las Cortes como diputado de este Exmo. Ayuntamiento de México," 1811, A. Ex-A., Elecciones de diputados a Cortes, vol. 870, no. 9.

7. "Decreto de las Cortes sobre que los Europeos y Americanos son iguales en derechos," October 15, 1810, A. Ex-A., Reales cédulas y órdenes, vol. 2979, no. 255; A. Ex-A., Actas de Cabildo, vol. 130, March 15, 1811, and vol. 131, July 31, 1812.

8. "Expediente relativo a la libertad de imprentas para que los ciudadanos puedan publicar sus pensamientos," A. Ex-A., Reales cédulas y órdenes, vol. 2979, no. 293.

9. A. Ex-A., Actas de Cabildo, vol. 130, January 23, 1811; Clarice Neal, "Freedom of the Press in New Spain, 1810–1820," in Benson, ed., *Mexico and the Spanish Cortes*, p. 88.

10. Ibid., pp. 88–91.

11. Arrangoiz, *Méjico desde 1808*, 1:145; "Expediente formada en virtud del superior oficio del virey con el que acompaña el Bando que mando publicar sobre los papeles sediciosos venidos de Sultepec," April 7, 1812, A. Ex-A., Historia, en general. vol. 2254, no. 64.

12. A. Ex-A., Actas de Cabildo, vol. 131, June 19, 1812.

13. Luis González Obregón, ed., *La constitución de 1812 en la Nueva España*, 2 vols. (Mexico: Archivo General de la Nación, 1912), 1:1; A. Ex-A., Actas de Cabildo, vol. 131, September 11 and 18, 1812.

14. The most easily available copy of the Constitution is in Hernández y Dávalos, *Colección de documentos*, 4: 50.

15. Benson, *La diputación provincial*, p. 21; See also David T. Garza, "Mexican Constitutional Expression in the Cortes of Cádiz," in Benson, ed., *Mexico and the Spanish Cortes*, p. 56.

16. Charles R. Berry, "The Election of the Mexican Deputies to the Spanish Cortes, 1810–1822," in Benson, ed., *Mexico and the Spanish Cortes*, p. 22; Benson, *La diputación provincial*; Garza, "Mexican Constitutional Expression," pp. 57–58; Charles W. Macune, Jr., "A Test of Federalism: Political, Economic, and Ecclesiastical Relations between the State of Mexico and the Mexican Nation, 1823–1835," (Ph.D. diss., University of Texas, Austin, 1970).

17. Roger L. Cunniff, "Mexican Municipal Electoral Reform, 1810–1822," in Benson, ed., *Mexico and the Spanish Cortes*, pp. 64–65.

18. A. Ex-A., Actas de Cabildo, vol. 131, September 24, October 5 and 9, 1812.

19. Audiencia to the Cortes, Mexico, November 18, 1813, AGI, Mexico 1664.

20. Spell, *The Life and Works of José Joaquín Fernández de Lizardi*, pp. 36–37.

21. A. Ex-A., Actas de Cabildo, vol. 131, October 29, 1812; "Sobre que se incorpore en la guía de forasteros a los Sres. Regidores del extinguido ayuntamiento perpetuo," March 24, 1813, AGN, Ayuntamientos, vol. 178.

22. A. Ex-A., Actas de Cabildo, vol. 131, November 3, 1812; Benson, "The Contested Mexico Election of 1812," pp. 336–50.

23. A. Ex-A., Actas de Cabildo, vol. 131, November 17, 1812.

24. Ibid., November 24 and 26, 1812; "Real orden de 6 de marzo de 1812 sobre la voz que han de tener los eclesiásticos en las elecciones de ayuntamientos constitucionales," AGN, Ayuntamientos, vol. 183.

25. A. Ex-A., Actas de Cabildo, vol. 131, December 1, 1812.

26. Audiencia to Cortes, Mexico, November 18, 1813, AGI, Mexico 1664; See also Calleja to Minister of Ultramar, Mexico, June 22, 1813, AGI, Mexico 1480.

27. Calleja to Minister of Ultramar, Mexico, June 22, 1813, AGI, Mexico 1480.

28. Los Guadalupes to Morelos, Mexico, December 7, 1812, AGI, Mexico 1482.

29. Benson, ed., *Mexico and the Spanish Cortes*, p. 8; A. Ex-A., Actas de Cabildo, vol. 131, December 14, 1812.

30. Audiencia to Cortes, Mexico, November 18, 1813, AGI, Mexico 1664; Venegas to Minister of State, Mexico, December 27, 1812, AGI, Mexico 1322; Calleja to Minister of Grace and Justice, Mexico, August 18, 1814, AGI, Mexico 1482; Benson, "The Contested Mexican Election of 1812," pp. 336–50.

31. Los Guadalupes to Morelos, Mexico, January 20, 1813, AGI, Mexico 1482.

32. "Comunicación de D. Francisco Galicia, fecha 3 de enero, al Sr. Rayón, avisandole de cual es el estado que guarda México," in Hernández y Dávalos, *Colección de documentos*, 4:2.

33. A. Ex-A., Actas de Cabildo, vol. 132, March 1, 1813.

34. Los Guadalupes to Morelos, Mexico, March 5, 1813, AGI, Mexico 1482.

35. Calleja to Minister of Grace and Justice, Mexico, June 16, 1813, AGI, Mexico 1322; A. Ex-A., Actas de Cabildo, vol. 132, April 7, 1813; Calleja to Minister of Grace and Justice, August 18, 1814, AGI, Mexico 1482; Audiencia to Cortes, November 18, 1813, AGI, Mexico 1664.

36. "Instrucción para facilitar las elecciones de diputados para las próximas Cortes generales del año de 1813," AGN, Ayuntamientos, vol. 168.

37. "Proclama del Sr. Calleja al tomar el mando de este virreynato," March 26, 1813, AGN, Impresos oficiales, vol. 35, no. 14.

38. "Manifesto del Virey Calleja dando una idea de la situación del país y de la revolución," June 22, 1814, in Hernández y Dávalos, *Colección de documentos*, 5:554.

39. A. Ex-A., Actas de Cabildo, vol. 132, September 27, 1813.

40. Benson, ed., *Mexico and the Spanish Cortes*, pp. 8–9.

41. Calleja to Minister of Ultramar, Mexico, June 22, 1813, AGI, Mexico 1480; Berry, "Elections of Mexican Deputies," p. 24.

42. Audiencia to Cortes, November 18, 1813, AGI, Mexico, 1664.

43. A. Ex-A., Actas de Cabildo, vol. 132, June 18, 1813.

44. Wilbert H. Timmons, "Los Guadalupes: A Secret Society in the Mexican Revolution for Independence," *HAHR* 30, no. 4 (November, 1950), 453–499. See also Timmons, *Morelos*, pp. 85–95; Ernesto de la Torre Villar, ed., *Los "Guadalupes" y la independencia*; and Anastasio Zerecero, *Memorias para la historia de las revoluciones de México*. The correspondence of the Guadalupes is available in AGI, Mexico 1482 and Indiferente general 110, and in the Latin American Collection, University of Texas Library, Austin.

45. Zerecero, *Memorias*, pp. 253–54; Timmons, "Los Guadalupes," pp. 453–99.

46. A. Ex-A., Actas de Cabildo, vol. 132, April 8, 13, and 21, 1813; Calleja to Minister of Ultramar, Mexico, March 24, 1814, AGI, Mexico 1483.

47. "Plan de comisiones de esta N.C. repartidas entre los individuos de su ayuntamiento remitido a S.E. y oficio de su aprovación," April 21, 1813, A. Ex-A., Ayuntamiento, Comisiones, vol. 406, no. 10; A. Ex-A., Actas de Cabildo, vol. 133, December 30, 1814, and vol. 134, February 27, 1815.

48. Law of June 23, 1813, in Basilio José Arrillaga, ed., *Recopilación de leyes, decretos, y circulares de los supremos poderes de los Estados-Unidos Mexicanos* (Mexico, 1850), p. 205.

49. A. Ex-A., Actas de Cabildo, vol. 133, January 1, 1814.

50. Ibid., April 4, 1814.

51. Audiencia to Cortes, November 18, 1813, AGI, Mexico 1664.

52. Pedro de la Puente to Minister of Grace and Justice, Mexico, December 15, 1812, AGI, Mexico 1664. For further information on the clergy's involvement in the rebellion, see Farriss, *Crown and Clergy in Colonial Mexico*; Karl M. Schmitt, "The Clergy and the Independence of New Spain," *HAHR* 34, no. 3 (August, 1954): 289–312. See also José Bravo Ugarte's articles entitled "El clero y la independencia," in the following issues of *Abside*: 5 (1941): 612–30; 7 (1943): 406–9; 15 (1951): 199–218.

53. "Una lista de los facciosos de varios puntos que dieron su voto al Cabecilla Morelos para que fuese electo Generalíssimo," AGI, Mexico 1482.

54. Calleja to Minister of Ultramar, Mexico, June 22, 1813, AGI, Mexico 1480.

55. Pedro de la Puente to Minister of Grace and Justice, Mexico, February 1, 1813, AGI, Mexico 1664.

56. Calleja to Minister of Ultramar, Mexico, April 6, 1815, AGI, Mexico 1488.

57. Audiencia to Antonio Cano Manuel, Mexico, December 7, 1813, AGI, Mexico 1664; Calleja to Manuel, Mexico, December 31, 1813, AGI, Mexico 1480.

58. Miguel Bataller to the Council of the Regency, Mexico, January 1, 1814, AGI, Mexico 1664; Ambrosio Sagarzurrieta to the Council of the Regency, Mexico, January 8, 1814, AGI, Mexico 1664.

59. Calleja to Minister of Grace and Justice, Mexico, March 15, 1813, AGI, Mexico 1480; Calleja to Minister of Grace and Justice, Mexico, January 24, 1814, AGI, Mexico 1484.

60. Calleja to Minister of Grace and Justice, Mexico, January 24, 1814, AGI, Mexico 1484. Osés later returned to the audiencia.

61. Calleja to Minister of Grace and Justice, Mexico, July 31, 1814, AGI, Mexico 1483; Audiencia to King, Mexico, October 29, 1814, AGI, Mexico 1483.

62. Raymond Carr, *Spain: 1808–1939*, p. 84.

63. "Decreto expedido en Valencia en 4 de mayo por D. Fernando VII," A. Ex-A., Historia, en general, vol. 2254, no. 73. The rebels replied to the annullment of the Cádiz Constitution by completing, under auspices of the Congress of Chilpancingo, their own Constitution of Apatzingán (promulgated in October, 1814), which they hoped would attract the support of the disaffected creole liberals. It failed to do so. Anna Macías, *Génesis del gobierno constitucional*, pp. 103–6, 170–71.

64. A. Ex-A., Actas de Cabildo, vol. 133, August 22, 1814; Calleja to Minister of Grace and Justice, Mexico, August 27, 1814, AGI, Mexico 1482.

65. Audiencia to King, October 29, 1814, AGI, Mexico 1483; A. Ex-A., Actas de Cabildo, vol. 133, September 19, October 10, November 25, and December 15, 1814.

66. A. Ex-A., Actas de Cabildo, vol. 133, December 17 and 19, 1814.

67. A. Ex-A., Actas de Cabildo, vol. 134, February 10 and 28, 1815, and vol. 135, July 29, 1816.

68. Ibid., vol. 134, February 28, March 29, 1815.

69. "Averiguación de la conducta del regidor D. Ignacio Adalid, con el cabecilla Eugenio Montaño," AGI, Indiferente general 1523; Calleja to the King, Mexico, March 25, 1814, AGI, Indiferente general 1523; "Consejo de Indias en Sala de Justicia," June 25, 1817, AGI, Mexico 1147; Calleja to Minister of the Indies, Mexico, April 6, 1815, AGI, Mexico 1488; "El Ayuntamiento de México informa a V.M. sobre la conducta y meritos del Alcalde de Corte honorario de este Rl. Audiencia D. José María Fagoaga," Mexico, March 31, 1815, AGI, Mexico 1488; Calleja to Minister of the Indies, Mexico, September 30, 1815, AGI,

Mexico 1488; "Testimonio del cuaderno de la causa instruída al Sr. D. José María Fagoaga sobre infidencia, año de 1815," AGI, Mexico 1488; "El consejo de Indias en Sala de Justicia," July 15, 1817, AGI, Mexico 1147. See also Ladd, "The Mexican Nobility," pp. 222–24.

70. Calleja to Minister of Grace and Justice, Mexico, August 18, 1814, AGI, Mexico 1482. The translation is from Ward, *Mexico in 1827*, 1:512–22.

71. Cabildo to Minister of Grace and Justice, Mexico, April 5, 1816, AGI, Mexico 2770; Alamán, *Historia de Méjico*, 4:308; Audiencia to Cortes, Mexico, November 18, 1813, AGI, Mexico 1664 (the translation is from Ward, *Mexico in 1827*, 1:497–509.

72. See Ocampo's discussion of the writings of José María Tornel, who gave as a chief cause for independence the failure of Spanish administrators to apply the reforms to Mexico. (*Las ideas de un día*, pp. 151–52.

73. Richard Herr, *An Historical Essay on Modern Spain*, p. 76. For more detail on this period, see Miguel Artola Gallego, *La España de Fernando VII*, vol. 26 in Ramón Menéndez Pidal, ed., *Historia de España* (Madrid: Espasa-Calpe, 1968); Artola, *La burgesía revolucionaria*; and Carr, *Spain, 1808–1939*.

74. Stanley G. Payne, *A History of Spain and Portugal*, 2:428; Miguel Artola, ed., *Memorias de Tiempos de Fernando VII*, 2 vols., Biblioteca de Autores Españoles, nos. 97 and 98 (Madrid: Ediciones Atlas, 1957), 1:lv; Carr, *Spain: 1808–1939*, 120.

75. Consulta of Junta of Pacification, Madrid, copy dated February 8, 1817, AGI, Estado 86, A.

76. See, for example, the reports that nearly fill AGI, Indiferente 1354.

77. Many of these exceptionally important opinions are found in AGI, Estado 87.

78. Memoria of Conde de Vistaflorida, Madrid, August 31, 1814, AGI, Estado 87; José García de León y Pizarro, *Memorias*, Alvaro Alonso-Castrillo, ed., 2 vols. (Madrid: Revista de Occidente, 1953), 1:264, 266–67; Calleja to Minister of Estado, Arcos de la Frontera, September 29, 1819, AGI, Estado 103; Carr, *Spain, 1808–1939*, 123.

79. Pizarro, *Memorias*, 1:278, 281.

80. Quoted Hamill, *The Hidalgo Revolt*, p. 220.

81. Ward, *Mexico in 1827*, 1:198; Ocampo, *Las ideas de un día*, pp. 157–63.

82. Friedrich, *Tradition and Authority*, p. 121.

83. "Cuaderno de contestaciones entre el Virey de Nueva España y el Obispo de Puebla," copy dated July 12, 1816, AGI, Estado 31.

84. "Letter from Jamaica," in Simón Bolívar, *Selected Writings of Bolívar*, 1:103–22.

85. Ferguson, "The Spanish Tamerlaine?," p. 206.

CHAPTER 5

1. Florescano, *Precios del maíz*, p. 191; John Tutino, "Hacienda Social Relations in Mexico: The Chalco Region in the Era of Independence," *HAHR* 55, no. 3 (August, 1975): 496–528; A. Ex-A., Actas de Cabildo, vol. 133, August 29, 1814; "El ayuntamiento constitucional de esta capital solicita permiso para extraer de los Arcos del Pósito los 8,000 pesos existentes," July 10, 1813, AGN, Ayuntamientos, vol. 243.

2. Florescano, *Precios del maíz*, p. 224.

3. Apodaca to Minister of Hacienda, Mexico, August 27, 1817, AGI, Mexico 1322.

4. "Producto de la recaudación de los ramos de la Real Hacienda, en la Aduana de México, durante los años de 1810, 1811, y 1812," Archivo General de Hacienda, Mexico (hereafter cited as A. G. Hac.), Aduanas, Legajo 117, no. 46; "Estados que presentan los productos de algunos ramos de la Real Hacienda, recaudada en la Aduana de México en los años 1816 al 1823," A.G.Hac., Legajo 117, no. 129.

5. "Reglamento para el abasto de carnes en la capital," April 13, 1811, in Hernández y Dávalos, *Colección de documentos*, 2:927.

6. "Sobre abasto del Valle y ciudad de México," AGN, Ayuntamientos, vol. 161; A. Ex-A., Actas de Cabildo, vol. 133, August 27, 1814.

7. Ibid., August 29, 1814; "Al Virrey de Nueva España, participandole haver aprobado S.M. los arbitrios impuestos a las carnes que se introducen a esta ciudad," Madrid, April 23, 1819, AGN, Reales cédulas, vol. 220, no. 161.

8. A. Ex-A., Actas de Cabildo, vol. 132, July 14 and 30, 1813.

9. Ibid., October 29, November 5, 6, and 8, 1813.

10. Calleja to Minister of Hacienda, Mexico, September 30, 1814, AGI, Mexico 1484.

11. "Representación dirigida al virey por la junta de policía y tranquilidad pública de la ciudad de México," December 31, 1811, in Hernández y Dávalos, *Colección de documentos*, 4:714.

12. "Oficio del Exmo. Sr. Virey de 21 de marzo ultimo, sobre que este Tribunal le informe lo que se le ofrezca en razón de las circunstancias del trafico de Veracruz," A.G.Hac., Consulado de México, Legajo 216, no. 3.

13. "Documentos concernientes el establecimiento del camino militar de Perote a Veracruz, año de 1813," AGN, Historia, vol. 338, no. 1.

14. "Contestaciones del Governador de Veracruz exponiendo infinitas dificultades para el establecimiento del camino militar," AGN, Historia, vol. 338, no. 5; "Aprovando el aumento del ceremonial con que se anuncia la llegada del correo de España," March 28, 1818, AGN, Reales cédulas, vol. 218, no. 193.

15. "Oficios y cartas de Apodaca al Sr. Ministro de Guerra," AGN, Historia, vol. 152, no. 2; A. Ex-A., Actas de Cabildo, vol. 138, June 21, 1819.

16. Venegas to Minister of Hacienda, Mexico, March 6, 1811, AGI, Mexico 1635.

17. Romeo Flores Caballero, *La contrarevolución*, pp. 28–65. For a description of the workings of the *capellanías* see Costeloe, *Church Wealth in Mexico*.

18. Ladd, "The Mexican Nobility," p. 61; Zamacois, *Historia de México*, 6:561–63, 7:813; A. Ex-A., Actas de Cabildo, vol. 134, March 29, 1815.

19. Ladd, "The Mexican Nobility," p. 101.

20. *Gazeta de México*, October 12 and 25, 1808; "Proclama en que el Sr. Garibay exhorta a los havitantes de este reyno a que cooperan con donativos a los socorros de España," April 20, 1809, AGN, Impresos oficiales, vol. 29, no. 2; *Gazeta de México*, July 7, August 11, 1809; Venegas to Minister of Hacienda, September 20, 1810, AGN, Virreyes, vol. 248, no. 4.

21. "Préstamo patriótico ejecutivo para despachar al navio inglés el *Beluarte*," A.G.Hac., Donativos y préstamos, Legajo 1, no. 7.

22. "Subscriptores y cantidades con que concurren al fondo que se esta formando con el objeto de premiar a los que descubrian y denuncien a los citados," A.G.Hac., Donativos y préstamos, Legajo 1, no. 1; Arrangoiz, *Méjico desde 1808*, 1:121, 144; A. Ex-A., Actas de Cabildo, vol. 130, March 29, 1811.

23. Royal Order, Seville, January 2, 1810, AHN, Estado 11; Calleja to Luis Salazar, Mexico, October 31, 1814, AGI, Mexico 1484; "Real orden sobre contribuciones para la guerra," Cádiz, January 31, 1812, A. Ex-A., Reales cédulas y órdenes, vol. 2979, no. 331.

24. "Bando sobre el préstamo patriótico de 20 millones de pesos fuertes," May 29, 1810, AGN, Impresos oficiales, vol. 30, no. 22; "Balanza del comercio de Veracruz en 1810," in Hernández y Dávalos, *Colección de documentos*, 4:871; "Reglamento formado por la Real Junta de préstamo patriótico para el govierno económico de los Consulados," August 23, 1810, A.G.Hac., Donativos y préstamos, Legajo 223, no. 6; "Sobre consultar al Virey se saquen 25,000 pesos a réditos para cooperar al préstamo patriótico," A. Ex-A., Hacienda, Créditos pasivos, vol. 2067, no. 70.

25. "Ordenes para el préstamo de dos millones de pesos con destino al urgente socorro de la peninsula," A.G.Hac., Donativos y préstamos, Legajo 1, no. 3; "Dos millones de pesos—Préstamo destinado para el socorro urgente de la peninsula," A.G.Hac., Donativos y préstamos, Legajo 1, no. 6.

26. "Circular acompañando exemplares del bando sobre exacción de 10% sobre el producto de los arrendamientos de casas," February 24, 1812, AGN, Impresos oficiales, vol. 33, no. 13. Morales has shown how complete the census for private property owners was, although it is not clear if institutions, such as convents occupied by members of their orders, were taxed. The completeness of the statistics, at any rate, suggests that this tax was not merely a dead letter ("Estructura urbana y distribución de la propiedad en la ciudad de México en 1813," pp. 363–402.

27. A. Ex-A., Actas de Cabildo, vol. 132, March 29, 1813; Apodaca to Minister of Hacienda, Mexico, April 30, 1817, AGI, Mexico 1493; Arrangoiz, *Méjico desde 1808*, 1:265.

28. A. Ex-A., Actas de Cabildo, vol. 131, September 7, 1812; Calleja's report to the Junta de Arbitrios, Mexico, July 24, 1813, AGI, Mexico 1322.

29. Arrangoiz, *Méjico desde 1808*, 1:204; "Prestamistas del pedido por el virey en marzo de 1813," in Hernández y Dávalos, *Colección de documentos*, 5:11.

30. Calleja to Minister of Ultramar, Mexico, December 31, 1813, AGI, Mexico 1322; the Spanish income tax is explained in a Royal Cédula, Cádiz, July 8, 1810, AGI, Indiferente general 677; "Circular y bando que se ha mandado publicar sobre la contribución directa para atender a los urgentes necesidades del Estado," December 19, 1813, AGN, Impresos oficiales, vol. 36; A. Ex-A., Actas de Cabildo, vol. 133, February 19, 1814; "Circular y bando publicado en esta capital sobre contribución directa general de guerra," October 14, 1812, AGN, Impresos oficiales, vol. 37; Audiencia to the King, Mexico, October 27, 1814, AGI, Mexico 1664.

31. A. Ex-A., Actas de Cabildo, vol. 134, January 3, 1815; vol. 133, July 8 and 22, 1814; Arrangoiz, *Méjico desde 1808*, 1:265; "Oficios de la superintendencia de la policía de México," AGN, Historia, vol. 459.

32. "Reglamento para la lotería forzosa," December 14, 1815, AGN, Impresos oficiales, vol. 38; José María Cordoncillo Samada, *Historia de la Real Lotería en Nueva España (1770–1821)*, p. 72.

33. "Comunicando estar satisfecho de las ventajas que se han obtenido para el Erario," Madrid, September 11, 1818, AGN, Reales cédulas, vol. 219, no. 149; "Aprobando las medidas tomadas a fin de extinguir la lotería—llamada forzosa," Madrid, May 10, 1820, AGN,

Reales cédulas, vol. 223, no. 33; "Oficios de Apodaca," Mexico, October 31, 1816, AGN, Historia 152.

34. "Estados de las rentas de esta N.C. y sus gravamenes con un informe sobre su origin, año de 1801," A. Ex-A., Créditos pasivos, vol. 2067, no. 54; "Varias adiciones puestas por el Sr. Regidor Francisco Urrutia a las cuentas de Propios desde los años de 1798 hasta 1807," A. Ex-A., Cuentas remitidas a la Contaduría de Propios, vol. 2234, no. 49. For more complete information see Anna, "The Finances of Mexico City," pp. 55–75.

35. "Orden de la Regencia del Imperio para que se remita un estado del ingreso de caudales desde marzo de 1816 hasta fin de octubre de este año," November 22, 1821, A. Ex-A., Hacienda, Aduana, vol. 2000, no. 13.

36. "Razón de lo recaudado en la Aduana de México en los años de 1817–1820," A.G.Hac., Aduana, Legajo 117, no. 84; "Estado que manifieste los rendimientos que el derecho municipal de mercados ha producido a la N.C. desde 1810 hasta marzo de 1816," AGI, Mexico 1489, no. 4; Apodaca to Minister of Ultramar, Mexico, September 30, 1820, AGI, Mexico 1679.

37. "El Real Tribunal del Consulado demanda 28,600 pesos . . . de los fondos de la N.C.," A. Ex-A., Créditos pasivos, vol. 2067, no. 109; "Sobre que la N.C. pague los réditos del capital de 50,000 pesos," AGN, Ayuntamientos, vol. 137; A. Ex-A., Actas de Cabildo, vol. 135, April 26, 1816; "Expediente formado en virtud de superior oficio del virey sobre que las ciudades de este Reyno deben contribuir a esta N.C.," A. Ex-A., Policía y Acordada, vol. 3620, no. 36.

38. Apodaca to Minister of Grace and Justice, Mexico, January 31, 1817, AGI, Mexico 1492.

39. "Sobre que se pasen al Exmo. Sr. Virey las cuentas de las rentas de esta N.C. para su aprobación," A. Ex-A., Ayuntamiento, Propios, vol. 411, no. 2; "Incidente del expediente sobre el paso de las cuentas de esta N.C. a la Contaduría de Propios," A. Ex-A., Cuentas remitidas a la Contaduría de Propios, vol. 2234, no. 53.

40. A. Ex-A., Actas de Cabildo, vol. 133, November 4, 1814; vol. 136, September 6 and 9, 1817; vol. 132, September 13 and 27, 1813; "D. Benito Larrañaga quexandose del nombramiento de Tesorero de la N. Ciudad hecho en D. José Ignacio Náxera," AGN, Ayuntamientos, vol. 183.

41. A. Ex-A., Actas de Cabildo, vol. 131, February 19, April 24, May 14, and June 8, 1812.

42. Ibid., vol. 133, October 17 and December 30, 1814, and vol. 134, February 27, 1815. Larrañaga's report is "Lista de las dependencias activas de la N.C.," August 20, 1813, A. Ex-A., Hacienda, Créditos

activos, vol. 2058, no. 34; Sánchez de Tagle's speech, Actas de Cabildo, vol. 134, April 22, 1815.

43. "Colección de los Generales que cada trimestre se dan al público del ingreso y egreso de caudales de esta N.C.," A. Ex-A., Hacienda, Cuentas municipales y de plaza, vol. 2000, no. 9; A. Ex-A., Actas de Cabildo, vol. 138, May 7, 1819, and vol. 672, April 2, 1821.

CHAPTER 6

1. Louisa S. Hoberman, "Bureaucracy and Disaster: Mexico City and the Flood of 1629," *Journal of Latin American Studies* 6, no. 2 (November, 1974): 211–30; see also Hoberman, "City Planning in Spanish Colonial Government," and Richard E. Boyer, *La gran inundación.*

2. Florescano, *Precios del maíz,* p. 163; for detail on some of the epidemics see Cooper, *Epidemic Diseases.*

3. *Diario de México,* May 20, 1813.

4. "Expediente formado en virtud de Superior Oficio sobre que se tome providencia de que se impenda la limpia de calles de esta ciudad," A. Ex-A., Limpia de ciudad, vol. 3243, no. 107.

5. "Expediente formado en virtud de oficio del Exmo. Sr. Virey sobre aseo y decoro de esta capital," October 12, 1810, A. Ex-A., Policía, en general, vol. 3629, no. 169; "Expediente instruído por el Sr. Intendente Corregidor," April 10, 1811, A. Ex-A., Limpia de ciudad, vol. 3242, no. 109; A. Ex-A., Actas de Cabildo, vol. 131, February 14, 1812; "Oficio del Sr. Intendente sobre que se trasladen a los arrabales de esta ciudad los ataudes . . . para evitar el contagio," February 20, 1812, A. Ex-A., Policía, Salubridad, vol. 3688, no. 6.

6. A. Ex-A., Actas de Cabildo, vol. 132, January 15, February 5 and 10, 1813.

7. Cooper, *Epidemic Diseases,* pp. 158, 163–64.

8. A. Ex-A., Actas de Cabildo, vol. 132, April 26, 28, and 29, July 24, 1813; Cooper, *Epidemic Diseases,* p. 165; "Medidas tomadas para evitar el contagio de las calenturas que padecen los habitantes suburbios de esta capital," AGN, Ayuntamientos, vol. 178; Calleja to Minister of Ultramar, Mexico, January 24, 1814, AGI, Mexico 1484.

9. "Medidas tomadas para evitar el contagio," AGN, Ayuntamientos, vol. 178; A. Ex-A., Actas de Cabildo, vol. 132, May 6, 10, and 28, 1813.

10. Ibid., May 11, 1813; *Gazeta de México,* May 28, 1813; Calleja to Minister of Ultramar, Mexico, January 24, 1814, AGI, Mexico 1484.

11. Cooper, *Epidemic Diseases,* p. 171; *Diario de México,* June 14, 1813.

12. "El ayuntamiento constitucional de esta capital solicita permiso para extraer de los Arcos del Pósito los 8,000 pesos existentes," July 10,

1813, AGN, Ayuntamientos, vol. 243; A. Ex-A., Actas de Cabildo, vol. 132, June 11, July 10 and August 14, 1813.

13. Ibid., May 6 and June 9, 1813; Cooper, *Epidemic Diseases*, p. 175.

14. "Providencias para que el asentista de la limpia D. Rafael Morales cumpla las condiciones de su contrata," June 18, 1813, and "Entrega del Asentista D. Rafael Morales por recisión de la contrata," June 30, 1813, A. Ex-A., Limpia de ciudad, vol. 3242, nos. 115 and 112; "Oficio de S.E. avisando a este ayuntamiento haver dado orden de que se entregue a esta N.C. todo lo perteneciente al Desagüe," A. Ex-A., Desagüe, vol. 741, no. 54.

15. "Bando sobre que ningun vecino de esta capital se escuse a recibir del ayuntamiento el encargo de darle parte de los defectos de policía," July 19, 1813, AGN, Impresos oficiales, vol. 35.

16. A. Ex-A., Actas de Cabildo, vol. 132, August 14, 1813.

17. "Sobre reparo del Río nuevo de la jurisdicción de Coyoacán, y medios para evitar las inundaciones que se temen en esta capital," A. Ex-A., Desagüe, vol. 741, no. 58; Hoberman, "Bureaucracy and Disaster," 221–30 (illustrates the use of Indian labor drafts in drainage work); A. Ex-A., Actas de Cabildo, vol. 133, February 18 and 28, March 5, 1814.

18. A. Ex-A., Actas de Cabildo, vol. 132, December 3, 1813.

19. Ibid., September 10, 1813. Calleja to Minister of Ultramar, Mexico, January 24, 1814, AGI, Mexico 1484; Navarro y Noriega, "Memoria sobre la población," AGN, Impresos oficiales, vol. 60, no. 48.

20. A. Ex-A., Actas de Cabildo, vol. 132, August 20, September 3, and September 10, 1813; "Ocurso de los boticarios sobre que se les satisfagan las cantidades que demandan procedidas de Medicinas," A. Ex-A., Hacienda, Créditos activos, vol. 2058, no. 32; A. Ex-A., Actas de Cabildo, vol. 133, September 12, 1814.

21. A. Ex-A., Actas de Cabildo, vol. 133, May 9, 20, and 23, 1814.

22. "Instrucción formada para ministrar la vacuña," May 17, 1814, AGI, Mexico 1488; A. Ex-A., Actas de Cabildo, vol. 133, July 15, August 1, 1814, and vol. 134, February 23, 1815.

23. "Expediente sobre los reparos del canal y otros puntos del Desagüe," A. Ex-A., Desagüe, vol. 741, no. 55.

24. A. Ex-A., Actas de Cabildo, vol. 134, May 8, September 15, 1815.

25. "Sobre que salga a la almoneda para su remate la contrata de la limpia de calles," A. Ex-A., Limpia de ciudad, vol. 3242, no. 117; Contract with Bustamante, January 29, 1819, A. Ex-A., Limpia de ciudad, vol. 3242, no. 119.

26. A. Ex-A., Actas de Cabildo, vol. 138, July 12, 1819; "Sobre que el Sr. Procurador general y Maestros mayores de ciudad informen las

causas de la inundación de las calzadas," A. Ex-A., Historia, Inundaciones, vol. 2273; Apodaca to Minister of Grace and Justice, Mexico, September 30, 1819, AGN, Virreyes, vol. 280, no. 220; "Expediente instruído sobre la limpia de Ríos de este presente año," A. Ex-A., Historia, Inundaciones, vol. 2273.

27. A. Ex-A., Actas de Cabildo, vol. 669, July 20 and 21, 1820.

28. "La junta de sanidad sobre haver resuelto imprimir y distribuir gratis el método curativo de la toz de los niños," October 25, 1820, A. Ex-A., Policía, Salubridad, vol. 3668, no. 7; A. Ex-A., Actas de Cabildo vol. 669, November 9, 1821, and vol. 672, February 15, 1821.

29. A. Ex-A., Actas de Cabildo, vol. 669, August 29, 1820.

30. "Lista de causas de la tercera Sala de esta audiencia territorial para el año de 1820," AGN, Impresos oficiales, vol. 60; A. Ex-A., Actas de Cabildo, vol. 133, August 8, 1814, and vol. 134, January 20, 1815; "Sobre provisión de las plazas vacantes de Guardas del alumbrado de esta capital," AGN, Ayuntamientos, vol. 243.

31. A. Ex-A., Actas de Cabildo, vol. 133, June 3, August 5, 1814; "Circular sobre el modo con que los gefes políticos deben proceder con los vagos y mal entretenidos y los que no tengan ocupación," October 11, 1820, AGN, Impresos oficiales, vol. 60, no. 68.

32. "Anselmo del Río pide se estudien y manden observar las Ordenanzas para el ramo de instrucción pública formadas por el," A. Ex-A., Instrucción pública, en general, vol. 2477, no. 168.

33. "Instrucción presentado por el Maestro Mayor de primeras letras para el arreglo de las escuelas," July 21, 1813, A. Ex-A., Instrucción pública, en general, vol. 2477, no. 185.

34. A. Ex-A., Actas de Cabildo, vol. 136, January 22, 1817.

35. "Expediente formado sobre el cumplimiento de la real cédula de 20 de octubre de 1817 relativa al establecimiento de escuelas en los conventos," AGN, Historia, Instrucción pública, vol. 499.

36. "Copia del expediente promovido por el Rector del Colegio de San Juan de Letrán sobre que se reuna a dicho colegio la escuela pia que sostiene el ayuntamiento," A. Ex-A., Instrucción pública, en general, vol. 2477, no. 214; Juan Batista Arechederreta to the King, Mexico, August 25, 1818, AGI, Mexico 1147; Apodaca to Minister of Ultramar, Mexico, November 30, 1820, AGI, Mexico 1502.

37. "Reales decretos sobre que se instruya al pueblo en la constitución y se formen noticias estadísticas y de la instrucción primaria y secundaria," A. Ex-A., Instrucción pública, en general, vol. 2477, no. 250.

38. "Carta de D. Pasqual Azpeitia dirijida al Sr. Alcalde primero," Mexico, July 5, 1820, A. Ex-A., Limpia de ciudad, vol. 3243, no. 123.

CHAPTER 7

1. Hamill, *The Hidalgo Revolt*, pp. 214, 215.
2. Apodaca to Minister of Ultramar, Mexico, January 8, 1821, AGI, Mexico 1680.
3. Alamán, *Historia de Méjico*, 4:308.
4. Calleja to marqués de Campo Sagrado, Mexico, September 6, 1816, AGI, Mexico 1322.
5. As Carol C. Ferguson emphasizes in "The Spanish Tamerlaine?," p. 264.
6. Manuel Palacio Fajardo, *Outline of the Revolution in Spanish America*, p. 343; "Oficios y cartas de Apodaca al Sr. Ministro de Guerra," Mexico, February 28, March 10, and July 31, 1817, AGN, Historia 152; Ward, *Mexico in 1827*, 1:164.
7. "Oficios y cartas de Apodaca al Sr. Ministro de Guerra," Mexico, reports of October 31, November 30, and December 31, 1816; January 23 and February 28, 1817; and March 15, 1818, AGN, Historia 152.

CHAPTER 8

1. See Margaret L. Woodward, "The Spanish Army and the Loss of America, 1810–1824," *HAHR* 48, no. 4 (November, 1968): 586–607; and Ferguson, "The Spanish Tamerlaine?," pp. 260–62.
2. Ferdinand to Alexander I, Madrid, June 21, 1821, AHN, Estado 2579.
3. Ferdinand to Alexander I, Madrid, August 10, 1822, AHN, Estado 2579.
4. Richard Herr, *An Historical Essay on Modern Spain*, p. 81.
5. "Sobre el reestablecimiento de la Constitución política promulgada en 1812," AGN, Impresos oficiales, vol. 60, no. 28.
6. A. Ex-A., Actas de Cabildo, vol. 139, May 31, 1820; "Circular y bando sobre la publicación solemne de la Constitución," Mexico, June 7, 1820, AGN, Impresos oficiales, vol. 43; "Cuenta general de los gastos erogados en la jura de la Constitución celebrado por la N.C. de México," June 17, 1820, A. Ex-A., Historia, Constituciones, vol. 2253, no. 9; Apodaca to Minister of Ultramar, Mexico, August 29, 1820, AGI, Mexico 1679.
7. "Real bando sobre elección de ayuntamientos constitucionales," June 14, 1820, AGN, Impresos oficiales, vol. 43; A. Ex-A., Actas de Cabildo, vol. 139, June 19 and 22, 1820, and vol. 669, June 23, 1820.
8. Ibid., vol. 669, June 23, 1820.
9. Villoro, *El proceso ideológico*, pp. 185–214.

10. A. Ex-A., Actas de Cabildo, vol. 139, June 10, 1820; vol. 669, July 21 and 27, August 2, 1820; Apodaca to Minister of Ultramar, Mexico, September 13, 1820, AGI, Mexico 1502.

11. "Sobre que de los fondos municipales se proporcionen 3,000 pesos a cada uno de los Señores diputados de esta provincia para su viaje de ida y vuelta," A. Ex-A., Elecciones, Diputados a Cortes, vol. 870, no. 18. The cabildo did finally scrape together 10,000 pesos.

12. "Proclama del Rey a los habitantes de Ultramar," Mexico, July 24, 1820, AGN, Impresos oficiales, vol. 43.

13. "Ordenando que deben ser separados de sus empleos todos aquellos que no vuelvan a jurar la Constitución de 1812," August 27, 1820, AGN, Reales cédulas, vol. 222, no. 121; "Circular con inserción de Real orden para que los empleados de las oficinas extinguidas sean colocados según su aptitud, con preferencia en las vacantes que ocurran," October 2, 1820, AGN, Impresos oficiales, vol. 43.

14. "Bando y circular con inserción de Real orden prohibiendo se reciban pruevas de nobleza en la admisión de individuos en los colegios, academias, o cuerpos militares," September 23, 1820, AGN, Impresos oficiales, vol. 43.

15. A. Ex-A., Actas de Cabildo, vol. 669, August 23, 1820. Many of the reform decrees are to be found in AGN, Impresos oficiales, vol. 60.

16. "Real decreto de 30 de abril en que se manda demoler y quitar todos los signos de vasalage de todos los sitios donde se encuentran," November 15, 1820, AGN, Impresos oficiales, vol. 60, no. 40.

17. Notice of receipt of report by Apodaca, Madrid, October 17, 1820, AGN, Reales cédulas, vol. 224, no. 93; "Contestaciones de los Sres. Regidores electos para el año entrante," A. Ex-A., Elecciones de ayuntamiento, vol. 862, no. 2; Apodaca to Minister of Ultramar, Mexico, January 8, 1821, AGI, Mexico 1680; "Aviso al público que las elecciones de los diputados a Cortes se han de celebrar en las casas consistoriales," March 10, 1821, AGN, Impresos oficiales, vol. 44.

18. See James M. Breedlove, "Effect of the Cortes, 1810–1822, on Church Reform in Spain and Mexico," and Neill Macaulay, "The Army of New Spain and the Mexican Delegation to the Spanish Cortes," in Benson, ed., *Mexico and the Spanish Cortes*, pp. 113–33, 134–52; and Apodaca to Minister of Ultramar, Mexico, January 31, 1821, AGI, Mexico 1680. On the fueros in general see Farriss, *Crown and Clergy in Colonial Mexico*, and Lyle N. McAlister, *The 'Fuero Militar' in New Spain, 1764–1800*.

19. For Odoardo's letter see Arrangoiz, *Méjico desde 1808*, 2:12–16.

20. "Sobre que el sistema constitucional pierde cada día mucho de su valor y eficacia por las conquistas reprimidas que hacen sus enemigos," Mexico, January 9, 1821, AGN, Ayuntamientos, vol. 178.

21. In this light, see Ocampo's discussion of the question. He concludes that this is an example of a phenomenon that occurs frequently in the history of ideas. Mexican liberals came to support independence because the reforms of the Constitution were not made applicable to Mexico, while Mexican traditionalists came to support independence to save religion. The same event provoked contrary positions, which in turn led to the same effect (*Las ideas de un día*, p. 153).

22. Ladd, "The Mexican Nobility," pp. 237–38.

23. Ibid., p. 239.

24. Rodríguez, *Emergence of Spanish America*, pp. 31–37.

25. Quoted from Manuel de la Bárcena, *Manifiesto al mundo de la justicia y la necesidad de la independencia de la Nueva España* (Puebla, 1821), in Ladd, "The Mexican Nobility," p. 240.

26. Ibid., p. 241.

27. "Plan de la independencia de México proclamada y jurada en el pueblo de Iguala en los días 1 y 2 de marzo de 1821," AGN, Impresos oficiales, vol. 60, no. 62.

28. Ocampo, *Las ideas de un día*, p. 49.

29. Iturbide to Apodaca, Iguala, February 24, 1821, AGI, Mexico 1680.

30. Ladd, "The Mexican Nobility," p. 230. William Spence Robertson discusses the confused provenance of the Plan of Iguala but arrives at no conclusion (*Iturbide of Mexico*, pp. 67–69).

31. Quoted in Ladd, "The Mexican Nobility," p. 231.

32. Ibid., p. 232; Rodríguez, *Emergence of Spanish America*, p. 39.

CHAPTER 9

1. Apodaca to Minister of Ultramar, Mexico, March 7, 1821, AGI, Mexico 1680; Apodaca to Minister of Ultramar, Guanabacoa, Cuba, November 17, 1821, AGI, Mexico 1680.

2. Public statements in AGN, Impresos oficiales, vol. 44; "A la proclama del Exmo. Sr. Virrey de Nueva España, el Cuerpo de artillería nacional," March 8, 1821, Archivo Histórico, Instituto Nacional de Antropología e Historia, Mexico, Antigua Colección, Tomo 2–31, fol. 14–51.

3. Iturbide to Apodaca, Iguala, February 24, 1821, AGI, Mexico 1680.

4. "Proclama del Conde del Venadito al vecindario de América para que no sigan los planes del Coronel D. Agustín de Iturbide," March 3, 1821, AGN, Impresos oficiales, vol. 44; Apodaca to Minister of Ultramar, Mexico, May 29, 1821, AGI, Mexico 1680.

5. Report of the Junta of War, meeting held March 5, 1821, AGI, Mexico 1680.

6. "Se ordena al ayuntamiento haga apresto de viveres para remitirlos al Ejército Realista con motivo de una exitativa de Iturbide a que sean secundadas sus miras por la independencia," A. Ex-A., Historia, en general, vol. 2255, no. 94; A. Ex-A., Actas de Cabildo, vol. 672, March 2 and 5, 1821; "Proclama del ayuntamiento de México a su vecindario para que no sigan el partido del Iturbide," March 3, 1821, AGN, Impresos oficiales, vol. 44.

7. "Orden superior en que se previene a todos los individuos de tropa urbana que se hayan separado del servicio, se presenten inmediatemente a los gefes de los cuerpos en que servieron," AGN, Impresos oficiales, vol. 60, no. 66.

8. A. Ex-A., Actas de Cabildo, vol. 672, March 8, 1821.

9. "Aviso al público que las elecciones de los diputados a Cortes se han de celebrar en las casas consistoriales," March 10, 1821, AGN, Impresos oficiales, vol. 44; A. Ex-A., Historia, en general, vol. 2255, no. 94; "Pedro José de Fonte, Arzobispo de México, al venerable clero secular y regular," March 19, 1821, AGN, Impresos oficiales, vol. 60, no. 67. The archbishop was so opposed to independence that he fled the country afterward. See also Francisco Sosa, *El Episcopado Mexicano, Biografía de los Illmos. Señores Arzobispos de México*; Wilfred Hardy Callcott, *Church and State in Mexico, 1822–1857* (Durham: Duke University Press, 1926); Mariano Cuevas, *Historia de la iglesia en México*, 5 vols. (El Paso: Editorial Revista Católica, 1928); and Luis Medina Ascensio, *La Santa Sede y la emancipacíon mexicana* (Guadalajara, 1946).

10. Arrangoiz, *Méjico desde 1808*, 2:52.

11. Apodaca to Minister of Ultramar, Mexico, May 29, 1821, AGI, Mexico 1680; A. Ex-A., Actas de Cabildo, vol. 672, May 31, 1821.

12. Ibid., June 1, 1821.

13. "Apodaca ordena que todos los que pueden sustenerse y uniformarse a sus expensas a tomar las armas desde la edad de 16 años hasta 40," June 1, 1821, AGN, Impresos oficiales, vol. 60; A. Ex-A., Actas de Cabildo, vol. 672, June 2, 1821.

14. "Apodaca ha resuelto se renueve el bando promulgado por Calleja de 26 de octubre de 1813," June 7, 1821, AGN, Impresos oficiales, vol. 60.

15. A. Ex-A., Actas de Cabildo, vol. 672, June 7, 14, 15, 16, and 22, 1821; "Apodaca ordena la colección de armas particulares," June 16, 1821, AGN, Impresos oficiales, vol. 60, no. 83.

16. See Timothy E. Anna, "Francisco Novella and the Last Stand of the Royal Army in New Spain," *HAHR* 51, no. 1 (February, 1971): 92–111.

17. Apodaca to Minister of Ultramar, Guanabacoa, Cuba, November 17, 1821, AGI, Mexico 1680.

18. Bustamante, *Cuadro histórico de la revolución mexicana*, 3:268–273.

19. "Renuncia que hace el Exmo. Sr. Virey Conde del Venadito en Novella y encargo de este del mano militar," A. Ex-A., Historia, en general, vol. 2255, no. 106; Apodaca to Minister of Ultramar, Guanabacoa, November 17, 1821, AGI, Mexico 1680.

20. A. Ex-A., Actas de Cabildo, vol. 672, July 7, 1821; Juan O'Donojú to Minister of Ultramar, Villa de Córdoba, August 31, 1821, AGI, Mexico 1680.

21. "Bando para el establecimiento de una junta presidida por Novella con toda autoridad para el restablecimiento de la disciplina militar," July 7, 1821; "Novella al ejército real," July 8, 1821; "Novella prohibe toda reunión sospechosa en casas particulares," July 13, 1821; and "Novella ordenando que todo ciudadano desde edad de 16 a 60 años los presenten dentro de 48 horas para servicio en defensa de la patria," July 16, 1821, all in AGN, Impresos oficiales, vol. 60. "Proclama de Novella a los egoistas," July, 1821, AGN, Impresos oficiales, vol. 44, no. 75.

22. A. Ex-A., Actas de Cabildo, vol. 672, July 28 and August 3, 1821; "Aviso al público que se haga un solemne Novenario a María de los Remedios," July 30, 1821, AGN, Impresos oficiales, vol. 60, no. 89.

23. Robertson, *Iturbide of Mexico*, p. 112.

24. "Tratados celebrados en la villa de Córdoba," August 24, 1821, AGN, Impresos oficiales, vol. 60, no. 100.

25. O'Donojú to Minister of Ultramar, Córdoba, August 31, 1821, AGI, Mexico 1680.

26. "Bando sobre números de caballos permitidos a los oficiales del ejército," August 4, 1821, AGN, Impresos oficiales, vol. 60.

27. A. Ex-A., Actas de Cabildo, vol. 672, August 9, 10, 15, and 16, 1821; "Oficio del Sr. Novella sobre que el ayuntamiento nombre dos individuos para la Junta que ha determinado establecer con el objeto de una contribución de cien mil pesos mensuales," A. Ex-A., Hacienda, contribuciones, vol. 2019, no. 6.

28. "El Sr. Novella convoca a todas las corporaciones para tratar sobre la llegada del Sr. O'Donojú," August 30, 1821, A. Ex-A., Historia, en general, vol. 2255, no. 87.

29. "Representación del Exmo. Ayuntamiento de Méjico al comandante accidental de armas de la misma ciudad Mariscal de campo D. Francisco Novella," September 2, 1821, Impresos oficiales, vol. 60, no. 103. The title was given when this letter was published two weeks later in Puebla by the Iturbide press. The rough draft of this exposition, only slightly differing from the final draft, is in A. Ex-A., Actas de Cabildo, vol. 672, September 3, 1821.

30. "Avisa haverse hecho un armisticio con el Ejército trigarante por seis días," September 7, 1821, AGN, Impresos oficiales, vol. 44, no. 77; "Un Puñado de verdades, a nuestros enemigos, por el Pensador Mejicano," Imprenta del Ejército Imperial, September 12, 1821, AGN, Impresos oficiales, vol. 60, no. 104.

31. Robertson, *Iturbide of Mexico*, pp. 125–26; "Resumen histórico de los acontecimientos de Nueva España, dada al Exmo. Sr. Capitán General de la Isla de Cuba y su ejército por el Ten. Coronel de Navarra Vicente Bausá," Havana, December 8, 1821, AGI, Mexico 1680.

32. "El Sr. Gefe político Mazo acompaña con oficio unos sobre extinción de pasaportes, licencias de andar a caballo, de haber recaido en él el mando político," A. Ex-A., Historia, en general, vol. 2255, no. 89; "Proclama del Exmo. Sr. O'Donojú exitando el reconocimiento de la Junta de Govierno del Imperio," Tacubaya, September 17, 1821, A. Ex-A., Historia, en general, vol. 2255.

33. "Oficio del Generalísimo D. Agustín de Iturbide avisando que el 27 de septiembre hará su entrada el Ejército Trigarante a esta capital," September 24, 1821, A. Ex-A., Historia, en general, vol. 2255, no. 104.

34. "Resumen histórico . . . de Vicente Bausá," AGI, Mexico 1680; "Carta escrito por un comerciante frances residente en la Havana acerca de los sucesos de Nueva España," Havana, November 16, 1821, AGI, Mexico 1680. Apodaca to Minister of Ultramar, Guanabacoa, November 17, 1821, AGI, Mexico 1680.

35. Ubaldo Vargas Martínez, *La ciudad de México, 1325–1960*, pp. 91–92.

36. Council of State minutes, Madrid, May 29, 1828, AGI, Indiferente 1564.

37. Ocampo, *Las ideas de un día*, pp. 284–319; for proof of the continuity of Spanish liberalism in this early period of independence see Rodríguez, *Emergence of Spanish America*, pp. 47–64, 229–34.

38. However, Ocampo argues that there were considerable elements of spontaneity, based in hero-worship, in the public's call for Iturbide to assume the Crown (*Las ideas de un día*, pp. 72–82).

Selected Bibliography

PRIMARY SOURCES

Archivo General de la Nación, México. *La constitución de 1812.* 2 vols. Mexico, 1912–1913.

———. "Descripción de la entrada del ejército trigarante en México." AGN *Boletín* 10: no. 3 (1947): 483–86.

———. *Documentos para la guerra de independencia 1810–1822: Correspondencia privada de Don Agustín de Iturbide y otros documentos de la época.* Mexico, 1933.

———. "Prisión del virrey Iturrigaray." AGN *Boletín* 12: no. 1 (1949): 83–140.

Bolívar, Simón. *Selected Writings of Bolívar.* Compiled by Vicente Lecuna; edited by Harold A. Bierck, Jr.; translated by Lewis Bertrand. 2 vols. New York: Colonial Press, 1951.

García, Genaro. *El Clero de México y la guerra de independencia: documentos del Arzobispado de México.* Vol. 9 in *Documentos inéditos o muy raros para la historia de México.* Mexico: Viuda de C. Bouret, 1906.

———. ed. *Documentos históricos mexicanos, obra conmemorativa del primer centenario de la independencia de México.* 7 vols. Mexico: Museo Nacional de Arqueología, Historia y Etnología, 1910–1912.

García Icazbalceta, Joaquín, ed. *Colección de documentos para la historia de México.* Mexico: Monografias Bibliograficas Mexicanas, 1925.

———, ed. *Nueva colección de documentos.* 5 vols. Mexico: Antigua Libreria de Andrade y Morales, 1886.

Gazeta de Mexico. (Title varies: *Gaceta, Gazetas, Gaceta del Govierno.*) Vols. 1–12, 1810–1821.

Hernández y Dávalos, Juan E., ed. *Colección de documentos para la historia de la Guerra de Independencia de México.* 6 vols. Mexico: José María Sandoval, 1877–1882.

Iturbide, Agustín de. *La correspondencia de Agustín de Iturbide, después de la proclamación del Plan de Iguala.* Archivo histórico militar mexicano, no. 1. Mexico: Taller Autográfico, 1945.

263

———. *Documentos para la historia de la guerra de independencia.* Publicaciones del Archivo General de la Nación, vols. 9, 11, 16, 23. Mexico: Talleres Gráficos de la Nación, 1923–1933.

———. *El Libertador, documentos selectos, colectados por P. Mariano Cuevas.* Mexico: Editorial Patria, 1947.

Miquel i Vergés, José María. *Diccionario de Insurgentes.* Mexico: Editorial Porrúa, 1969.

Recopilación de las leyes de Indias. 3 vols. Madrid: Consejo de la Hispanidad, 1943.

SECONDARY SOURCES

Alamán, Lucas. *Historia de Méjico desde los primeros movimientos que prepararon su independencia en el año de 1808 hasta la época presente.* 5 vols. 1849–1852. Reprint. Mexico: Editorial Jus, 1942.

Anna, Timothy E. "An Essay on the Mexican Viceroys during the War of Independence: The Question of Legitimacy." In *Historical Papers 1975,* edited by Peter Gillis, pp. 59–78. Ottawa: Canadian Historical Association, 1976.

———. "The Finances of Mexico City during the War of Independence." *Journal of Latin American Studies* 4, no. 1 (May, 1972): 55–75.

———. "Francisco Novella and the Last Stand of the Royal Army in New Spain." *Hispanic American Historical Review* 51, no. 1 (February, 1971): 92–111.

———. "The Last Viceroys of New Spain and Peru: An Appraisal." *American Historical Review* 81, no. 1 (February, 1976): 38–65.

Archer, Christon I. "Pardos, Indians and the Army of New Spain: Inter-relationships and Conflicts, 1780–1810." *Journal of Latin American Studies* 6, no. 2 (November, 1974): 231–55.

———. "To Serve the King: Military Recruitment in Late Colonial Mexico." *Hispanic American Historical Review* 55, no. 2 (May, 1975): 226–50.

Arrangoiz y Berzábal, Francisco de Paula de. *Méjico desde 1808 hasta 1867, relación de los principales acontecimientos políticos que han tenido lugar desde la prisión del Virrey Iturrigaray hasta la caída del segundo imperio.* 4 vols. Madrid: A. Pérez Dubrull, 1871.

Bancroft, Hubert Howe. *History of Mexico.* 6 vols. New York: Bancroft Co., n.d.

Bayle, Constantino. *Los cabildos seculares en la América española.* Madrid: Sapienta, 1952.

Benson, Nettie Lee. "The Contested Mexican Election of 1812." *Hispanic American Historical Review* 26, no. 3 (August, 1946): 336–50.

————. *La diputación provincial y el federalísmo mexicano.* Mexico: Colegio de México, 1955.

————. ed. *Mexico and the Spanish Cortes, 1810–1822: Eight Essays.* Latin American Monographs, no. 5. Austin: University of Texas Press, 1966.

Brading, D [avid] A. *Miners and Merchants in Bourbon Mexico, 1763–1810.* Cambridge: At the University Press, 1971.

————. "Government and Elite in Late Colonial Mexico." *Hispanic American Historical Review* 53, no. 3 (August, 1973): 389–414.

————. *Los orígenes del nacionalismo mexicano.* Translated by Soledad Loaeza Grave. Mexico: Secretaría de Educación Pública, 1973.

Bravo Ugarte, José. "El clero y la independencia." *Abside* 5 (1941): 612–30, 7 (1943): 406–9, 15 (1951): 199–218.

Burkholder, Mark A. "From Creole to *Peninsular*: The Transformation of the Audiencia of Lima," *Hispanic American Historical Review* 52, no. 3 (August, 1972): 395–415.

————, and D. S. Chandler. "Creole Appointments and the Sale of Audiencia Positions in the Spanish Empire under the Early Bourbons, 1701–1750." *Journal of Latin American Studies* 4, no. 2 (November, 1972): 187–206.

Bustamante, Carlos María. *Campañas del General D. Félix María Calleja del Rey, comandante en gefe del Ejército Real de Operaciones, llamado del Centro.* Mexico: Aguila, 1828.

————. *Cuadro histórico de la revolución mexicana.* 6 vols. 2d ed., corr. and aug. Mexico: J. M. Lara, 1844.

Calderón de la Barca, Fanny. *Life in Mexico, the Letters of Fanny Calderón de la Barca, with New Materials from the Author's Private Journals.* Edited and annotated by Howard T. and Marion Hall Fisher. Garden City, N.Y.: Doubleday, 1966.

Campbell, Leon G. "A Colonial Establishment: Creole Domination of the Audiencia of Lima during the Late Eighteenth Century." *Hispanic American Historical Review* 52, no. 1 (February, 1972): 1–25.

Carr, Raymond. *Spain, 1808–1939.* Oxford: Clarendon Press, 1966.

Carreño, Alberto María. "Hidalgo, Morelos, y el Capitán José María Landa." *Boletín de la Sociedad Mexicana de Geografía y Estadística* 76 (July–December, 1953): 47–60.

————. *La real y pontificia universidad de México, 1536–1865.* Mexico: Universidad Nacional Autónoma de México, 1961.

Carrera Stampa, Manuel. "Planos de la ciudad de México," *Boletín de la Sociedad Mexicana de Geografía y Estadística* 68 (1949): 263–427.

Castillo Ledón, Luis. *La fundación de la ciudad de México, 1325–1925.* Mexico: Editorial Cultura, 1925.

————. *Hidalgo, la vida del héroe*. 2 vols. Mexico: Talleres Gráficos de la Nación, 1948–1949.

Castro, C. *México y sus alrededores*. Mexico, 1869.

Cavo, Andrés. *Los tres siglos de México durante el govierno español*. Notes by Carlos María Bustamante. 4 vols. Mexico: Luis Abadiano, 1836–1838.

Cooper, Donald B. *Epidemic Diseases in Mexico City, 1761–1813*. Latin American Monographs, no. 3. Austin: University of Texas Press, 1965.

Cordoncillo Samada, José María. *Historia de la Real Lotería en Nueva España (1770–1821)*. Seville: Escuela de Estudios Hispano-Americanos, 1962.

Costeloe, Michael P. *Church Wealth in Mexico, 1800–1856*. Cambridge: At the University Press, 1967.

Crahan, Margaret E. "Spanish and American Counterpoint: Problems and Possibilities in Spanish Colonial Administrative History." In Richard Graham and Peter H. Smith, eds., *New Approaches to Latin American History*, pp. 36–70. Austin: University of Texas Press, 1974.

Cuevas, Mariano. *Historia de la iglesia en México*. 5 vols. El Paso: Editorial Revista Católica, 1928.

Dealy, Glen. "Prolegomena on the Spanish American Political Tradition." *Hispanic American Historical Review* 48, no. 1 (February, 1968): 37–58.

Diario histórico de los sucesos acaecidos en México desde el 15 hasta el 30 de Septiembre de 1808. Edition of the *Voz de México*. Mexico, 1863.

Di Tella, Torcuato S. "The Dangerous Classes in Early Nineteenth-Century Mexico." *Journal of Latin American Studies* 5, no. 1 (May, 1973): 79–105.

Domínguez, Jorge S. "Political Participation and the Social Mobilization Hypothesis: Chile, Mexico, Venezuela, and Cuba, 1800–1825." *Journal of Interdisciplinary History* 5, no. 2 (Autumn, 1974): 237–66.

Dusenberry, William H. "The Regulation of Meat Supply in Sixteenth-Century Mexico City." *Hispanic American Historical Review* 28, no. 1 (1948): 38–52.

Dyer, Louise. "History of the Cabildo of Mexico City, 1524–1534." *Louisiana Historical Quarterly* 6 (1923): 395–477.

Farriss, N. M. *Crown and Clergy in Colonial Mexico, 1759–1821: The Crisis of Ecclesiastical Privilege*. London: Athlone Press, 1968.

Fehrenback, Charles Wentz. "Moderados and Exaltados: The Liberal Opposition to Ferdinand VII, 1815–1823." *Hispanic American Historical Review* 50, no. 1 (February, 1970): 52–69.

Ferguson, Carol C. "The Spanish Tamerlaine?: Félix María Calleja,

Viceroy of New Spain, 1813–1816." Ph.D. dissertation, Texas Christian University, 1973.

Fernández de Lizardi, José. See Lizardi.

Fisher, Lillian Estelle. *The Background of the Revolution for Mexican Independence*. Boston: Christopher Publishing House, 1934.

———. *Champion of Reform, Manuel Abad y Queipo*. New York: Library Publishers, 1955.

———. *Viceregal Administration of South American Colonies*. University of California Publications in History, vol. 15, no. 1. Berkeley: University of California Press, 1926.

Flores Caballero, Romeo. *La contrarevolución en la independencia: Los españoles en la vida política, social y económica de México (1804–1838)*. Mexico: Colegio de México, 1969.

———. "La consolidación de vales reales en la economía, la sociedad, y la política novohispana." *Historia mexicana* 18 (1969): 334–78.

Florescano, Enrique. *Precios del maíz y crisis agrícolas en México (1708–1810)*. Mexico: Colegio de México, 1969.

Friedrich, Carl J. *Tradition and Authority*. New York: Praeger, 1972.

Galindo y Villa, Jesús. *Historia sumaria de la Ciudad de México*. Mexico: Editorial Cultura, 1925.

García, Genaro. *Leona Vicario, heroína insurgente*. Mexico, 1910.

Gibson, Charles. *The Aztecs Under Spanish Rule: A History of the Indians of the Valley of Mexico, 1519–1810*. Stanford: Stanford University Press, 1964.

González, Luis, comp. *El Congreso de Anáhuac de 1813*. Mexico: Camara de Senadores, 1963.

González Obregón, Luis. *Las calles de México, leyendas y sucedidos*. 2 vols. Mexico: Ediciones Botas, 1936.

———. *México viejo, noticias históricas, tradiciones, leyendas y costumbres, 1521–1821*. Rev. ed. Mexico: Viuda de C. Bouret, 1900.

———. *La vida en México en 1810*. Mexico: Viuda de C. Bouret, 1911.

Guthrie, Chester L. "Colonial Economy, Trade, Industry, and Labor in Seventeenth-Century Mexico City." *Revista de historia de América* 7 (December, 1939): 103–33.

Hale, Charles A. "The Reconstruction of Nineteenth-Century Politics in Spanish America: A Case for the History of Ideas." *Latin American Research Review* 8, no. 2 (Summer, 1972): 53–73.

Hamill, Hugh M., Jr. "Early Psychological Warfare in the Hidalgo Revolt." *Hispanic American Historical Review* 41, no. 2 (May, 1961): 206–35.

———. *The Hidalgo Revolt: Prelude to Mexican Independence*. Gainesville: University of Florida Press, 1966.

————. "Royalist Counterinsurgency in the Mexican War of Independence: The Lessons of 1811." *Hispanic American Historical Review* 53, no. 3 (August, 1973): 470–89.

Hamnett, Brian R. "The Appropriation of Mexican Church Wealth by the Spanish Bourbon Government: 'The Consolidación de Vales Reales,' 1805–1809." *Journal of Latin American Studies* 1, no. 2 (November, 1969): 85–113.

————. *Politics and Trade in Southern Mexico, 1750–1821*. Cambridge: At the University Press, 1971.

Hardoy, Jorge. *Pre-Columbian Cities*. London: George Allen and Unwin, 1973.

Haring, C. H. *The Spanish Empire in America*. New York: Harcourt, Brace and World, 1952.

Herr, Richard. *An Historical Essay on Modern Spain*. Berkeley: University of California Press, 1974.

Hoberman, Louisa. "Bureaucracy and Disaster: Mexico City and the Flood of 1629." *Journal of Latin American Studies* 6, no. 2 (November, 1974): 211–30.

————. "City Planning in Spanish Colonial Government: The Response of Mexico City to the Problem of Floods, 1607–1637.' Ph.D. dissertation, Columbia University, 1972.

Howe, Walter. *The Mining Guild of New Spain and Its Tribunal General, 1770–1821*. Cambridge, Mass.: Harvard University Press, 1949.

Humboldt, Alexander von. *Ensayo político sobre Nueva España*. Prologue, selection, and notes by Luis Alberto Sánchez. Santiago de Chile: Ediciones Ercilla, 1942.

Izquierdo, José Joaquín. *Montaña y los orígenes del movimiento social y científico de México*. Mexico: Ediciones Ciencia, 1955.

King, James F. "The Colored Castes and the American Representation in the Cortes of Cádiz." *Hispanic American Historical Review* 33, no. 1 (February, 1953): 33–64.

Ladd, Doris M. "The Mexican Nobility at Independence, 1780–1826." Ph.D. dissertation, Stanford University, 1971.

Lafuente Ferrari, Enrique. *El Virrey Iturrigaray y los orígenes de la Independencia de México*. Madrid: Consejo Superior de Investigaciones Científicas, 1941.

Lavrin, Asunción. "The Execution of the Law of *Consolidación* in New Spain: Economic Aims and Results." *Hispanic American Historical Review* 53, no. 1 (February, 1973): 27–49.

————. "The Role of the Nunneries in the Economy of New Spain in the 18th Century." *Hispanic American Historical Review* 46, no. 4 (November, 1966): 371–93.

Lemoine Villicaña, Ernesto. *Morelos, su vida revolucionaria a través de sus escritos y de otros testimonios de la época.* Mexico: Universidad Nacional Autónoma de México, 1965.

Liceaga, José María de. *Adicciones y rectificaciones a la historia de México que escribio D. Lucas Alamán, formadas y publicadas en Guanajuato, año de 1868.* 2d ed. Mexico: L. Alvarez y Alvarez de la Cadena, 1944.

Lizardi, José Joaquín Fernández de. *El Pensador Mexicano, 1812–1814.* 3 vols. Mexico, n.d.

———. *El Periquillo Sarniento (The Itching Parrot).* Translated by Katherine Anne Porter. Garden City, N.Y.: Doubleday, Doran and Co., 1942.

López Cancelada, Juan. *Conducta del Exmo. Sr. Don José Iturrigaray durante su govierno de Nueva España.* Cádiz, 1812.

Lynch, John. *The Spanish American Revolutions, 1808–1826.* New York: W. W. Norton, 1973.

Macías, Anna. *Génesis del govierno constitucional en México: 1808–1820.* Translated by María Elena Hope and Antonieta Sánchez Mejorada de Hope. Mexico: Secretaría de Educación Pública, 1973.

Macune, Charles W., Jr. "A Test of Federalism: Political, Economic, and Ecclesiastical Relations between the State of Mexico and the Mexican Nation, 1823–1835." Ph.D. dissertation, University of Texas, Austin, 1970.

McAlister, Lyle N. *The 'Fuero Militar' in New Spain, 1764–1800.* Gainesville: University of Florida Press, 1957.

Marroqui, José María. *La Ciudad de México.* 3 vols. Mexico: J. Aguilar Vera, 1900–1903.

Martin, Luis. "Lucas Alamán, Pioneer of Mexican Historiography: An Interpretative Essay." *The Americas* 32, no. 2 (October, 1975): 239–56.

Mexico, La Junta Directiv⁻ del Desagüe. *Memoria histórico, técnica y administrativa de las obras del Junta directiva del desagüe del Valle de México, 1449–1900, publicada por orden del desagüe del Valle de México.* Mexico: Oficina Impresora de Estampillas, 1902.

Mier, Servando Teresa de. *Historia de la revolución de Nueva España, antiguamente Anáhuac, o verdadero origen y causas de ella con relación de sus progresos hasta el presente año de 1812.* Mexico, 1822.

Mora, José María Luis. *México y sus revoluciones.* 3 vols. Paris: Librarie de Rosa, 1836.

Morales, María Dolores. "Estructura urbana y distribución de la propiedad en la ciudad de México en 1813." *Historia Mexicana* 25 (January–March, 1976): 363–402.

Moreno, Frank Jay. "The Spanish Colonial System: A Functional Approach." *Western Political Quarterly* 20 (June, 1967): 308–20.

Morse, Richard M. "The Heritage of Latin America." In *Politics and Social Change in Latin America: The Distinct Tradition,* edited by Howard J. Wiarda, pp. 25–69. Amherst: University of Massachusetts Press, 1974.

Núñez y Domínguez, José de. *La virreina mexicana: Doña María Francisca de la Gándara de Calleja.* Mexico: Imprenta Universitaria, 1950.

Ocampo, Javier. *Las ideas de un día: el pueblo mexicano ante la consumación de su independencia.* Mexico: Colegio de México, 1969.

O'Gorman, Edmundo. "Reflexiones sobre la distribución urbana colonial de la ciudad de México." In *Seis estudios históricos de tema mexicano,* edited by Edmundo O'Gorman, pp. 13–40. Xalapa, Veracruz: Facultad de Filosofia y Letras, Universidad Veracruzana, 1960.

Palacio Fajardo, Manuel. *Outline of the Revolution in Spanish America; Or an account of the origin, progress and actual state of the war carried on between Spain and Spanish America.* London: Longman, Hurst, Rees, Orme, and Brown, 1817.

Patterson, John Clarke. "José María Morelos, Mexican Revolutionary Patriot." Ph.D. dissertation, Duke University, 1930.

Payne, Stanley G. *A History of Spain and Portugal.* 2 vols. Madison: University of Wisconsin Press, 1972.

Pierson, W. W. "Some Reflections on the Cabildo as an Institution." *Hispanic American Historical Review* 5, no. 4 (November, 1922): 573–96.

Pike, Fredrick B. "The Municipality and the System of Checks and Balances in Spanish Colonial Administration." *The Americas* 15, no. 2 (October, 1958): 139–58.

Poinsett, Joel R. *Notes on Mexico, Made in the Autumn of 1822 by a citizen of the United States.* Philadelphia: H. C. Carey and I. Lea, 1824.

Priestley, Herbert I. "Spanish Colonial Municipalities." *Louisiana Historical Review* 5, no. 2 (April, 1922): 125–43.

Robertson, William Spence. *Iturbide of Mexico.* Durham: Duke University Press, 1952.

Rodríguez O., Jaime E. *The Emergence of Spanish America: Vicente Rocafuerte and Spanish Americanism, 1808–1832.* Berkeley: University of California Press, 1975.

Romero Flores, Jesús. *México, historia de una gran ciudad.* Mexico: Ediciones Morelos, 1953.

Rydjord, John. *Foreign Interest in the Independence of New Spain: An Introduction to the War for Independence.* Durham: Duke University Press, 1935.

Santiago Cruz, Francisco. *El Virrey Iturrigaray, Historia de una Conspiración.* Mexico: Editorial Jus, 1965.

Schmitt, Karl M. "The Clergy and the Independence of New Spain." *Hispanic American Historical Review* 34, no. 3 (August, 1954): 289–312.

Simpson, Lesley Byrd. *Many Mexicos*. 4th rev. ed. Berkeley: University of California Press, 1967.

Smith, Peter H. "Political legitimacy in Spanish America." In *New Approaches to Latin American History*, edited by Richard Graham and Peter H. Smith, pp. 225–55. Austin: University of Texas Press, 1974.

Sosa, Francisco. *El Episcopado Mexicano, Biografía de los Illmos. Señores Arzobispos de México, desde la época colonial hasta neustros días*. 3d. ed., corr. and rev., note and appendix by Alberto María Carreño. 2 vols. Mexico: Editorial Jus, 1962.

Soustelle, Jacques. *Daily Life of the Aztecs on the Eve of the Spanish Conquest*. Translated by Patrick O'Brian. Harmondsworth, England: Penguin, 1964.

Spell, Jefferson Rea. *The Life and Works of José Joaquín Fernández de Lizardi*. Philadelphia: University of Pennsylvania, 1931.

Teja Zabre, Alfonso. *Vida de Morelos*. 3d ed. Mexico, 1959.

Thompson, G. A. *The Geographical and Historical Dictionary of America and the West Indies, Containing an Entire Translation of the Spanish Work of Colonel D. Antonio de Alcedo*. 5 vols. London: George Smelton, 1812.

———. *Atlas to Thompson's Alcedo*. London: George Smelton, 1819.

Timmons, Wilbert H. "Los Guadalupes: A Secret Society in the Mexican Revolution for Independence." *Hispanic American Historical Review* 30, no. 4 (November, 1950): 453–99.

———. *Morelos: Priest, Soldier, Statesman of Mexico*. El Paso: Texas Western College Press, 1963.

———. "José María Morelos: Agrarian Reformer?" *Hispanic American Historical Review* 35, no. 2 (May, 1956): 183–95.

Torre Villar, Ernesto de la, ed. *Los "Guadalupes" y la independencia, Con una selección de documentos inéditos*. Mexico: Editorial Jus, 1966.

———. *La Constitución de Apatzingán y los creadores del estado Mexicano*. Mexico: Universidad Nacional Autónoma de México, 1964.

Tutino, John. "Hacienda Social Relations in Mexico: The Chalco Region in the Era of Independence." *Hispanic American Historical Review* 55, no. 3 (August, 1975): 496–528.

Valle-Arizpe, Artemio de. *Historia de la ciudad de México, según los relatos de sus cronistas*. Mexico: Editorial Pedro Robredo, 1939.

———. *La muy noble y leal ciudad de México, según relatos de ataño y hogaño*. Mexico: Cultura, 1918.

———. *Virreyes y virreinas de Nueva España*. 2 vols. 2d ed. Mexico: Editorial Jus, 1947.

Vargas Martínez, Ubaldo. *La ciudad de México, 1325–1960*. Mexico, 1961.

Velázquez, María del Carmen. *El Estado de guerra en Nueva España, 1760–1808*. Mexico: Colegio de México, 1950.

Viera, Juan de. *Compendiosa narración de la ciudad de México.* Prologue and notes by Gonzalo Obregón. Mexico: Editorial Guaranía, 1952.

Villoro, Luis. *El proceso ideológico de la revolución de independencia.* Mexico: Universidad Nacional Autónoma de México, 1967.

———. *La revolución de independencia: ensayo de interpretación histórica.* Mexico: Universidad Nacional Autónoma de México, 1953.

Ward, Henry George. *Mexico in 1827.* 2 vols. London: H. Colburn, 1828.

Woodward, Margaret L. "The Spanish Army and the Loss of America, 1810–1824." *Hispanic American Historical Review* 48, no. 4 (November, 1968): 586–607.

Zamacois, Niceto de. *Historia de México, desde sus tiempos mas remotos hasta nuestros días.* 18 vols. Barcelona: J. F. Parres, 1876–1888.

Zárate, Julio. *La Guerra de Independencia.* Vol. 3 in *México a través de los siglos,* edited by Vicente Riva Palacio. Barcelona, 1888–1889.

Zerecero, Anastasio. *Memorias para la historia de las revoluciones de México.* Mexico: Imp. del gobierno a cargo de J. M. Sandoval, 1869.

Acknowledgments

THIS BOOK owes whatever imagination or perceptiveness it might possess to more people than can be listed here. The works that have most influenced me are reflected in the notes. The documentary sources are found in the rich archives of Mexico and Spain, to whose directors and staffs I am grateful for making those national treasures available. Financial support to undertake the archival research came from the Duke University Council of Hispanic Research and the Committee on International Studies, which provided two grants to visit Mexico, and from the Canada Council, which provided several grants to visit Spain and a Leave Fellowship to allow me to write the manuscript. The book has been published with the help of a grant from the Social Science Research Council of Canada, using funds provided by the Canada Council. My wife, I need not tell anyone who knows her, was a source of constant support and aid.

If any one person can be singled out for his contribution to this study, it is the late John Tate Lanning, who originally suggested the topic and then followed its development for years. He provided an example of scholarly excellence and independent thought that I will long cherish.

Index

275